MW01060974

MAKING
BODIES
MAKING
HISTORY

MAKING
BODIES
MAKING
HISTORY

Feminism & German Identity

Leslie A. Adelson

University of Nebraska Press
Lincoln and London

Library of Congress Cataloging-in-
Publication Data

Adelson, Leslie A. Making bodies,
making history:
feminism and German identity /
Leslie A. Adelson. p. cm. –
(Modern German culture and literature)
Includes bibliographical
references and index. ISBN 0-8032-1036-1
1. German literature –
20th century – History and criticism.
2. German literature –
Women authors – History and criticism.
3. Women in literature.
4. Feminism and literature – Germany.
I. Title. II. Series.
PT405.A17   1993   830.9′9287—dc20
92-37873 CIP

for Dora

Contents

Acknowledgments

This book has been a long time in the making. Chapter Two was the first to be written. Originally published in *Signs: Journal of Women in Culture and Society* 13 (1988): 234–52 with the title "Racism and Feminist Aesthetics: The Provocation of Anne Duden's *Opening of the Mouth*," it is reprinted here with the permission of the University of Chicago Press. © 1988 by the U. of Chicago. All rights reserved. I have altered the title and notation system so as to conform with the other sections of the book and have added some information in notes 3, 8, 16, and 27. Most of Chapter One was written in spring 1988, although an earlier version of some portions of this chapter was first published as "Contemporary Critical Consciousness: Peter Sloterdijk, Oskar Negt/Alexander Kluge, and the 'New Subjectivity'" in *German Studies Review* 10 (1987): 57–68. These arguments are reprinted here with the permission of the German Studies Association. Chapter Three followed in summer 1990 and Chapter Four in summer 1991. Whenever possible I have cited from published English translations of original German texts. In those instances in which such translations are either not available or unknown to me, I have provided my own translations.

The research for this project could not have been undertaken, nor the book written, without the generous support, graciously administered, of the Alexander von Humboldt-Stiftung in Bonn and the Ohio State University's College of Humanities and Office of Research and Graduate Studies. In this regard I owe special thanks to Professor Jörg Schönert of the University of Hamburg, who was kind enough to serve as my academic sponsor during my tenure as a Humboldt Fellow in 1987–88, and to Dean G. Micheal Riley and former Associate Dean Marvin R. Zahniser, both of the Ohio State University. Their principled support of feminist scholarship has been exemplary. Professor David P. Benseler, former Chair of the Department of German of the Ohio State University, has played a comparable role in my professional development. For his unflagging encouragement I am deeply grateful. Many thanks are due Virginia Hull of Columbus, Ohio, for her magnanimous contributions that have allowed and encouraged women scholars to pursue innovative research in the humanities. I would also like to convey my sincere appreciation to all those colleagues here and abroad who have written any number of letters of recommendation and evaluation on my behalf, thereby enabling me to obtain much-needed research support as well as tenure at the associate rank. Since the names of some of these colleagues are known to me while those of others are not, I shall name none of them here but thank them all. The research reflected in this study was further facilitated by material made available to me by the Zeitungsausschnittsammlung der Bibliotheken der Stadt Dortmund; my thanks go too to this collection's conscientious staff. For their willingness to read some or all of the earlier drafts of this study and to share their critical insights with me, I am indebted to Steve Giles, Lynne Layton, Biddy Martin, Torsten Meiffert, Karen Remmler, Linda Haverty Rugg, Arlene Teraoka, Jörg Schönert, and the late Henry J. Schmidt. While I believe that I have benefited enormously from the wisdom of these respected colleagues, responsibility for any errors of judgment or analysis lies in my hands alone. To my colleagues in my home department go my thanks for kindnesses received and lessons learned. Susan Farquhar, Gloria Hartwell, and Treva Sheets of the office administrative staff merit my compliments and gratitude for their good-humored and expert assistance in keeping the department and my computer running.

As the making of this book has been embedded in the making of my life, I am also profoundly beholden to those steadfast spirits who have taught me much about love and survival. To these dear people I can only hint at my appreciation: Angela Disse and Bill Panning, for restoring me to faith; Peggy Berger and Paul Linden, for truly extraordinary friendship and wisdom literally beyond words; Peggy Purple Murray, Kari Lokke, and Christine Rinderknecht, for being sisters to my soul; Fred Sack, for always caring; Hugo Bekker, for his compassion and his laugh; J. J. Reneaux and Max Reinhart, for Thanksgiving long ago and all the talking tales since; Holger Iburg, for giving me a place to stay and for sharing his gift of earnest curiosity; my aikido partners in Columbus, Flat Rock, Hamburg, and Cincinnati, for endless patience and opportunities galore; the Bieri clan, for welcoming me into their heartwarming fold; my sister and brother, for believing me; Phyllis and Sid Weinberg, for standing by me in hours of need; Eddie, Phil, Sara, and Jimmy Allen, for always being there. A word of especially grateful acknowledgment belongs to leb, partner in building bridges, my one and only diving buddy, for plumbing the everyday depths with me, for whipping up those miracle meals, for letting me cry and making me laugh, and for turning the radio down while I tried to write. Without my mother's hard work and strong influence on my life I daresay that this book would never have been written. I would gladly exchange it for the chance to see her face again. My father's legacy is dustier but has also been far-reaching. Some lessons are too vast for words to hold them. To all those who have taught me, knowingly or unwittingly, I pay my respects. My great-aunt Dora Weinstein, Lithuanian immigrant and long-time maker of ladies' decorative feathers, died believing that she was less worthy as a human being because she could not read or write. To her I dedicate this book. If she were able to read it, she would perhaps realize that she had been misled. The written word alone can make us neither great nor free. In all humility I offer my own words to those wise enough to know that the human heart requires more.

Introduction

In many ways various attempts to negotiate the complex relationship between material reality and discursive signification have long been, and remain, at the heart of feminist scholarship and politics. (Judith Butler's *Gender Trouble* and Diana Fuss's *Essentially Speaking* are two recent, especially sophisticated examples.) Indeed, one could argue that there is no feminist issue or cause that does not reflect, in either spoken or unspoken terms, constitutive assumptions about "real women's lives" and the normative meanings ascribed to them. This applies to constructs of femininity, sex, gender, and sexuality as well as to women's purported roles in history and culture. Battles over reproductive rights serve as only one indicator that the relationship between the material world and its discursive signification is contested on and through the signified and signifying ground of women's bodies. This holds equally for debates concerning women's access to speech in patriarchal societies, inasmuch as women's bodies have been posited alternatively as a medium for putatively authentic, prediscursive "speech" or as a socially inscribed site of speechlessness. *Some* conceptualization of embodiment is crucial to any feminist enterprise. The particular manifestations of such conceptualization will, however, vary widely in response to historically, politically, and culturally differentiated exigencies and the discursive traditions in which they are articulated.

In this sense it would be misleading to assume that feminism is inherently international. While one may contend that it has been adapted and applied in a variety of international contexts, one should not infer from this that feminist positions arise in a global vacuum. Just as no woman is "all and only woman" (Spelman 1988: 187), no feminist theory is all and only feminist theory. The critical reflections to be presented here seek not to apply a universal concept of gender identity to the particular context of West German culture of the 1970s and 1980s, but rather to elaborate ways in which the particular construction of a specific historical context necessarily and constitutively informs the construction of a particular mode of theorizing feminism. This does not mean that this study has no implications outside a German context. Nevertheless, the questions raised here can at best elicit only comparable questions in other fields. The responses to such questions will be inflected by cultural, political, historical particularities implicit in their making. One of the challenges of the present undertaking is to render explicit some of the means by which gender identity is constructed and contested in the contemporary German context.

Yet "gender identity" is a misnomer to the extent that it implies a single vector (albeit one conventionally defined in binary terms) along which identity could be produced and represented. The concept of positionality developed and deployed in the pages to follow allows us instead to pursue the production of gender as simultaneously and inextricably intertwined with configurations of race, nationality, class, ethnicity, and other signifying social practices through which power is manifested. And although feminist theories have been particularly impelled to examine these often elusive connections, attempts to negotiate the intricate interplay of materiality, embodiment, and signification are by no means confined to the realm of feminist scholarship.

This investigation of making bodies making history therefore seeks to delineate some of the ways in which other critical theories do or do not account for the positionality of embodied relationships to power and discourse. Although broad-based variants of poststructuralism and hermeneutics offer many useful insights, even these insights lose luster if they function as general, universal principles of which specific cultural contexts are understood to be merely illustrative rather than constitutive. In the case of the first Federal Republic of Germany (or even of the second, more recently constituted one) no trenchant analysis of bodies, power, and discourse can ensue if the specific contours of recent postwar German history are elided. While the twentieth-century obsession with the Third Reich tends to highlight only a murderous "German" relationship to bodies and discourse, sociopolitical developments of the contemporary period (the latter half of the postwar era) reflect influences that are both multifaceted and international as well. In this sense critical theories that strive to illuminate conditions of a postmodern world can be seen to apply to a German context, but—and this is important—only in historically, socially, and culturally specific ways (see Santner 1990 in this regard). This call for particularity means both that the legacy of the Third Reich must be addressed and that it must not be reified.

In order to invoke such requisite specificity, it is necessary to turn once again to the practice of feminist theory, for it is here that the identity of difference has been most rigorously pursued and ardently disputed. Questions of identity and constructions of difference as they are enacted in German-language prose texts by authors such as Anne Duden, TORKAN, and Jeannette Lander bear intrinsically on the broader political issues surrounding competing models of contemporary German identity and constructions of German history. Over the last twenty years literary representations of the human body in German literature have served less as metaphors for the nation as a whole, functioning more as sites of contested individual identities. These constructions of cultural heterogeneity go far beyond cultural pluralism, however, to inform the politics of making German history. If we ask how literary representations of difference reflect or enact the historical embodiment of contested and conflicted identities, then an awareness of imbricated constructs of race, gender, and ethnicity can only sharpen our understanding of how German national cultural identity or history is produced and represented.

The textual analyses presented in the second, third, and fourth chapters demonstrate that attention to particular constructions of gender identity enables us to renegotiate constructions of German identity. They also demonstrate that attention to specific constructions of German identity compel us to reevaluate the inevitable complexity of gender production. As neither "German" nor "gender" constitutes a single axis along which identity could be produced or defined, constructs of race, ethnicity, and religion will also be explored as only some of the vectors along which identity is articulated in the contemporary German context. These and other constitutive factors do not arise in isolation from one another's influence, nor is their relationship one of simple or sequential juxtaposition. In this vein the analyses provided here raise crucial questions regarding alternative conceptualizations of "German" culture as well as feminist models of minority discourse. Furthermore, historically generated constructions of "women" and of "Germans" are implicated in constructing contemporary German history and figuring German national identity. Related questions of subjective agency and historical determination, of responsibility and accountability, have long plagued both German Studies and Women's Studies. In both contexts these questions demand to be reformulated in terms of historically constituted positionalities and their subjective effects. This study attempts to provide such reformulation by elaborating contemporary theoretical positions on embodiment and signification in the first chapter and then, in the subsequent chapters of textual analysis, delineating possibilities for the often disparate traditions of Germanist and feminist scholarship to be both mutually enriched and significantly revised.

1 | Of Bodies, Secrets, and the Making of Histories

Bodies guard their secrets well and divulge them at every turn. Certainly more eloquent proponents than I have contended that the body itself has been a well-kept secret in the history of Western civilization. And yet what is history if not the accounts of human bodies in and over time? History without bodies is unimaginable. How odd then that the grand abstraction of history would seem to obliterate the very concrete stuff of which it is made. But just how concrete or real *are* the bodies of history? This question is neither rhetorical nor facetious but crucial to the study at hand. If we are willing to contemplate the body as a secret of history (Horkheimer and Adorno locate what they call the "night side" of history *underground*),[1] then we must also be willing to entertain history as an even better-kept secret of the body. The alleged dichotomy between historical abstractions and the concrete bodies whose stories they tell rests on the exclusion of human subjects from both poles: history becomes its own subject in the abstraction, and bodies are mere objects on what Hegel calls the "slaughterbench" of history. It is by now *no* secret that a common link between poststructuralist and contemporary Marxist theories of culture and language is a series of problems concerning the transcendental subject of the European Enlightenment.[2] While poststructuralists tend to want to do away with "the subject" or "history" altogether, Marxist and hermeneutic theorists have been at pains to rethink these terms, particularly the former, in such a way as to avoid the trappings of hegemonic subject-identity while still allowing for agents of social emancipation or, at the very least, struggle.[3] The only point of agreement seems to be that "the subject" and "history" are *constructs*. The nature and process of their construction remain subject to broad debate.

All in all, a rather strange beginning for a book on contemporary West German prose. Everyone knows that there are no real bodies in literature but, at best, images of real bodies or, perhaps more precisely, images of bodies imagined to be real.[4] The fact that human bodies in literature are not concrete but "mere" images is, however, more problematic than the realization that a chair, a weapon, or a torrential downpour is not real or even referential. For any notion of a subjective agent in history is necessarily housed in images of the human body, and these images are in turn intrinsically related to concepts of subjectivity. If we think this body away from the literary text, all other images are rendered meaningless.[5] Biases thus reveal themselves in terms considered highly suspect in poststructuralist circles: subjective agents, history, meaning. To these terms accrue no permanently or metaphysically fixed identity or authority. They do, however, seem useful in the sense implied by Edward Said (1983: 3–4) when he argues against a fashionable obsession with "textuality" and "discourse" that has often posited these phenomena in opposition to history. While the significance of deconstructive discourse analysis for contemporary critical theory (in all its variations) should not be underestimated—there are many traces of it in the book about to unfold—this study is undertaken in the belief that there is an assuredly multifaceted reality of human bodies that does not exist outside discourse and is yet not by any means subsumed by it.[6]

In the West German context the Frankfurt School of Critical Theory has been faulted for overemphasizing ideology while paying insufficient critical attention to the role of the body in twentieth-century history and, further, for denying the human body any possible role in effective political resistance to structures of domination.[7] Indeed, Horkheimer and Adorno's intransigent consignment of the

modern body to the status of corpse (1972: 234)—however understandable given the historical circumstances in which they wrote—
would certainly seem to preclude any viable notion of subjective
agency in history. A comparable criticism is made of the French social
theorist and structuralist Michel Foucault, who is on the one hand
praised for placing the body at the center of politics and on the other
hand taken to task for his homogeneous conception of the body as
well as for a structural critique that does not allow for what Nina Auerbach has called "the messiness of experience." Foucault, it is argued, fails to accommodate the possibility that some untidy bits of human experience might conceivably elude the deadly dominion
exercised by the power of discourse or, for that matter, the discourse
of power.[8] At times a heady enthusiasm for deconstruction makes it
indeed difficult to distinguish between what is meant by these two
concepts. All power is seen to reside in discourse, and discourse is
seen as all-powerful. The conflation of these terms rides roughshod
over the complex specificity of human bodies—socialized, engendered, historically signified and, at the same time, real, that is, not
merely products of discourse or objects of institutionalized power. By
this I mean that bodies as physical organisms are not ontologically reducible to discourse as such or to institutionalized functions ascribed
to them.[9] And yet neither discourse nor power functions without the
human bodies through and by which they are mediated.

Although Julia Kristeva and Jacques Lacan are often lauded either for stressing the heterogeneity of human experience and signification or for accounting for bodily functions in the cultural assigna-
tion of the subject, their psychoanalytical orientation addresses psychological drives and conflicts at a very early age more than the
bodies of society as sensory environments privy to both interior and
exterior space over a lifetime.[10] It seems that if we are to challenge
"*the ideology of the subject* (as male, white, and middle-class) by develop-
ing alternative and different notions of subjectivity" (Huyssen 1984:
44), then we must begin by more thoroughly rethinking the role
played by bodies in the constitution of social subjects. Not long ago
two unconventional West German studies approached the issue of
contemporary critical consciousness by grounding that consciousness as well as its political consequences in the human body. A com-

parison of Peter Sloterdijk's more philosophically oriented *Critique of Cynical Reason*, which appeared in German in 1983 and in English in 1987, with Oskar Negt and Alexander Kluge's 1981 social theory of history, *Geschichte und Eigensinn*, will help us understand more clearly how we might fruitfully think of bodies as sites of social experience and political resistance.[11] Alternatively, it will also show us what pitfalls to avoid.

Both works can be seen—see themselves, in fact—as an attempt to reinstate the human body to its rightful place in critical theory; to do so entails for both a certain distancing from the Critical Theory of the Frankfurt School. Sloterdijk ascertains a kinship with Adorno and Critical Theory to the extent that the latter proceeded dialectically without the "victor's fantasies" that, Sloterdijk alleges, mar other theories of modernity (373, 375). He notes further, however, that Critical Theory claimed "a provisional ego (Ich)" as the locus of criticism, albeit one defined and born in pain (xxxiii). Sloterdijk rejects this accession to negativity as being incapable of effective social resistance. For Sloterdijk, the critical agent capable of duping or foiling the cyclops of our times should be properly called not the "nobody" of Homeric tradition, but the "yesbody" (73). (Sloterdijk uses the English word in the German original [156].)

This agent of critical resistance that affirms life with his body is Sloterdijk's "kynic," a term derived from his analysis of the role of cynicism in the history of the Enlightenment. Cynicism is "*enlightened false consciousness*" (5), that fresh vitality that has betrayed its original goal of resisting oppression, unmasking deception, and attaining freedom. In what he characterizes as the ongoing, unequal dialogue between those who exercise institutionalized power and those who exercise none, Sloterdijk ascertains throughout modern history the two "constants" (218) of cynicism and its opposite, kynicism. The originally intended subject of the Enlightenment becomes "the subject," now in quotation marks, primarily concerned with self-preservation against everyone and everything perceived as other in a reality that has become the source of all possible deceptions. The "subject" that must barricade itself to survive in the face of such threats becomes instead a paranoid "self-preservation ego" (355). This leads, according to Sloterdijk, to an approximation of the ego to a rigidified, externalized thing: a weapon. At the height of modernity we have, he contends, "the identity of subjectivity and armament" (379). The atomic bomb is in this analysis the concrete, technical representation of what has become of the subject in industrially developed countries (131, 325, 346, 354, 379).[12]

As the intended counterpoint to such a "self-preserving" ego, Sloterdijk's kynic rejects by definition any *"fixed form"* of ego identity (61). Not representing but actually living "self-embodiment in resistance" (218), Sloterdijk's kynic somehow mysteriously manages to elude those market forces or other institutionalized forms of social organization that have otherwise secured subjectivity as an armed state. In fact, Sloterdijk's examples of kynics are all steeped in sociohistorical contexts, which become muted when he abstracts from them his "constants" of cynic and kynic. The faith he articulates in such unscathed, vital human forces furthermore implies the kynic's capacity to erase, individualistically, the boundaries between public and private spheres without, however, attaining to public power himself. Let us recall for a moment that Sloterdijk's prime example of the kynic (albeit certainly not his only one) is Diogenes masturbating in the marketplace. The free space of monadic resistance so conceived is, to be sure, problematic, not least of all because of the circumstances of modern existence that Sloterdijk himself rightly attacks. Although he cites a modern split between the experience of the self and that of the world (63, 537, 543–44) as pivotal to the dilemma of contemporary identity, he does not argue for a theory or a praxis that actively mediates between the two. Instead, he implicitly posits the kynic as a monadic entity beyond the dictates of oppressive social identities but also outside any collective capable of organized resistance to social domination. He would have us believe that the kynic is a nonsubject with no fixed social identity but at one with his own body. This body becomes both the agent and the vehicle of resistance, as Sloterdijk perceives it.[13]

The body plays a very different role for Negt and Kluge in *Geschichte und Eigensinn,* as does, consequently, the notion of identity.[14] A comparison of Sloterdijk's and Negt and Kluge's treatment of tongues alone reveals that Sloterdijk, in contrast to Negt and Kluge, has no concept of experience as work or process. The famous photograph of Einstein sticking out his tongue illustrates Sloterdijk's section on "Tongue, Stuck Out" (141–42), but the picture bears no caption or identification. The reader is given no textual clue as to who the person in the picture is or what the circumstances were in which he (Einstein) assumed this pose. The text itself emphasizes the capacity of the body—in this case, of the tongue—to say no, "where words alone are not enough" (142). In this context, if we may be so generous to call it that, the tongue functions as a *symbol* of resistance. For Negt and Kluge, on the other hand, the tongue is an organ of *orientation,* one that mediates between interior and exterior space.

> Ob etwas zu mir paßt, ob es roh oder gekocht ist, ob es mich vergiftet, das prüft sie intim. Sie beteiligt sich an der *Sprache,* alle ihre Gewohnheiten sind kollektiv. Es gibt Landschaften in Deutschland, in denen hat sich der Freiheitsgedanke nicht entwickelt, wohl aber die Eßlust—die Intelligenz ist in die Zunge abgewandert.

> [Intimately, the tongue tests whether something suits me, whether it is raw or cooked, whether it will poison me. The tongue participates in *language,* all its habits are collective. There are landscapes in Germany in which the idea of freedom has not been developed but the pleasure in eating has—intelligence has wandered into the tongue.] (1005)

But Negt and Kluge do not accord the tongue (or any other organ, for that matter) the capacity to yield orientation. Orientation, they argue, depends on the production of a public sphere that links what is public with what is intimate (1005). For Negt and Kluge, the body is an ever open door to experience of the self and the world; indeed, their analysis does not allow for the distinction between the two since they exist not as entities unto themselves, but as mutually constitutive components of social reality as process.

> Uns interessiert die Natur der Zellen, die Haut, die Körper, das Hirn, die fünf Sinne, die darauf aufgebauten gesellschaftlichen Organe: Lieben, Wissen, Trauern, Erinnern, Familiensinn, Hunger nach Sinn, die gesellschaftlichen Augen, die kollektiven Aufmerksamkeiten. Einiges davon gibt es wirklich;

anderes davon existiert als nicht ausgeübtes Vermögen, als Protest oder Utopie.

[We are interested in the nature of cells, the skin, bodies, the brain, the five senses, the social organs predicated on them: loving, knowing, grieving, remembering, sense of family, hunger for meaning, social eyes, collective awareness. Some of this really does exist; some of the rest exists as latent capability, as protest or utopia.] (45)

The body is seen concretely as that through which all human experience is filtered, processed, and pursued; it is at once personal and social. Never privy to a fixed, permanent identity, it can sometimes be the battleground for conflicting social antagonisms in the same person (782). This understanding of multiple, conflicting subjectivities within the same body is something for which Sloterdijk does not fully allow. It is, however, central to Negt and Kluge's theses on what it means to be a subject. At the same time, it should be noted that they studiously eschew such simplistic terminology. They speak of *Arbeitskräfte* (labor power, in the broadest sense), not "subjects."

How is it then that Negt and Kluge cite the very real need for identity, identity as a "category of survival" (502–3)? Like Sloterdijk and other theorists of the 1980s, Negt and Kluge reject what has come to be known as the classical configuration of identity.

Einer kann sich identisch verhalten; dies ist aber die Summe seiner Schwankungen, Nicht-Identitäten, und eines Restes an Notwehr hiergegen, in dem sich beharrliches, identisches Festhalten an einem Rest oder einem Vorbehalt zeigt. Dies wäre im klassischen Sinne Nicht-Identität, nämlich nach der Vorstellung, in der innerhalb der gebildeten und besitzenden Oberschicht im 18. und frühen 19. Jahrhundert sich das Konzept der Persönlichkeit herausgebildet hat, die zwischen Außenwelt und ihrem inneren Souverän integrierte. Das hat es auch in der Oberschicht und im Zeitraum der Klassik nur unter enormen Kosten (d.h. Ausgrenzungen) gegeben. . . . Radikale Versuche zur Identität kosten das Leben oder Teile der Kommunikation

(Hölderlin, Kleist). Für die proletarische Klasse sprechen wir nirgends von solcher Identität.

Soweit wir von Identität handeln, sprechen wir von einer Eigenschaftskette, die sich im Zustand radikaler Bedürfnisse befindet, also der Substanz nach: von Nicht-Identität.[15]

[One's behavior can be marked by identity. But this is the sum of one's waverings, nonidentities, and a residue of self-defense against this nonidentity. Such self-defense manifests itself in holding on tight, doggedly and identically, to something that is left over or held in reserve. In the classical sense this would be nonidentity, that is to say, in the sense that the concept of personality developed in the educated and propertied upper strata in the eighteenth and early nineteenth centuries was understood as integrating the outer world and the personality's inner sovereignty. Even in the upper crust and during Classicism this was possible only at enormous expense (i.e., exclusionary maneuvers). . . . One pays for radical attempts at identity with one's life or aspects of communication (Hölderlin, Kleist). When speaking of the proletarian class, we never mean this kind of identity.

To the extent that we deal with identity, we mean a chain of characteristics in a state of radical needs, in essence then: nonidentity.] (376)

This being the case, Negt and Kluge ask, not so rhetorically: "But who has an image of paradise, false belief, or its opposite, if nation, consciousness, and feelings of identity cannot be the subjective carriers of such things?" Their own reply: "The carriers are living, i.e., subjective splinters" (395). This is indeed a radical challenge to traditional (bourgeois liberal) notions of individuals capable of subjective agency. As Negt and Kluge see it, identity becomes a "category of something lacking" (376). It cannot be attained, affirmatively, by merely filling in the gaps of existing structures. The fact is that these social theorists do not allow, categorically, for "individual resistance" or even "individual subjectivity" but stress the collective conditions for the social production of identity. The common assumption that subjectivity consists of all things private (wishes, hopes, feelings, and the like) merely reproduces, they argue, structures of domination (784). While Negt and Kluge do not credit the emancipatory consciousness of solidarity per se with as much potential for radical social change as Herbert Marcuse (1980) would, they do seem to share the latter's conviction that there is a "realm of freedom"—even beyond mere resistance—within social givens. One should say more properly, *moments* of freedom, not *from* social constraints but *in* social process. After all, if the carriers of ideas of paradise or consciousness are not subjects but "subjective splinters," it stands to reason that there are no whole (monolithic) lives—such as Sloterdijk's kynic might embody—but only moments in constantly shifting subject-object relationships that attest to self-regulation in the face of domination. An analysis of the "social side of identity" (Negt and Kluge 1981: 503) must take these shifting relationships into account. It should perhaps be noted that the splintering of the subject is not itself an emancipatory goal for Negt and Kluge but a term of analysis. Unlike many poststructuralists, they accord these diverse and sometimes contradictory moments the capacity for *meaningful* contributions to the effective undermining of institutionalized power.[16]

Both *Critique of Cynical Reason* and *Geschichte und Eigensinn* are informed by a critique of social and theoretical processes that systematically silence or exclude facets of reality. The distinction between subjects and subjectivity on the one hand and society and social processes on the other is only one such exclusionary maneuver. "Das was vorgibt Realität zu sein, unter diesem Namen auftritt, ist fiktiv. Es ist unter Trennung von wesentlichen Anteilen der Geschichte erbaut. Es ist aber Geschichte darin versteckt" [That which pretends to be reality, appears under this name, is fictitious. Its construction excludes essential elements of history. But history is hidden in it] (Negt and Kluge 1981: 32; see also 505). History is, however, not only the silenced partner in what passes as contemporary reality; it is also the silenced partner in what passes for subjectivity. The body has long been a silenced partner in both. The present is, as Walter Benjamin has stressed in *Illuminations,* an *experience* that the historical subject has with the past (1980: 259–60). To what extent do Sloterdijk, Negt, and Kluge allow for the body of such experience? Like the authors of

Geschichte und Eigensinn, Sloterdijk is mindful of that which tradition excludes or severs from our reception of history. "The historical is reduced to what has been finished and what has only passed but is not yet over—the unfinished, the imperfect, the inherited evil, the historical hangover" (293).[17] But experience? Citing as positive examples the contemporary emancipation movements for women and for homosexuals, Sloterdijk maintains that the history of that which has been left or written out of history can be written only by those who have been so excluded (293). While there is certainly much to be said for that, Sloterdijk's analysis includes no concrete sense of what that process of reinstatement would entail in terms of social experience. *How* history is appropriated remains unclear. Memory is accorded similarly nebulous status in Sloterdijk's study. Indeed, memory does not seem to be constitutive or even particularly significant for Sloterdijk's now-oriented kynic. Winston Smith's tormentor in George Orwell's *1984* (1949: 222) tells him he is "non-existent" because the state has rendered him "outside history." Sloterdijk does not so much posit the kynic outside history as he posits history outside the kynic.

Unlike Sloterdijk, Negt and Kluge ground their discussion of exclusionary maneuvers in an analysis of material processes of social relations. They note that *Geschichte und Eigensinn* begins where their earlier work, *Öffentlichkeit und Erfahrung* (The Public Sphere and Experience, 1972), ended: "That is, with the materialist question of organization" (Negt and Kluge 1981: 32). For them, history is a set of relationships that must be treated as concrete because these relationships are concrete. "The experiences that set us into motion must pass through not only our minds but also our bodies, nerves, senses, feelings; it must be possible to work on the relationship of history *as something concrete*" (1981: 777; my emphasis). Here again experience is regarded as work: a collectively, historically determined process undertaken by real persons. Just as subjectivity is historically determined, Negt and Kluge contend, so is history subjectively determined. The individual reception ("im individuellen Lebenslauf") of the historical determination of subjectivity they call "die Bedingung dafür, daß Subjektivität als geschichtlich bestimmte [*sic*], als subjektiv-objektives Verhältnis wiederangeeignet werden kann" [the prerequisite that allows for subjectivity to be reappropriated as historically conditioned, as a subjective-objective relationship] (783). Without the individual participation of those "subjective splinters," history remains objectified, beyond experience (783). The organization of contemporary West German society does not, however, encourage the unabashed and unimpeded active appropriation of history, as Negt and Kluge make clear by characterizing history in terms of a series of long-distance senses, the activation of which cannot be simply reduced to the work of the five senses oriented to immediacy ("short-distance" senses).

Die Nähesinne arbeiten, an den Fernsinnen ist nicht gearbeitet worden. Sie bilden vor allem keine Gesellschaft. Das ist politisches Problem der Gegenwart und Verzerrung des Grundverhältnisses zur Geschichte. Es existiert kein menschliches Verhältnis zur Geschichte, wenn daran nicht gearbeitet wird; ein sachliches Verhältnis ist überhaupt keines. Das Problem liegt daran, daß nicht einmal die Sensibilität unterstellt werden kann, daß dies als ein Problem empfunden wird. Es sich als Problem vorzustellen setzt bereits Arbeitskraft der Phantasie voraus.

[*The short-distance senses are at work, the long-distance senses have not been worked on. Above all, they do not form society. This is a political problem of the present and a distortion of the fundamental relationship to history.* No human relationship to history exists if it is not worked on. An objective relationship is none at all. The problem is that we cannot even assume a sensibility that would experience this as a problem. Imagining such a problem already demands the labor power of fantasy.] (597)

While *Critique of Cynical Reason* and *Geschichte und Eigensinn* both reject traditional notions of personal identity and subjective agency as inherited from the European Enlightenment and the era of bourgeois individualism, their authors are nonetheless motivated by a concern for human emancipation from structures of domination. The main difference between the two works is that Sloterdijk posits resistance or freedom in the embodiment of an attitude: a gesture. For Negt and Kluge, these things can never be embodied in this frozen sense, since they always take the form of sociohistorical, that is to say, subjective-objective *processes*. And yet it is clear that they posit the body as the site in and through which these tensions are played out. Of particular interest here is furthermore the designation of history as a bodily sense, a sensory relationship to something not directly accessible or, for that matter, reducible to the five classical senses and yet somehow dependent on them for its mediation (*Fernsinne,* long-distance senses; 597). This radical expansion of our understanding of both history and the body stands in marked contrast to the emphasis on the senses in two recent West German sociological anthologies (Kamper and Wulf 1982, 1984). The articles in *Schwinden der Sinne* (The Diminution of the Senses) and *Wiederkehr des Körpers* (The Body Returns) tend to take their cue from Baudrillard's notion that the human body recedes from the landscape of postmodernism. One notes here a kind of last-ditch retreat to individual senses, particularly to those that allow for perception of things close at hand (or accessible to one's ear, nose, or tongue). Sight, for example, is dismissed as a dominant and hence oppressive sense, an organ of control (remember Foucault's analysis of prison surveillance techniques in *Discipline and Punish*). Although the authors of these studies may well track the histories of the different senses, they do not, in contrast to Negt and Kluge, allow for history itself as a long-distance sense.[18]

Nonetheless, the explicit concern from which Kamper and Wulf's anthologies ensue is not easily dismissed. Do our sensory activities resist domination, they ask, or reinforce it? Will they set us free or are they the means of our enslavement? Such questions are specific to Western culture in the latter half of the twentieth century, to that phase of late capitalism in which not only is the reified body found in the realm of alienated industrial labor, but the physically fit body, the body beautiful, and physical pleasure itself have been rigorously commodified.[19] While the choice to focus on categories of individual senses rather than on the interrelationship of the various senses in given bodies in specific social circumstances hardly allows for an emancipatory subject in whose body diverse senses work together, the question as to resistance to or reinforcement of structures of domination implies another one, one that promises more tantalizing results. This is the question as to what extent the body is subject of or subject to the cultural process of signification. Whereas Negt and

Kluge offer much to challenge traditional notions of consciousness, experience, the subject, and history, aside from the question of class they leave the problem of signification curiously untouched. This lacuna is particularly striking when the topic turns to women's bodies, as feminist theory has generated so many studies of the ways in which these engendered bodies are at once real as well as the locus of cultural inscriptions of "femaleness" (see, for example, Suleiman 1986).[20] Without glossing over the gender-specific functions of inscription to which male and female bodies are subjected, one can argue that the classical conception of the subject (white and male) also relies on an inscription of the body. This is, to be sure, an inscription that reduces the body to the manservant/handmaiden of consciousness, but an inscription nonetheless. Feminist theory enacts an important intervention here by suggesting that only a "feminist theory of self" that accounts for embodiment, "which must include a theory of the social significance of embodiment," can also account for the imbrications of sexism, racism, classism, and homophobia (Spelman 1982b: 128).[21] When Kamper (1985: 133) distinguishes between the speaking body and the bespoken body, he draws our attention to the body as subject and/or object. Unfortunately, this is as far as Kamper is able to go. As his terms of discussion are more impassioned than analytical, we must look elsewhere for more detailed insight into the complex and contradictory functions of "human" bodies in late twentieth-century culture.[22]

TWO

The Body and Society: Explorations in Social Theory (1984) is Bryan S. Turner's critical reckoning with both Marxist and structuralist traditions for their inadequate accounts, however divergent, of the body as social construct. The central term of Marx's own analyses is, as Turner and countless others point out, labor. Admittedly, this implicates the human body, and Marx is often cited for his comment that the human senses are the products of all previous history. But to speak of labor in the Marxian sense is not by any means to exhaust the function of bodies in the constitution of society. Turner in fact criticizes the Marxist tradition into the present day for not fully allowing for an *embodied* agent of social change (248).[23] Structuralists, on the other hand, indulge in "discursive reductionism," ignoring the question of an embodied human agent while focusing instead, if at all, on a particular function of the body—namely, pleasure (245). Turner's critique of these influential strains of social theory is embedded in a more general attack on the legacy of Cartesian sociology, which at best grants that people *have* bodies but not that they *are* bodies. In some schools of sociology a social actor is not even necessarily a real living person (32).[24] Turner writes, therefore, to uncover the secret history of the body in social theory (34). From his premise that the government of societies is predicated on the regulation of bodies, individually and collectively, he goes on to discuss the fourfold nature of this regulation: "The reproduction of populations in time, the regulation of bodies in space, the restraint of the 'interior' body through disciplines, and the representation of the 'exterior' body in social space" (2).[25] Of particular interest to the present study are the last two elements. For here, as throughout his treatise, Turner speaks of bodies as interiors (not to be confused with consciousness) and exteriors, both being subject to social regulation, the first primarily through restraint and the second mainly through representation. Hence we read that the "body is a material organism, but also a metaphor" (8), "both a thing and a sign" (55), physiological and "drenched with symbolic significance" (54). The fact that the body is never wholly one (materiality) or the other (discursivity) allows Turner to maintain that resistance to structures of domination is always possible. "Bodies may be governed, but embodiment is the phenomenological basis of individuality" (251). If we substitute "subjective agency" for the ideologically cumbersome "individuality," we can glean much from Turner that is useful in rethinking the function of the body in history.

And yet feminist theory offers a necessary refinement to Turner's theses.[26] Citing Featherstone (1982), Turner distinguishes between the interior of the body as a physical environment and the body's exterior as a field of cultural representation. In other words, representation or social signification (as differentiated from the restraint or control of discipline such as, for example, diet) is seen as targeting the physical exterior of our selves. Feminist cultural criticism, however, has long distinguished between real women on the one hand, with both interior and exterior bodies, and on the other hand cultural projections of femaleness not only onto the exterior of female bodies but also onto a notion of inner being peculiar to "woman." This "inner being" is not identical to the physical environment of the female body's interior, but it certainly relies on the latter (e.g., ovaries, uterus, mammary glands) for its alleged legitimation. Judith Butler's *Gender Trouble* (1990) contends that even the designation of certain interior organs and spaces as "female" is already marked by the law of compulsory heterosexuality.[27] What is important here is that the interior environment of women's bodies is no less subject to processes of cultural signification than their exteriors. Turner's differentiations between the body as material organism and as symbolic construct are therefore not quite refined enough to account for the representative engendering of female bodies. This much then becomes clear: a discussion of the mediation between bodies as material realities and bodies as discursive constructs must also acknowledge that the mediation may be further deflected by distinctions, contradictions, or tensions between interior and exterior spaces, neither of which in turn can be justifiably considered wholly private or thoroughly constructed. "The body is at once the most solid, the most elusive, illusory, concrete, metaphysical, ever present and ever distant thing—a site, an instrument, an environment, a singularity and a multiplicity" (Turner [8]). Whereas Butler rejects any "corporeal ground" of gendered identity, her argument is designed to counter the assumption that one's "sex" can be understood as a real, factual, or "natural" state of "being" (1990: 141, 146). We can agree that one's purported anatomical "sex" does not constitute an ontological ground for gender without, however, concluding that bodies are not also, among many other contradictory possibilities, "solid" and "concrete." That is to say, bodies constitute a nonontological, material ground for action at specific moments in time. Such ground is, moreover, subject to diachronic shifts as well as synchronic instability. A critical consideration of the body, especially of the body in literature, will perforce rely on a mingling of semiotics and social theory, for both offer insight into the nature of materiality and the construction of subjective agents of history.

THREE

Particularly from the ever-expanding corner of feminist theory, one discerns critical dismay over what Kaja Silverman (1983: viii) has characterized as the ambivalent relationship of the female subject to semiotics. The overvalorization of language is considered by some to be inadequate to account for women as subjects rather than objects or victims (e.g., Newton and Rosenfelt 1985). Since all subjects require bodies, one's suspicions are aroused that the prioritization of language over sensory experience poses a more general problem as well. The Lacanian psychoanalytic theory of culture—extremely controversial among feminist theorists—is praised in one study, however, precisely for resolving the idealist underpinnings of structuralism by providing a *materialist* account of the double nature of "the subject" as both social individual and ideological space. Rosalind Coward and John Ellis's relatively early, remarkably lucid analysis, *Language and Materialism: Developments in Semiology and the Theory of the Subject* (1977), attacks what the authors regard as the Marxist failure to allow for the part language has in constructing the subject. Only psychoanalytic theories of signification, they argue, can successfully address this lacuna. In emphasizing the doubly "subject-ed" nature of the subject, which they refer to as "it" (2), Coward and Ellis underscore three issues: materiality, signification, and the fact that the subject is always produced *in process*. Their aversion to the metaphysical splitting of subject from object and to the ultimately ideological notion of any kind of "coherent" or fixed subjectivity leads them to favor, along with Barthes and Derrida, "structuration" over "structure," the latter dismissed as too rigid an analytical term. They speak of the social individual occupying a "plurality of sometimes conflicting subject positions, given in a plurality of representations" (68). This sounds indeed reminiscent of Negt and Kluge when they speak of conflicting social antagonisms existing in the same person (782). The resemblance, however, is deceptive, for these respective theories rest on very different notions of materiality in social process.

For their analysis of the "primacy of contradiction over identity" (86), Coward and Ellis rely on Lacan's and Kristeva's notions of *positionality* in the signifying practice. Positionality, however, is not to be confused here with immutable fixity of position. "Signifying practice

. . . provides, through psychoanalysis, what the Marxist notion of ideological practice elides: it shows the constitution of a necessary positionality, which is the language-using subject (Lacan calls this the symbolic). But it also shows how that positionality only appears in an ideological formation; it hence shows the nature of the movement of subjective contradictions, the moment of individual practice, of action" (80–81). Echoing these thoughts, Coward and Ellis contend that the "process of positioning-displacement-positioning is precisely Kristeva's ideal of textual practice" (151). For this French semiotician, "there is only the discursive space of the subject in relation to a contradictory outside and ideological articulations" (155). Positionality thus becomes, for Coward and Ellis, a matter of shifting representations, activated by the signifier (122). To be sure, they seek to contribute to a materialist understanding of the constructed nature of the human subject, but for them the materialist dialectic is one "between history, language and ideology" (92). The human body in history is curiously missing from this "materialist" account. Not entirely absent from their study, the body does figure in Coward and Ellis's explorations of Lacan's theses on positionality, which are built on his reading of the mirror phase and the castration complex (134). Yet this narrow optic reduces the body to particular drives and to specific forms and meanings of sensory perception at a very early age. The initial attention to the body yields quickly to the focus on signification, after which the concrete body loses rapidly in significance. The "materiality" of which Coward and Ellis speak is one of signifiers, not of bodies privy to social experience and cognition. Although Negt and Kluge cannot be said to explore questions of signification and discourse as part of the social landscape they otherwise so painstakingly traverse, the bodies of their "subjective splinters" never disappear from *Geschichte und Eigensinn*. Their concept of an economy of experience (*Erfahrungsökonomie* [782]) allows for the body as the site of cognition, the organ of historical experience, and the field onto and on which multiple, sometimes contradictory social antagonisms are projected and enacted.[28] This plurality of subjectivities is, clearly, an *embodied* one.

It is no mere coincidence then that Negt and Kluge's earlier work on the public sphere as political praxis (1972) should play a support-

ing role in Teresa de Lauretis's 1984 treatise on the cultural assigna-
tion of meaning for women in the realm of film and cinematic theory.
To avoid conflating the cultural construct of "woman" with women as
real persons, she argues, film theory must allow for women as social
subjects who are not simply objects in and of film production. Disput-
ing the claim that Lacan provides a dialectical materialist theory of
the subject or of signification (189 n. 31), she challenges the prioritizing of language as a universal model. (In a different context altogether Peter Dews [1987] provides a more systematic analysis of
Hegelian influences in Lacan's work than that at which de Lauretis
only hints.) In de Lauretis's view, to be sure, semiotics must address
the ever-shifting construction of meaning "across a plurality of discourses" (32). She draws on Umberto Eco's concept of sign-functions
for a more dynamic sense of signification than that which linguistics
provides (hence her criticism of both Lacan and Kristeva), but Eco
fails, she contends, to acknowledge the body of the subjects under
construction or "the heterogeneity of historical process" (176). The
body of experience, she implies, does not succumb to the alleged hegemony of dominant codes (this is where she takes Foucault to task
for his reading of the body in the discourse of power). Experience
needs to be redefined as "a *process* by which, for all social beings, subjectivity is constructed" (159). To support a definition of experience
that allows for subjectivity that is at once steeped in materiality and
constantly engaged in dynamic sign-functions, de Lauretis relies on
the semiotic theory of Charles Sanders Peirce, specifically on his notion of bodily habit in semiosis. "The point of my return to Peirce, rereading him through Eco, was to restore the body to the interpreter,
the subject of semiosis. That subject, I have argued, is the place in
which, the body in whom, the significate effect of the sign takes hold
and is real-ized" (182–83). The political and theoretical concerns at
the heart of *Alice Doesn't* thus come very close to those of the present
study, although de Lauretis looks at the production of women as subjects in film, while the analyses to follow here address the body as a socioaesthetic construct in the literary genre of prose writing. (See
Chapter Three, below, for further elaborations on the importance of
de Lauretis's later publications.)[29]

FOUR

More than a matter of mere "representations" in a web of signifiers and signifieds, positionality thus becomes a mark of physical experience, which does not by any means render it identical to the physical body. Positionality *characterizes* the body of social experience as well as the sign-functions of which it partakes, but we cannot say that positionality *is* the body, since it always implies a complex physical and significatory relationship to structures of power. To illustrate the point that the positionality of human bodies partakes of social discourse without ever being completely reduced to a set of merely discursive signs, I would like to draw on Elaine Scarry's compelling interdisciplinary investigation, *The Body in Pain: The Making and Unmaking of the World* (1985). Scarry examines the ways in which bodies figure in torture and war: as vehicles and sites of immediately physical experience and as signs in the discourse of power. Although she traces how real bodily pain is translated into what she calls the fiction of power (27), there is never any doubt—in the case of torture there can be no doubt—that the body in pain does not vanish in a discursive puff of smoke but remains, itself, painfully real. "This book is about the way other persons become visible to us, or cease to be visible to us. It is about the way we make ourselves (and the originally interior facts of sentience) available to one another through verbal and material artifacts, as it is also about the way the derealization of artifacts may assist in taking away another person's visibility" (22). If we as theorists acknowledge the body only as discursive sign, then we assume a role comparable to that which Scarry ascribes to the torturer, who becomes all voice, the arbiter of language, as the prisoner and his or her world become all body (51, 57).[30] "It is the intense pain that destroys a person's self and world, a destruction experienced spatially as either the contraction of the universe down to the immediate vicinity of the body or as the body swelling to fill the entire universe. Intense pain is also language-destroying: as the content of one's world disintegrates, so the content of one's language disintegrates, so that which would express and project the self is robbed of its source and its subject" (35). Having "no referential content" (5), physical pain is identical to itself in a "reversion to a state anterior to language" (4), while the *meaning* of that pain is orchestrated by the powers that perpetrate it, not the body experiencing it.

Scarry's evaluation of the structuration of torture and its political significance highlights some points that are relevant to the discussion of the body as regards the constitution of subjective agency. First, we see that the very concrete body of experience does not *mean* one consistent thing but is itself involved as well as implicated in the *construction* of meaning in specific, politically charged contexts. Clearly, the discursive representation of the body must not be mistaken for the body of experience, however intricately imbricated the two may be. This should remind us of Turner's insistence that human beings both are bodies and have bodies. The second point, that for the person being tortured the "dissolution of the boundary between inside and outside gives rise to . . . an almost obscene conflation of private and public" (53), is reminiscent of the subjective-objective processes of production cited by Negt and Kluge for all social circumstances. It is likewise a dramatic illustration of Turner's implied contention that, while the body may not be wholly subsumed or erased by the discourse of power,[31] it is never private but always socialized. The third point concerns the construction of agency through the tortured body. As Scarry demonstrates, the real motive for torture is not in all cases the informational content of confession but rather the unmaking of the prisoner's world and the making of power.[32] What this means is that torturers *accord* their prisoners no agency while *ascribing* certain forms of agency to them. This lie, as Scarry calls it, "mimes something real," that is, that "the person in great pain experiences his own body as the agent of his agony" (47). Scarry proceeds to elaborate the way in which torture first exacerbates the distinction between the self and the body only to obliterate the self by negating everything in the prisoner's universe but the sheer physical experience of pain:

> What the process of torture does is to split the human being into two, to make emphatic the ever present but, except in the extremity of sickness and death, only latent distinction between a self and a body, between a "me" and "my body." The "self" or "me," which is experienced on the one hand as more private, more essentially at the center, and on the other hand as participatory across the bridge of the body in the world, is "embodied"

in the voice, in language. The goal of the torturer is to make the one, the body, emphatically and crushingly *present* by destroying it, and to make the other, the voice, *absent* by destroying it. (48–49)

Scarry's explanation of "the double experience of agency" (52)—the torturer as well as the prisoner's own body experienced as agents of the painful unmaking of the world—thus underscores the complex construction and experience of the body as subject and/or object. The tortured body is experienced as the object of the torture inflicted on it, while it may also experience itself as the agent of its own distress. "Agent" in this context, as delineated by Scarry, more closely resembles a weapon than a social subject. The self, before it is annihilated in torture, is conceived quite literally as a desperately transcendental subject, an "I" that at that moment craves disembodiment but can assert itself, if at all, only against the body experiencing pain.

Not surprisingly, Scarry's finely honed theoretical analysis of such criminally substantialized experience helps to refine our understanding of a process often cited in the experience of concentration camp prisoners. When Turner points out "that it would be ludicrous to say 'I have arrived and I have brought my body with me'" (7), he is emphasizing the ineluctable embodiment of the self. What he is not thinking of at this juncture are those situations in which persons may be driven to *conceive* of their selves as absolutely disembodied because of the horrors to which their bodies are being subjected. As will be shown, this only apparently contradicts Turner's position. Having been imprisoned in the concentration camps of Dachau and Buchenwald for a year in 1938–39, Bruno Bettelheim describes in *The Informed Heart: Autonomy in a Mass Age* (1960) how he survived the forced transport from one camp to the other. "I have no doubt that I was able to endure the horrors of the transport and all that followed, because right from the beginning I became convinced that these dreadful and degrading experiences were somehow not happening to 'me' as a subject, but only to 'me' as an object" (127). Since Bettelheim has just before this told us of receiving a bayonet wound and a severe blow to the head, it is clear that the "me" he experiences as an object is his body, while his subject-me is posited outside his body—

indeed, outside the brutal reality of the camp. Bettelheim observed this same splitting between self and body, between "a figure to whom things happened and the prisoner who observed in detachment" (161), in other prisoners whose incarceration had not yet exceeded three years. "Whereas new prisoners tried to retain their attitude toward the world of the camps as being nonreal, to old prisoners it was the only reality" (162). In Scarry's terms the old prisoners and especially the "walking corpses" (commonly referred to as "*Muselmänner*") have experienced the unmaking of their world, such that their tortured body is the only reality they know. For the others, the self conceived as disembodied represents a kind of temporary haven for the victims of camp brutality. And yet one notes a revealing shift in Bettelheim's narrative when he speaks of the body not only as object but as subject. "To survive, not as a shadow of the SS but as a man, one had to find some life experience that mattered, over which one was still in command" (147). For Bettelheim, this survival tactic consisted of the decision to eat and to defecate whenever possible. "To have some small token experiences of being active and passive, each on one's own, and in mind as well as body—this, much more than the utility of any one such activity, was what enabled me and others like me to survive" (148). Similarly, reports that female concentration camp prisoners sometimes continued to menstruate when amenorrhea was more common cite this bodily function as a sign of self-assertion (Heinemann 1986: 20). The fact that the body that hurts, hungers, menstruates, digests, and defecates is experienced and *interpreted* as both subject and object supports Turner's contention that the social self is inescapably embodied. Furthermore, as Scarry has shown, the body itself—and not merely its representations—is involved in varying and shifting constructions of agency.[33]

FIVE

"The experiences that set us into motion must pass through not only our minds but also our bodies, nerves, senses, feelings; it must be possible to work on the relationship of history as something concrete" (Negt and Kluge 1981: 777). History does not happen *to* people; it is a function of the relationships among human bodies, which are themselves historically constituted, and the concretized structures of social organization in which they interact. While history is always predicated on human bodies as organs of experience, that experience in turn becomes historical once it is interpreted as such, that is to say, once it assumes a place in a narrative of history. Recently, much scholarly debate has focused on the extent to which history is fundamentally narrative or, as Hayden White would say, "an essentially *poetic act*" (1973: x).[34] Without taking issue with the notion that history requires narrativity to be perceived as such (and hence does not exist outside narrative), I would like to point out that the emphasis on narrativity as a grounding or as a function of historical consciousness tends to displace or render of somehow peripheral interest the fact that historical consciousness is perforce mediated first and foremost through sentient bodies. German National Socialism, for example, has been the subject of countless interpretive analyses as to its causes, nature, and consequences, but what motivates these studies is not the historical abstraction of National Socialism but the fates of *embodied* social subjects. The abbreviation "six million" is as effective as it is, one might surmise, not merely because the figure is astronomical or frequently repeated, but because it signifies in no uncertain terms the ineluctable embodiment of history.[35] Thus we see that historical processes and relationships are rooted in concrete, sentient experience, while narratives of history comprise *interpretations* of bodily experience. When Agnes Heller characterizes histories as "*criminal cases*" (1982: 124), demanding that historiography show empathy and the theory of history partiality for "those who suffered the most" (125, 298), she in effect pays homage to the embodiment of history. "We are history" (191), she asserts as she rejects the metaphysical notion that history happens *to* us or rules *over* us. We should, however, bear in mind that to say that we are historicity, as Heller does (3), is not by any means to reduce history to the simple equivalent of the human body or its sentient functions. History, Heller stresses, is a construct. Her analysis of the interpretive nature of this construct will be useful to our examination of the ways in which bodies and histories are constructed in literary texts.

Heller's *Theory of History*, which has as its subject both historiography and the philosophy of history, might also be considered a semiotics of history, since for Heller the past persists in the present only through signs, which must first be identified as such and then read. (This is *not* to say that the *experience* of history is essentially textual.) "We *choose* our history (or histories) from among many" (296), the plurality of pasts and the messages we seek in them having emerged together with civil society (92). In Heller's assessment historiography deals with what is past while the philosophy of history deals with the past in the present (81, 88). The *theory* of history she presents regards history as a medium with which to understand the present (20), the purpose of this endeavor being the future (14) (the need for utopia is an acknowledged factor in Heller's mapping of the construction of histories). This all sounds rather amorphous until we consider the distinctions she makes among three types of past, present, and future, respectively. For the past, she discerns past history, historical past, and the past-present age. Comparably, the future is comprised of future history, the historical future, and the future-present age (43). To clarify further, past history is "all events and happenings . . . whose consequences are no longer alternative in character, as well as events which do not threaten us or fill us with hopes" (44). The historical past designates a sociocultural structure in which we no longer reside, whereas the past-present age is "the historical past *understood* by the present (or eventually, past history understood by the present). The past-present age is an age whose symbols and values have become *meaningful* for us. It can threaten us or fill us with hopes even if it is beyond our power to alter it" (44). The distinctions among the three types of present follow analogous lines of differentiation.

> Present history encompasses all events and happenings whose consequences are alternative in character, and also events which can threaten us or fill us with hope; events to which we can relate both practically and pragmatically. Historical present is the cultural structure that we are "inside." The present-present age is the sum total of meaningful objectivations, systems of belief, and values which are essential to our way of life; which direct and "steer" our attitudes to our world. (44)

Gradually, we discern that the three levels of distinction here correspond roughly to the flow of events and activities, the structures of sociocultural life, and the ascription of meanings and values. Each of the time frames (past, present, future) takes place on all three levels (flow, structure, meaning). "Indeed," Heller insists, "we live in three presents (and distinguish between three pasts and three futures). This does not mean that all humans *equally* live in all three presents, but that we all more or less *live in all three*. Equally we can (and do) reconstruct the past from the viewpoint of all three presents. This is how we construct the future" (45). These differentiations are thus analytical, not surgical.

Detailing what she means by history as a dynamic construct, in flux and subject to constant re-vision, Heller's model thus helps us refine our understanding of the different ways in which the past figures or ceases to figure in the present. Although it has been argued above that this theory of history respects the embodiment of the historical process, Heller also makes it clear that we cannot know the past directly; we can know it only through testimony (138, 145). In other words, "a theory of history cannot come to grips directly with historical consciousness, but only with its reflections: it has to reflect on reflections" (51). History thus becomes a mediation of signs interpreted as messages from the past. But Heller herself astutely queries: "How can the past absorbed in the fabric of our present be recognized as past at all?" (201). In fact, she contends that the questions we ask of the past are inevitably questions of our presents. Whereas the historiographical norm is to elicit from the past questions that are properly its own, this norm can at best be approximated but never fulfilled "because the resurrection of the dead is accomplished by those living in the present and the past can only speak with the tongue of the present" (89).[36] If this is true for historiography, which genuinely strives to communicate with the past, it is doubly true for the philosophy of history, which Heller accuses of asking only those questions of the past to which it already knows the answers, that is, questions that are really questions of the present merely masquerading as questions of the past.

While she distinguishes between "speaking with the tongue of the present" (historiography) and "spelling out the message of the present" (philosophy of history) (89), we see that whereas our presents are always inscribed with historical traces, we ascribe meaning to the past only when we seek in it answers to our own questions. This is why Heller's category of the past-present age (the historical past as it arouses our hopes and fears, through symbols to which we ascribe meaning) is crucial to the discussion of the bodies of history as constructed in literary texts. What are the historical questions of the present to which these bodies tender answers, even or especially when these bodies are posited as belonging to the historical past? Concluding his study *Difference and Pathology: Stereotypes of Sexuality, Race, and Madness* (1985), in which he (among other things) critically explores analogies between historical and biological models in the post-Darwinian era, Sander L. Gilman cites Walter Benjamin's fifth thesis on the philosophy of history. While Benjamin alerts us to the irretrievable disappearance of those images of the past in which the present fails to recognize itself, Gilman cautions us not to underestimate the shadow cast by these receding images on the images of ensuing presents (239). Gilman's use of the word "palimpsest" in this context is salutary for our own discussion, as it allows for two ways in which history figures in the present. The images and structures by and in which we live have histories, as Gilman elaborates, *and* the past persists as an encoded message to be read or ignored. *Which* messages we choose to read and *how* we decode by encoding them in our own tongue (to borrow Heller's figure of speech) depend on which questions we ask of our presents in selecting our history or histories from among many. History is thus predicated on the experience of sentient bodies, while the past can be read in the present only through signs. Whenever we ascribe meaning to images of the past, we in effect seek and sometimes find answers to questions that are, in fact, germane to our presents.[37]

Lest Heller's emphasis on history as a plurality of constructs (and dynamic ones at that) be mistaken for a postmodernism of historical relativism, a word or two should be said about the status of moral judgment in Heller's theory of history. Since most of us bear at least some responsibility for the criminality of our histories, she contends, it is "more moral" for us not to moralize historiography. This does not, however, lead to a case for "neutrality." "The partiality for those who suffered the most is not moralizing. Those who suffered the most cannot be regarded as the morally better ones; they usually are not. They cannot claim moral approval but they can claim *empathy*" (124–25). While historiography makes moral judgments by comparing what historical actors have done with what they could have and should have done (121), it allows us to communicate with the dead only "on the basis of *our* morality" (126). The philosophy of history, on the other hand, essentially precludes the possibility of moral choice inasmuch as freedom is annihilated once it is ontologized (263). Heller therefore accuses Marx, for example, of having sacrificed a theory of history to the philosophy of history (269, 274). Although *A Theory of History* does not explicitly address the nature of social conflicts, Heller makes no bones about her own socialist consciousness (the belief in socialism as a *possibility* [294]). Her plea for what she calls planetarian responsibility bespeaks, further, moral choices in how the peoples of the world treat each other and the ecosystem in which we live. History with a capital *H* is morally dismissed as "the product of Western European civilization," its march having meant for most other peoples "the march of armies ready to destroy their culture and way of life" (282). Sadly enough, this is not just a figure of speech. A life element in modern society rather than a mark of its dysfunction (288), instability and heterogeneity thus emerge in Heller's theory not as a kind of inverted postmodernist telos, but as a precondition for exercising greater freedom and making "more moral" choices. "Modern society is characterized by *alternatives*. These alternatives are borne by the actors of *this* history" (284). In this sense we may read Heller's notions of instability and contradiction as further elaborations on Turner's theory of the body in society and Negt and Kluge's theory of the subjective-objective processes of historical relationships. All three theories posit human agents of history that are subject to social construction while retaining a capacity for choice that defies the hegemony of dominant structures (or even structurations). The fact that these choices are themselves historical does not render us any less the subjects of our respective histories.

SIX

My excursions into the realms of sociology, semiotics, and history have been guiding us on a slow boat to West Germany, where history has been a subject of heated dispute. That history would have been a topic in the 1980s comes as no surprise, given that 1985 marked the fortieth anniversary of the liberation of the concentration camps, the end of the Third Reich, and the cessation of World War II and that 1989 signaled both the fortieth anniversary of the founding of the two modern postwar German states and the end of the division between them. What is striking is not so much *that* these dates were commemorated as *how* they were commemorated and what meanings are inscribed in these commemorations. The period of German history from 1933 to 1945 is indeed a bone-chilling example of what Heller means by a past-present age: a historical past that we seek to understand, through the ascription of meaning, an age that continues to fill us (in this case) with dread even though we are helpless to alter it. Though events of past history are not themselves changed when we remember, deny, or even rewrite them, the significance they attain in the present-present age does shift as different parties ascribe different meanings to them, while respective histories are chosen for their capacity to answer questions of the present. West Germany alone has yielded far too much evidence of this in recent years to be explored in depth here. One need only recall public discussion of the memorial ceremony at the Bitburg cemetery in 1985, the museums of German history planned for West Berlin and Bonn, the documentary exhibit at the Prinz-Albrecht-Straße 8, and Berlin's year-long celebration of seven hundred fifty years of history in 1987. The year 1986 marked the onslaught of the by-now infamous "Historians' Debate" (*Historikerstreit*), a deluge of newspaper articles and, subsequently, books in which German historians argue over the meaning (in historical terms) that can be legitimately ascribed to the Nazis' systematic genocide of the Jews.[38] By contesting the uniqueness of this murderous program, the neoconservatives feel free to contend that National Socialism was an understandable response to the perceived spread of Communism. Quick to dispute the details of these arguments, the more liberal historians are also pointedly aware that what is really at issue in this debate is the *interpretation* of history (of a past-present age, in Heller's vocabulary), the purpose of which is to construct an identity for the West German historical present (see Friedländer 1986; Habermas 1987; Kocka 1987; Mommsen 1987; Wehler 1988).

Specifically, the interpretation of the fate suffered by the embodied six million is qualified by the neoconservatives so as to allow them to establish an essentially continuous tradition (of anti-Communism) from the 1920s into the present.[39] If one reads twentieth-century German history this way, then the Federal Republic of Germany (the one that existed until October 3, 1990) emerges as the sole legitimate heir of the greater German legacy *and* West Germany ties one more knot in the U.S.-dominated Western alliance. Furthermore, this neoconservative reading tends to erase the distinction between dead Jews and their Nazi murderers,[40] since both are seen, ultimately, as victims of the Communist threat (Bitburg in a nutshell). An analogy has been drawn between the numerical abstraction to which living Jews (and, one might add, other concentration camp victims) were subjected preparatory to their murder and the conceptual abstraction to which their memory is subjected by neoconservative historians in this debate (Brumlik 1987: 81). While I caution that *all* historical interpretation is an abstraction, I agree that in this case the *particular* embodiment of past history is sacrificed in order to make room for a specific interpretation of the present-present age.[41]

The interest in history manifested in contemporary West German literature must be seen in this broader context, in which different interpretations of a past-present age are used to construct divergent understandings of the present. I say "must," not because literary texts of the period all deal explicitly with the Third Reich (many do while many others do not), but because any contemporary piece of fiction that produces images of history—even of historical periods other than the Third Reich—is in effect constructing answers to present-day dilemmas.[42] While one might surmise that those prose texts showing no ostensible interest in any historical time other than the present produce *no* images of history, I hope to demonstrate that, both in texts with obviously historical themes and those without, the socioaesthetic construction of the body unlocks many secrets about a dilemma that is at once contemporary and historical: the constitution of subjective agents of history in West German culture and society. It is surely no mere coincidence that the two most frequently encountered *topics* in contemporary literature (when I speak in this abbreviated fashion, I am referring, unless otherwise indicated, to West German literature) are in all probability history and the human body. Patrick Süskind's long-standing bestseller *Perfume: The Story of a Murderer* (1985) in effect capitalizes on this phenomenon by combining both fascinations in a novelistic account of murder and bodily odors in eighteenth-century France.

SEVEN

Although the textual analyses to be presented in subsequent chapters are not confined to those pieces highlighting German history from 1933 to 1945, one may well conjecture that this period is proportionately the one most commonly treated in contemporary West German prose. One might add that this preponderance is nothing new in the tradition of postwar literature (see Futterknecht 1976; Wagener 1977). Following Heller's argument that historical images always reveal more about the needs of the present than about the past proper, it also makes sense to say that the questions asked of the Nazi era over time will shift in form and function as the needs of the present change. Judith Ryan (1983) has reassessed some common aesthetic approaches to the Third Reich in a variety of postwar German novels. Noting how much of the critical debate has hitherto centered on the appropriateness of realist or, alternatively, metaphoric modes in reconstructing the years of horror (18–19), she shifts the focus of debate (hoping to salvage respect for modernist techniques in the process) by reformulating the critical question. "If keeping alive the memory of Auschwitz is to make any sense, it will surely be as a reminder of the problematic nature of human culpability. What responsibility do we bear as individuals and how much freedom do we have to exercise it?" (20). These are the questions that guide her readings of selected German novels from the 1940s into the 1970s.

As Ryan herself points out, the growing emphasis on individual responsibility in the novel corresponded to a historical reevaluation of the theories of mass guilt (*Kollektivschuld*) so commonly cultivated immediately following the war (14). The mascot accompanying Ryan's quest for narrative structures capable of questioning the individual's role in history (in a way that accounts for moral responsibility) is borrowed from *Ästhetik des Widerstands* (The Aesthetics of Resistance) by Peter Weiss (1975–81). In Weiss's novel the figure of

Heracles, missing from the Pergamon frieze in a Berlin museum, prompts three working-class boys involved with the antifascist resistance to contemplate their own possibilities, in 1937, for taking effective action against the National Socialist regime. Although Ryan later finds the aesthetic structure of this novel to be a cumbersome and inadequate answer to the questions she has asked of postwar German literature (164), Heracles resurfaces again and again in her own text as a symbol for a meaningful "blank spot" (15). "Remembering the past means at the same time reconstructing the past—searching for missing pieces, filling in gaps, re-creating lost images" (13). The element of class struggle in both political conflict and artistic production, which is so prevalent in the three boys' ruminations about Heracles, recedes into the background as Ryan appropriates this figure from Weiss's novel for her own purposes. *The Uncompleted Past* posits the missing Heracles, more generally, as the cipher for aesthetics that engage the reader in an active questioning of historical circumstance and moral alternatives to passivity. "The problem was not where to find appropriate models, but where to locate the meaningful blanks. It was how to make readers aware of the missing figure, how to help them find the place where it might have stood and begin to construct the image that had never quite been realized" (21). Clearly, this project must have been particularly compelling for those who lived through the Third Reich as adults.

EIGHT

Ryan's focus and methodology may well be appropriate to postwar German novels into the 1960s. What I take issue with is the assumption that the emphasis on individual responsibility, as delineated in *The Uncompleted Past,* is also a suitable one for dealing with West German prose of more recent vintage. With reference to those novels with aesthetic structures that she deems adequate to the task of reconstructing the moral dilemmas of the Nazi past, Ryan goes on to assert that, "in a wider context, they also provide a model for literature whose aim is to initiate and develop responses to other political changes that dramatically call a people's self-understanding into question" (22). This prescriptive posture, with which the book also concludes, emerges as highly problematic when we consider how it is that Ryan reduces what she acknowledges as a "complex issue" to the bipolarity of "determinism versus freedom" (14). As indicated earlier in the discussion of the body as social construct, the contemporary dilemma of subjective agency is characterized not by determinism *versus* freedom but by determinism simultaneous *with* freedom. Ryan's quest for morally desirable positions in literature adheres to an outdated notion of subjects who are, to be sure, influenced by, yet somehow distinct from, the world that constructs them, that is, ultimately transcendent. Presumably, this would be the deconstructionist criticism of *The Uncompleted Past*. And yet what does this charge import for the ethical imperative? Can we, with any semblance of legitimacy, claim that this is an invalid concern on Ryan's part? Heller's voice reverberates here, making the case for the freedom to make moral choices, for empathy and partiality for "those who suffered the most." But Heller's philosophical arguments attain cogency only when we think them together with the materialist social theories of the body espoused by Turner and Negt and Kluge. What Ryan fails to account for is the *constitution* of the subject from whom she demands moral choices. She tends to equate the novel of consciousness with the novel of conscience, without seeing that the construction of the subject's body is also constitutive for historical consciousness. This does not nullify the ethical concern, but it decidedly complicates Ryan's key term ("individual responsibility"). It also renders possible its reformulation.

Take, for example, the absent Heracles. Ryan reads him as a symbol of missing heroes, whereas in the museum scene in Weiss's novel his name functions as an image (in the text) of a missing image (erased from the surface of the frieze) of a missing body (the embodied subject on whom resistance is predicated). The highly mediated nature of this meaningful "blank spot" should serve us as a reminder that aesthetic constructions of the ethically minded subject are also a function of body images and that these images are, furthermore, threads of a social fabric in which real bodies are simultaneously discursive and material or, in other words, constructed without being merely passive objects of construction. To focus on consciousness and conscience alone is to see the bodies of history only as the latter's victims, as objects of history. Of an age traumatized by the public knowledge and filmic images of so many dead and tortured bodies (I am thinking specifically of documentary footage of the concentration camps), the first twenty years or so following the war could be expected to see the bodies of history in this light. But as the experiential shock of German National Socialism has been gradually submerged (I would not presume to say "diminished") under the very different structures of experience that come with the progressive entrenchment of advanced capitalism, the brutal victimization of the human body has given way to its mundane commodification.[43] Certainly, both raise serious questions as to the status of the people who have and are these bodies. Are they objects or subjects of history? Or are they both, and if so, how? My point is that the body is relevant *in different ways* for the discussion of subjective agency in the first twenty years and in the subsequent twenty years of the Federal Republic. Ryan overlooks this when she implies that the fundamental problem ("individual responsibility") poses itself in a historically constant way and hence that the aesthetic solutions for dealing with the Third Reich in the 1950s and 1960s might be appropriate for dealing with more contemporary problems as well. Alternatively, one can argue that the particular prominence of bodies across the spectrum of contemporary West German prose has displaced the moral categories so prevalent in the literature of the first two decades after the war.

Indisputably, bodies are also present (and important) in this earlier period. Who can forget Adrian Leverkühn's syphilitic body or Oskar Matzerath's gnomic one? As countless critics have elaborated, however, these bodies tend to serve as symbols or allegories for political, economic, or national issues. Oddly enough, a novel by one of the captains of postwar literature, whose style is often considered less sophisticated and more simplistically allegorical than that of Thomas Mann or Günter Grass, reveals ever so slight traces of a different writing of the body in 1959. Tellingly, it is the body of resistance (to fascism) that is rendered more than mere object of history or allegorical symbol in Heinrich Böll's *Billiards at Half-Past Nine*. Schrella, standing in front of the house that used to belong to his family on his temporary return from exile, experiences something just shy of memory in the skin of his thumb as he rings the brass doorbell (1962: 216, 221): in

Negt and Kluge's terms, skin as an organ of orientation. Of the nameless youth who risked his life to bring Robert Fähmel's parents news of their son in exile, we learn that only the stoop on which he used to stand remains—"his feet touched it."[44] If we replace "nameless" with "missing" and the stoop with the paw of a lion skin, it is not difficult to recognize a predecessor to Weiss's Heracles here. Belaboring the point, one could also note that the little act of anarchy (Nägele 1977: 197) in slicing the abbey-shaped cake at the end of the novel makes practical sense only if one assumes that the pieces of cake are then to be eaten: a politically significant act predicated on a bodily function. There are obviously limits to just how far this point may be stretched with Böll, for *Billiards* only sporadically and tentatively explores alternative images of the body. Yet these brief forays should alert us to a shifting paradigm.[45]

NINE

What I propose then is this: Once we begin to examine the different ways in which bodies are constructed and in which body images function in contemporary West German prose, some of the secrets of the subjective agents of history in our time will be revealed. Since we have already established that the abstractions of "the subject" and "history" are variable products of both discursive praxis and material experience, an understanding of the discursive status of the body in literature is crucial to comprehending the construction of history at work in these texts. The postmodernist preoccupation with the difficulty, impossibility, undesirability of saying "I" (claiming the imperial rights of the subject) is released from the falsely dichotomized alternative between subject and object as soon as the body comes into sharper focus. For the body is so many things all at the same time. Sometimes the victim of history, it is always the object of historical construction, the site of historical experience, the arbiter of all cognition, and the material ground of freedom. It is a thing and a sign, an inside and an outside, a boundary constantly crossing itself. To dismiss the binary opposition between subject and object in this manner is to rethink the notion of political opposition. If the body, from which neither we nor our cultural projections of the subject can escape, is both within and outside the reach of dominant orders, then resistance to oppression is a matter not of missing heroes beyond the invisible walls of culture but of everyday mortals: you and me, your neighbors on the planet and mine.

The question as to how literature constructs "the individual's role in history" (Ryan 1983: 20) is therefore not primarily a moral issue but a political one. For it cannot be answered without recourse to the social implications of aesthetic constructs of power. In this context the delineation of the sometimes contradictory functions of today's body requires two additional elaborations, each of which will be guiding the analytical expeditions into the texts to which subsequent chapters are devoted. First, it would be a grievous error to overlook the fact that, although real bodies all share in discursivity and materiality, they do not by any means do so uniformly. This is where a rigorous discussion of feminist positionalities, partaking of both discursivity and materiality, will prove particularly useful in scrutinizing not only historicized and racialized constructions of gender, but also engendered and racialized constructs of German history and national identity. Bodies are constructed in different ways for different social groups, these differences often being a function—at least in part—of interlocking formations characterized by race, gender, class, ethnicity, and nationality. To ignore the multiplicity of socialized and aestheticized bodies and the tensions of difference that set them into motion would be to subject the material bodies I have invoked to yet another crude abstraction. While we have already ascertained that the body in literary texts exists only as aesthetic construct, and feminist scholarship has long since established that "woman" is a projection of sociohistorical discourse, it remains to be said that race, too, will be explored here as what one African American scholar has characterized as a fiction (Gates 1986: 4–5) or, as one Afro-German writer has argued, a politically charged "hypothetical construct" (Opitz 1986: 89).[46]

That the body and its social characteristics should be so heavily constructed brings us to a second elaboration, which concerns the literary techniques used to project various images of the body. If the novels of the earlier postwar period relied primarily on the body for its metaphoric or allegorical value, what aesthetic alternatives do we find in more recent prose, and what can we learn from them about the subjective agents of our present history? In the West German context of the last twenty years one could argue that the body in literature functions no longer as the mere object (victim) of history or as an allegorical emblem for the nation (or its moral conscience) but rather as the heterogeneous site of contested identities. One of the questions to be pursued in this study is how literary representations of difference reflect or enact the historical embodiment of contested and conflicted identities.

The fact that I have chosen here to explore these questions in prose texts by Anne Duden, TORKAN, and Jeannette Lander is not meant to indicate that women (as a group) write differently from men (as a group). Since terms and concepts relevant to the issue of positionality have figured predominantly and with increasing frequency in feminist theories of literature and culture, however, it seems most fruitful to begin with these theories and some German-language texts that challenge their presuppositions (in every sense of the word "challenge").[47] This will necessitate a closer look at *specific* ways in which gender is produced and represented concurrently with— albeit not parallel to—constructions of race, class, ethnicity, and nationality. This procedure cannot help but raise vital questions concerning the constitution of both contemporary German culture and feminist models of minority discourse. The 1990 "unification" of the two German states founded in 1949 has served as only one forceful reminder that postwar contestations of "German" identity (construed in terms of both personal and national identity) have always been about the making and remaking of German history. While some might argue that a detailed interrogation of concepts of feminist theory, minority discourse, and cultural heterogeneity is of merely peripheral interest to the field of contemporary German Studies, the analytical excursions on which we are about to embark are undertaken with the alternative understanding that this type of investigation has vital implications for precisely this field. The body is my starting point, a resting place that prompts me to move on, my own boundary as well as my vehicle for crossing it. Although I would not say that the bodies in the texts I am about to discuss know no bounds, I contend that they are delimited only by what we are and are not able to discern in their configurations. One might say: This is history in and of our making.

2 | Anne Duden's *Übergang*
Racism and Feminist Aesthetics: A Provocation

The contemporary West German discussion of what it means to write a text appropriate to women's experience began with the 1975 publication of a slim volume entitled *Shedding,* in which Verena Stefan explores the various power structures inherent in the relationship between a young physical therapist and her lover, a male Marxist activist.[1] Specifically, it was Stefan's critical focus on the limitations of sexist language and male-oriented sexuality that attracted the attention of West German feminists. What has generally gone unnoticed, however, is that this historically important text also perpetuates racist stereotypes regarding the sexual sensibilities of blacks. The protagonist is sorely disappointed to learn that her black male lover is no less sexist than her white boyfriend, a disappointment that stems from two assumptions: that one oppressed group is automatically more sensitized to the sufferings of any other oppressed group and that black people in general are *by nature* more "in their bodies" than whites (Stefan 1978, esp. 28). The common denominator here is a blindness to the historical specificity of various manifestations and imbrications of sexism and racism in very different social contexts. The protagonist does not wonder, for example, why white American women as a whole did not all denounce the institutionalized enslave-

37

ment of black men and women. Since the author never subjects the protagonist's experiences or her interpretations of them to any form of critical distancing, what has passed as a watershed feminist critique in West Germany explicitly asserts that sexism goes deeper than racism or economic oppression—an assertion that does not account for the very real possibility that specific manifestations of feminism may be implicated in systems of oppression not determined by gender alone.

The fact that racist stereotypes exist in a book that was of such initial importance to the contemporary West German discussion of feminist aesthetics may be an unfortunate coincidence. The textual significance accorded yet another racist premise in a more recent, far more complex text by another German woman writer suggests, however, that it behooves us as feminist critics to examine the potentially racist abuses and implications of some aspects of feminist aesthetics. By analyzing the varying functions of blackness in Anne Duden's *Opening of the Mouth,* originally published in German in 1982, as they relate to the notion of negativity in feminist theories of women's culture, we can explore how it is that a racist image becomes the pivot on which a text that aspires to feminist aesthetics comes to turn.[2] What bearing do the textual complexities of *Opening of the Mouth* have on the more general questions we do and do not ask regarding the relationship between racism and feminist aesthetics?[3]

Duden's tendentially positive appropriation of blackness on behalf of a female subjectivity evidences, on the one hand, a close affinity to generally held premises about *écriture féminine*. On the other hand, however, the racist core-image of this text underscores the issue of positionality vis-à-vis the dominant order for author, character, and reader alike. Ignoring the racism of the text's central image allows for a reading that is all too compatible with a "universal" understanding of what it means to write a text we might be tempted to call woman-centered. The racism in Duden's aesthetic, once it is named, forces us to acknowledge that the experience of femaleness is historically, socially, and racially specific. The political recognition of differences among women in the same or different cultures and societies thus suggests a far more rigorously differentiated understanding of feminist aesthetics than is often practiced.[4]

Duden's creative debut on the literary scene met with high praise from both establishment literary critics and feminists.[5] Only in rare instances, however, did the reviewers mention that the central episode, in which the protagonist, her brother, and two friends suffer an apparently unprovoked attack by a group of GIs in a West Berlin discotheque, involves a group of *black* GIs.[6] The attackers are never named, their faces never described, their motivations never analyzed, nor are their numbers ever properly counted. They are characterized only by ruthless, unexplained violence, which takes the form of "a moveable but impenetrable wall" (57). This highly questionable equation of a group of faceless blacks with what functions implicitly in the text as indiscriminate evil is rendered all the more problematic by the consequences of this attack for the female narrator. The brick that smashes through the windshield as she tries to drive herself and her companions to safety literally destroys the lower half of her face, necessitating a long hospital stay and the painful reconstruction of the part of her that violence has decimated. What we have here, one might contend, is the affirmation of the racist stereotype that black men pose an inherent danger to white people and to white women in particular.

Yet if Duden does affirm this prejudice, she fails to reproduce it in its pure form. The sexual connotations of this particular stereotype would lead one to expect a sexual assault on Duden's protagonist. It is, however, not her vaginal opening but her mouth that is violated. She is, quite literally, *ent-mündigt* (the unconventionally hyphenated version of the German term implies that she has been deprived of her mouth as well as of her right to speak for herself).[7] The focus of the cultural critique articulated by the text is thus not woman's sex in the narrow sense of the term but her gender (the experience of which is, of course, based on her sex).[8] The threat of indistinguishable darkness, perceived as a threat to life itself (60) and embodied by the black GIs, is thus linked and likened to the protagonist's inability to speak.

Before closely examining how blackness relates to speechlessness in *Opening of the Mouth*, it is useful to recall some of the more common premises found in feminist theory regarding the problems women encounter in finding a voice of their own. What follows does not by any means pretend to be a complete account of feminist theories of language, which are both varied and complex; rather, it sketches some of the steps leading from the understanding of language as oppression to the manifestation of the female body as a voice that cannot be silenced, even by language. This progression is crucial to the textual analysis at hand since it is around the function of the body in Duden's text that, first, a feminist notion of negativity as opposition to the dominant order crystallizes, and, second, the issue of what I call positionality asserts itself, thereby throwing into question that very assumption of feminist negativity as opposition. In this instance it is the racist core-image of the text that insists that we acknowledge the weight of positionality. For the purposes of this volume, negativity as opposition, manifestations of a feminist "bodyspeak," racist imagery, and positionality must all be thought *together,* or else none of the above will be properly understood in context.

Feminist critics of Western patriarchal literature see language as a phallocentric system that controls and dominates women as "other." Many women writers and theorists speak to, and beyond, these barriers by giving voice to women's bodies. Stefan's *Shedding* is an early, admittedly problematic, attempt at this. In "The Sex Which Is Not One," Luce Irigaray's famous arguments against "fixed, immobilized" meanings and identities are based on the implications of female organs for female sexuality and subjectivity (Irigaray 1980). Hélène Cixous notes, "Women must write through their bodies," a conviction also expressed by writers such as Adrienne Rich and Christa Reinig.[9] As Elaine Showalter points out, however, in her review of the biological perspective of feminist criticism, "there can be no expression of the body which is unmediated by linguistic, social, and literary structures" (Showalter 1982: 19). Woman's body can nonetheless be said to assume particular significance in the context of feminist writing, since the cultural notion of femaleness (*Weiblichkeit*) is inscribed on it. As Sigrid Weigel argues, "Woman . . . *embodies* femaleness, that is to say, her body is defined and pinpointed as the locus of femaleness in the male order" (Weigel 1984a: 109). This clearly indicates something of a double bind for the woman trying to write through her body. On the one hand, feminist theory cites that body as resistant or in opposition to the dominant system of order and signification. On the other hand, and at the same time, that body is a cultural construct through and on which that system is inscribed. Analyzing images of women in the tradition of bourgeois literature, Weigel has concluded that "the actual battlefield is the female body" (Weigel 1983a: 142). The same might be said, I would argue, albeit for different reasons, of the female body in feminist texts.

In the unconventionally materialist social theory of Oskar Negt and Alexander Kluge the body is seen concretely as that through which all human experience is filtered, processed, and pursued; it is at once an organ for both personal and social orientation. Never privy to a fixed, permanent identity, they contend, it can sometimes be the battleground for conflicting social antagonisms in the same person (Negt and Kluge 1981: 782). This allowance for multiple, conflicting subjectivities within the same body comes very close to some instances of feminist theory that owe more to poststructuralism than to dialectical materialism (see, for example, Irigaray 1980). Negt and Kluge do not, however, address the specific cultural value assigned to the female body as the embodiment of femaleness. Feminist writing may well provide the meeting ground between theories that assume the primacy of material relations and those that assume the primacy of discourse and signification. The female body is a material organ of woman's own (self-determined) orientation *as well as* the locus of her cultural signification. What this means concretely for the feminist author is that the female body must be charted as both friendly and enemy territory.

This, of course, renders *opposition* to dominant structures of language and signification problematic. The Lacanian designation of woman as lack or absence, the negative to the phallocentric positive, must be distinguished from the negative perceived as opposition (resistance) to the dominant order. It is the former to which Cixous refers when she asserts, "We have no womanly reason to pledge allegiance to the negative" (Cixous 1980: 255). Kristeva means oppositional subversion when she claims that "a feminist practice can only be negative" (Kristeva 1980: 137).[10] Weigel assesses this type of negativity as opposition to the "claim of universality" from which women's experience and self-articulation have traditionally been excluded and warns repeatedly against the dangers of filling in the real gaps of women's experience with the projected presence of utopian images (see Weigel 1984a: 107; 1984b: 9, 11; 1985: 59, 74; 1986).

This danger of positively occupying a negative movement (movement in the sense of passage or, if one will, *Übergang* or "transition") has its unfortunate counterpart in the tendency to celebrate oppositional negativity for women in a way that confuses the negative with absence or silence, which is, after all, the space that patriarchy has accorded women all along. It is, for example, extremely problematic when Susan Gubar extrapolates from Isak Dinesen's short story "The Blank Page" to imply that resistance in general, for women, articulates itself on a blank page and, further, that women writers should "contribute to the blank pages of our future history" (Gubar 1982: 93). The distinction we make between women and "woman" as a cultural construct in traditional male discourse (see Martin 1982; 1983: 212) must also be kept in mind when we grapple with femaleness in women's literature. Weigel cautions against what she perceives as Cixous's and Irigaray's tendency to mystify and hence dehistoricize femaleness and urges us to differentiate more carefully among real women, images of women, and utopia (Weigel 1984a; 1985: 77–78). We are further cautioned not to define femaleness in literature as writing characterized predominantly by discontinuity and rupture. Weigel thus takes up Cixous's notion of the impossibility of defining "a feminine practice of writing" but warns us against making this resistance to definition into yet another metaphor for femaleness (Weigel 1986; Cixous 1980: 253).

The negative or oppositional value of feminist writing is both circumscribed and complicated by the positionality of the woman author with regard to the dominant order. Inge Stephan and Sigrid Weigel refer to her position as one of "simultaneous exclusion and participation" (Stephan and Weigel 1983: 5; see also Martin 1983: 213–14). Assessing the relevance of Foucault's work for feminist theory, Biddy Martin similarly stresses the need to "deconstruct monolithic concepts of *the* oppressor and *the* oppressed" (Martin 1983: 210; 1982). Not surprisingly, both Weigel and Martin argue for a "doubled strategy" based on their understanding of women's "double existence" (Martin 1982: 13; Martin 1983: 212; Weigel 1985). This cuts deeper than Cixous's call for women writing their selves "to break up, to destroy; and to foresee the unforeseeable, to project" (Cixous 1980: 245) because it speaks for the historical contextualization of writing strategies for women. Feminist writing strategies are necessarily bound to the extraliterary struggle for social and cultural self-determination, a struggle that requires some working notion of historical agency for women.[11] Accepting negativity as a mere metaphor for simplistic opposition to dominant structures of signification and subject-hood would deny women this agency, relegating them to their own form of nonspeech and confining them to a "safe" corner from which they can oppose but not change the dominant order. When Weigel speaks of feminist utopia as "imaginable and testable only in a fragmentary fashion," it is not in allegiance to the negative as lack but in awareness of women's double existence both inside and outside language and ideology (Weigel 1984a: 107).[12] Any utopian undertaking must take this double existence into account.[13]

How then does this understanding of a "concrete utopia" (to borrow a phrase from the German philosopher Ernst Bloch) relate to images of blackness in *Opening*?[14] On one level, blackness is used to represent the female protagonist's exclusion from the patriarchal order of signification, an exclusion that Duden intermittently inverts into *positive* images of blackness: this yields negativity as opposition. On another level, however, we must realize that women are both included and excluded from dominant orders *in different ways* depending on factors such as race, class, age, religion, sexual preference, and national context. This demands that we acknowledge how the factor of positionality effectively challenges any simplistic or universalized assumption of negativity as opposition for women. Duden's protagonist is not Everywoman. She is a white, German, non-Jewish woman who, having been a young girl during World War II, feels herself victimized by her culture and yet realizes that she belongs to "the species of those responsible" (64), that is, responsible for the genocide of the Jews. How much of her experience is German, how much of it female, how much of it white? It is to Duden's great credit that she does not allow us to isolate surgically one from the other, for it is only historically, in the context of these other factors, that gender can be experienced. While certain images of blackness may adequately depict some aspects of the protagonist's existence as a woman in West German society, the specifically racist image of the black GIs reflects back only the whiteness of her own skin and experience.[15] As a white German woman she is caught in the cross fire of racial tensions in a culture whose present sensibilities with regard to race are determined by responses to the Nazi past, the presence of black American soldiers stationed in West Germany and West Berlin, and the continued employment of the so-called guest workers from countries such as Turkey, Yugoslavia, Italy, and Greece.[16] The conditions under which Duden's protagonist experiences "simultaneous exclusion and participation" vis-à-vis the dominant order cannot be considered identical to those experienced by an Afro-German woman reading this text or by the sister of a black GI reading it. Neither can I, as a white, American, Jewish woman find the terms of my own existence mimetically reflected in the experience of Duden's female protagonist or in the images of blackness that she has appropriated. It is only in particular shards of the mirror she holds out to me that I am able to recognize myself at all. The shock of simultaneous recognition in and alienation from this feminist text is what makes the images of blackness in *Opening* and the issue of positionality they suggest both deeply unsettling and potentially productive.

The chapter that lends its title to Duden's book in the German edition is situated in the middle of a series of shorter texts, all of which challenge the traditional distinction between inner and outer space by rendering that barrier so ambiguous as to be meaningless. This spatial ambiguity is echoed in a more general dissolution of boundaries. In one text it rains up as well as down, in another everything fuses into "a gigantic unit," and in a third the narrator cannot distinguish between noise and silence (38, 48, 98). It is significant that Duden asserts the primacy of space over temporality. There are enough intertextual allusions for us to assume that the different figures and narrative voices in this series of texts refer to "the same person," but, if so, we are compelled to see her as a composite of multiple subjectivities. As Duden herself writes in one text: "I and I, we hear each other" (44). "Heart and Mouth," a story that precedes "Transition," might well refer to the psychological and physical aftermath of the attack that does not occur until three stories later. Duden's refusal to adhere to linear time or to single, clearly delineated identities allows her images of spatial ambiguity to speak more forcefully than they otherwise might. Duden makes us listen to the silence of women's experience by making us feel the fullness of the empty space traditionally accorded us.[17]

The ambiguity between inner and outer space in "Transition" is developed primarily through the "bodyspeak" of the female protagonist and through her ambivalent attitudes toward darkness and light. "The Country Cottage," the first story in the series, relates the experience of a woman housesitting in the countryside. Initially, the blinding white light outside the house, the seemingly endless darkness inside, and the discomfort she experiences making the transition from one to the other (13–14) cause her to lose all sense of orientation. "I couldn't focus my gaze on anything any more" (14). Gradually, there is an approximation of the light conditions inside and outside the house (23) until one night, when the woman becomes obsessed with her fear of an intruder who might be lurking in the darkness outside the lit house, waiting to do her harm. "The darkness immediately opened up—especially behind me—like a bottomless sack which, billowing and lurching, was lying in wait to throw itself over my head and thus throw me right out of control and fell me once and for all" (27). She is finally able to lock herself into the bedroom, hoping to sleep in spite of her fears. "Instead the impenetrable darkness towered omnipotently around me and over me" (27). Not any human attacker but darkness itself emerges as the real invader here. While darkness is seen as life-threatening in "The Country Cottage," it is perceived as desirable in "The Art of Drowning." "During the day I mainly keep myself busy by waiting for it to get dark again. In the dark the invisible behaves more casually and naturally" (124). In the context of women's relegation to absence, darkness is considered the home of that which has been rendered invisible, that is, women's experience and subjectivity. The following passage reads almost like a direct contribution to the feminist commentary on the patriarchal order: "Compared with the prevailing peace, the light and the order, however, the darkness is too weak and too short. It has long been no effective alternative. But perhaps the day will come when it will no longer be light" (124).

The ambivalence toward darkness finds its most critical articulation in "Transition," the same text in which the death threat associated with loss of contours or dissolution of boundaries is most trenchantly conveyed. The text actually begins not with the injury to the woman but with an attack on her brother, who is beaten at night by a group of black GIs. The same group, "a dark, man-high wall" (59), waits outside the discotheque to attack the car in which its victims try to flee. The sister's subsequent injury brings her to the hospital, where she sees her anesthetist as a "black face" (66) against the neon hospital light. "He belongs to them. They want to kill me" (66). Here blackness is clearly reserved for perceived threats to her life, although the customary distinction between helper and attacker is negated by their shared blackness. Elsewhere, however, she perceives the darkness of night as her ally (68). In a reversal of what is generally considered normal, she claims: "The emergency lighting extinguished any orientation" (73).

By the same token, the injured woman's reaction to the partial destruction of her face is not what we might expect. We as readers are spared few of the unpleasant details either of her injury or of the reconstruction of her mouth. Going to feel her lips after being hit, she feels instead "torn and burst pulp and loose teeth hanging in it" (60). The nurse at the hospital gives her a basin to catch the "stream of blood, slime and saliva," and, were she to lie down, she would be suffocated by all these fluids that would flow back into her (61). Tellingly, the narrative voice shifts from the third to the first person at the point of the operation. While the account of the attack is narrated in the third person, the first person asserts itself when the doctor begins to reconstruct the formless mess she has where her face should be. This is, however, not the same first person that would have spoken had it been given a voice before the attack. "With a bloodless, precise cut the doctor separated me from what was" (62). "What was" was society's imposition and the woman's assumption of an identity inappropriate to her own subjectivity. One is tempted to call this a reversal of the familiar Freudian dictate: *Wo Ich war, soll Es werden* (Where ego was, id shall be). But the narrative voice speaks as *Ich* (I), not as *Es* (id). She does not relinquish her claims to an *Ich* altogether but problematizes her choices by welcoming the destruction of her mouth.[18] "The hole, the trap was to be stopped up, scarcely had it been ripped open. Yet in fact I could consider it fortunate that now, finally, my anatomy too had cracked, that my body could begin to catch up on what had until then been reserved only for my brainhead: following the limitless chaos of the world along all its secret pathways and everywhere where it made itself noticeable, to let it break into me then, and rage in me. Basically, I was relieved" (63). The terror we would normally associate with such an attack is experienced instead when medicine attempts to repair the damage. "The terror would abate to the degree in which what was broken could not be mended and intactness could not be restored" (63), an image that binds her former face, the attackers, and the medical personnel in a collusion of constriction. That which is soft and formless resists the penetration of the phallic "muzzle protector"; she considers herself "impaled" (75–76). Each stage of the "recovery" brings with it a growing sense of confinement. Her mouth is literally wired shut for weeks: "A feeling of inescapable narrowness, as though I were shut into myself and the key had been taken away" (84). She does not want to accept this: "That constantly something would be forced together in me that wasn't supposed to be. An exasperated, frantic speechlessness wanted to scream itself hoarse" (84). Duden's text speaks the speechlessness that refuses its own negation but struggles to find words to speak. For this reason the female protagonist suffers her injury as both pain and opportunity.[19] Her iv is both "gallows" and "umbilical cord" (67). The positive value of her effacement lies in the negativity not of nonidentity but of antiidentity in the dominant scheme of things. The narrative voice rejects identification; the I she does claim lies outside the *image* that others seek to recognize as her (see 69). Her physical disfigurement thus represents an approximation between the inner space of her subjectivity and the outer space of its representation.

This is how darkness portrayed as threat emerges as a source of potential liberation. The standard association of darkness with absence (of light) and silence is inverted when the woman fills that darkness with her own presence and her struggle for self-articulation. At least, this is one possible reading of "Transition." The black holes of history that mine the German protagonist's childhood experience of World War II and later postwar Germany are similarly illuminated by her physical responses to her most recent *Ent-mündigung*. She is constantly battling bouts of nausea. The vomit and blood in her stomach are the fluids inside her that resist the confinement delineated by the contours of the body. As Kristeva says of nausea and vomit, "'I' am in the process of becoming an other at the expense of my own death" (Kristeva 1982a: 3). And yet the protagonist can hardly be said to enjoy her vomit. Her mouth wired shut, she feels it rise and fall inside her as she struggles to keep it down and dreams a scream that can be neither released nor returned (85). This ambivalence toward her vomit has to do with the parallels between the functions of her mouth and her recollections of history.

The flashbacks scattered throughout "Transition" are adult recollections of childhood impressions in which the war and its aftermath figure predominantly. "Outside was the war, that no one wasted words on, that no one described as such" (70). Silence negates the war as it does female subjectivity. Not surprisingly, then, the narrative voice notes a kinship with a historical presence denied: "I the war" (70). The mouth becomes an organ of orientation for the young girl, for whom seeing is swallowing. "I swallowed whole battles away, mountains of corpses of the conquered. . . . I put away what they had put up with. I only did it, I couldn't have said anything about it, as language itself was what was being eaten and swallowed. And I was like a tablet which is uninterruptedly being written on, but not a single letter remains and can be gleaned: the body the unwritten page. Proof for the disappearance of wars" (71). This female body is left as a blank page on the surface only.[20] Inside it is filled with the unarticulated trauma of war, silenced by social convention. Her individual speechlessness is thus indicted along with a collective speechlessness peculiar to the German national experience. As Negt and Kluge have noted, no bodily organ alone has the capacity to yield orientation. Orientation, they contend, stems from the production of a public sphere that links what is public with what is intimate (Negt and Kluge 1981: 1005). Duden writes: "The vacuum mouth became the most important organ." But because there is no public sphere to acknowledge what that female mouth has swallowed, the mouth has only one choice: "to take in and swallow down inwardly. The opposite didn't work" (65). The woman's inner space becomes the site where unarticulated, unappropriated history, both individual and collective, is deposited and left to fester. "I grew up, as though nothing had happened. Only somewhere, unlocatable and unfathomable, something was getting worse and worse" (71). "It slowly became manifest that all those individually overpowered and aborted moments of my life had secretly remained in my body" (80–81). The "vacuum mouth" has become a "mouth of ruins" (83). Rather than building up from the rubble, this *Trümmerfrau* ("woman of ruins") has been condemned to swallow it. (*Trümmerfrauen* were German women who literally cleaned up much of the rubble after the war.) The nausea with which she is plagued is thus also historical: she gags on her own unarticulated experience of the Third Reich and World War II. What has been swallowed revolts inside her.[21]

In this historical sense, too, the attack on her person causes that which has been repressed into controllable form to resume movement. Her housing or casing has been crushed (82), much as the snail shells in her path are crushed by the woman in "The Country Cottage" (17). The woman in "Transition" knows that in all statistical probability medicine will restore her appearance to "normal," but she also knows that what this most recent attack has set into motion cannot and should not be stopped. "What had just happened simply could not be handled yet, neither by memory nor by suppression. . . . What had happened had already almost totally become something invisible, was shapeless and unpredictable. What to do with it?" (81–82).[22] The text flatly refuses to provide answers to this question. The woman feels no relief whatsoever once her wires are removed. "I could open my mouth again but that was just what I was trying to avoid, because it was as though I had to stem stones apart" (91). During the final removal of the tracks that had been laid in her mouth during surgery, she experiences her head as a kind of inverted "construction site," where beams creak and ceilings cave in (91–92). Once again the distinction between construction and destruction is dissolved. The female subject experiences herself as the *object* of both the attackers' destruction and the doctor's reconstruction. The initial destruction allows for the integration between inner and outer space that would be the prerequisite for her self-construction. The medical reconstruction, on the other hand, imposes order from without. No wonder that the woman leaves the doctor's office with a "hollow thank you" (*Übergang*, 101; the official English translation reads "muttered a thank you very much" [*Opening*, 92]). Note, however, that it is not the attack that the protagonist welcomes but the movement precipitated by it.[23]

Yet Duden carefully eschews the glorification of movement for its own sake. Once the pain and physical discomfort subside, the reconstructed woman is left with the emotional residue of the attack. The ending, anything but optimistic, reverts to the image of blackness as a source of death and silence. The protagonist returns from shopping in the "wintry darkness," passes the second, "inner courtyard," and enters the "pitchdark entrance to the lift" (93). Darkness reigns as we realize that this woman identifies with the darkness that fills the inner courtyard. The dark spaces that she has had to traverse are in fact her own, but given the dissolution of boundaries between inner and outer space, we must realize that this inner space is not private but social. "I have laboriously made my way through it, where in fact nothing should move; several times I had the impression the whole world, like this inner courtyard, was empty of people, sold into slavery" (94).

How then does this qualify as "concrete utopia"? The answer lies in the assertion of an "I" that resists external definitions but stops short of celebrating discontinuity for discontinuity's sake. The dark courtyard is described as "a terrain of ruins that has not yet been cleared. The choking sadness so often, the states of pain, the numbness, the sheer boredom of taking one step after another, and the constantly recurring uneasiness, the hunt, the grip on the throat, tighter and tighter. . . . I don't want to have to go through rooms or to buildings like that any more" (93). This "I" anticipates a brighter present without projecting misleadingly positive images onto the present, the future, or the past. As Weigel writes of Inga Buhmann's *Ich habe mir eine Geschichte geschrieben* (I Wrote Myself a Story, 1977): "The detours would be wrong ways only if they were not grasped as *transit*, if the woman contented herself in her development with conquering male spaces."[24] Duden clearly does not conquer the spaces she has us traverse. The transition invoked by the title is one of constant movement and exploration. Its destination cannot be ascribed to any one place since the woman herself is both in and outside the dominant order. The protagonist in Duden's text is thus a working subject, and therein lies the "concrete utopia."

If the analysis ends here, we are left with the impression that the racism in the image of a group of faceless blacks characterized as unmitigated evil is itself mitigated when feminist aesthetics appropriates this image of blackness for its own.[25] Evil becomes good, absence assumes presence, and silence speaks. This is, of course, an oversimplification of the binary oppositions, which do not, as such, play a role in "Transition." Nonetheless, it can be argued that an attack by a group of black GIs allows the female protagonist to assert her subjectivity somewhere between the positive-negative pull of the dominant order and that which it negates. Blackness, one might conclude, cannot be all bad or badness all black. Indeed, a dreamlike recollection of harassment by a group of young, *blond* youths is fused with an image of blacks in a way that momentarily binds black and white together in a conspiracy of evil (77, 79). Yet this poses no effective challenge to the fundamentally racist image of the black attackers. They do have other qualities besides being black and evil; they are also Americans, soldiers, and males. And yet none of these latter qualities is stressed or reinforced throughout the text as only blackness is. Prompted in part by Barbara Smith's contention that "much feminist scholarship has been written as if black women did not exist," Adrienne Rich writes in a lengthy essay: "I no longer believe that 'colorblindness'—if it even exists—is the opposite of racism; I think it is, in this world, a form of naiveté and moral stupidity" (Rich 1979: 300; B. Smith 1977). I have asked myself to what extent *Opening* is tainted with the "white solipsism" (Rich) indicted by Smith and Rich. In other words, does the fact that Duden's text claims blackness *on behalf* of female subjectivity excuse it from the charge of racism?

Whereas images of blackness and darkness are scattered throughout *Opening*, the GIs are the only human figures onto whom blackness is permanently projected. This has striking consequences when we consider that dark spaces are after all not the same as dark men or women.[26] I have already discussed the relationship between the darkness inside the protagonist and the darkness outside her. What does it mean for the dissolution of the boundaries between inner and outer space for this darkness to be projected, as a fixed characteristic, onto a group of human beings? By citing black GIS as aggressors, Duden fuses blackness, otherwise treated positively in the text in its association with the oppressed, with the qualities of the oppressor (male, "impenetrable wall"). While blackness in its other forms can be treated as both the repository of hope and the instrument of its destruction, the particular linkage in the black GIS yields black human beings who function in the text *only* as evil.[27] Duden in fact has the attackers represent what men traditionally fear in women: darkness, loss of self, threat to life. Yet the GIS do pose a real threat to the woman. She is attacked, one might argue, by the male projection of woman projected back onto another group of men. The woman is caught here between the dominant (white) order and the blackness that comes back to haunt it.

"Caught" is a good word for her situation because the two identifying characteristics that the narrative voice cannot flow into and out of are her gender and her race. This constitutes a textual thorn in the theory of oppositional negativity for women. If the story is not about the narrator's relationship to blacks as persons, and it is not, then why use them as a symbol? The particular role of black persons in the text forces the issue of positionality in a way that the other, metaphorical images of blackness in and of themselves do not. The story would surely read differently if the narrator herself were black. A writer like Toni Morrison can use images of "nightshade" and "blackberry" to refer to black experience in a way that is blocked to Duden as a white woman writer.[28] Any appropriation of blackness on her part is necessarily predicated on the experience that white skin brings in a predominantly white society, even if the white woman consciously rejects the dominant order.[29]

Although the race of the female persona is never named, it is clear from the context that she is a white woman in a culture that identifies itself as white. Foreign and appropriated by the text as a symbol of unabashed evil, the black GIS can pose a serious threat to her because they embody what has been severed, silenced, effaced, and repressed. This holds for her personal history as a woman as well as for the missing collective coming to terms with the (Nazi) past (*Vergangenheitsbewältigung*), in which her life as a German is bound. And yet this symbol of the "evil" blacks can function only on the basis of her "privilege." In spite of all the black holes of her history, the narrator is white and can speak only from that perspective. Not all cows are black or even gray in the night in which Duden erases the boundaries between inner and outer space.[30] For her own dark spaces (absences), the narrator lets stand a dark presence (the GIs), but by giving this presence a human form, she reinforces the racist premise of her privileged position—one from which, however, she clearly derives no satisfaction and certainly no identity. While she speaks from the disrupted vantage point of an oppressed gender, the inversions that *Opening* enacts in the relationship between oppressor and oppressed rely on a symbolism that qualifies the narrator as privileged. She is, to be sure, *injured* by the blacks who attack her and her companions, but she is *oppressed* by her entrapment in the privileged position that allows the symbol to function at all.

This particular manifestation of positionality is, furthermore, culturally specific to the West German context. The female protagonist, who realizes that she belongs to "the species of those responsible" for the genocide of the Jews (64), has too much historical consciousness to equate her own victimization as a woman with the victimization of the Jews by the Nazis. This non-Jewish German woman is precluded from appropriating Jewishness as a symbol or as a vehicle with which to express her own, culturally and socially determined victimization. Blackness, on the other hand, would *seem* to provide a more neutral medium with which both to articulate and to challenge this victimization. Such appropriation is, however, *textually* prohibited by the racist image of the black GIs, which essentially undermines the feminist, racially "neutral" expectations evoked by the text. While the piece provides a historical context for its discussion of Jews, there is no comparable context provided explicitly by the text for its treatment of blacks or blackness. Nevertheless, even though the central attack is depicted by the narrator as unprovoked, it seems logical to assume that racial tension must be at least a contributing factor. And yet this assumption is a misleadingly simplistic one if we too glibly conclude that the blacks attack the Germans *because* they are white or that the racist image of the GIs is *merely* a function of the protagonist's white skin per se. We need to know what it means to be black- or white-skinned in any given context. What is missing here is an articulation of the historical context in which the manifestation of racial conflict acquires historically and socially particular meaning. The GIs' own racial awareness has surely been shaped primarily by experiences in the United States, and yet these figures function in the story outside that context. It is their skin color, not the context of their lives, that links the incident both to the textual imagery of blackness and to the life history of the white German protagonist. Although feminist readers may be eager to emphasize the femaleness of the woman's injuries, the latter have just as much to do with the protagonist's being a German who grew up during the Third Reich as with her being a woman. While we may reasonably assume that extratextual racial tension between Afro-Americans and Germans continues to bear traces of the ideology of the "master race," it would be patently ridiculous to contend that the soldiers in the story enact or in any way speak for the vengeance of the Jews. The cross-cultural *specificity* of racial conflict in this particular context is very clearly *not* woven into the texture of the story, which is why the exact relationship of this German woman, Jews, and black GIs remains so disturbingly murky. And yet the unequivocally racist imagery with which the attack at the discotheque is depicted signals that the apparent racial neutrality of the textual appropriation of blackness is bogus. In other words, the racist image of the GIs points a finger at a sociohistorical context that the text itself does not elaborate. In that sense the real "dark presence" of the text is not the group of GIs, nor is it even the collective history of the Germans who were somehow part of the Third Reich. We have seen how the movement of the protagonist's vomit traces the progression from suppression and repression into consciousness and articulation. The presence that *remains* in the darkness in this text are the social and historical forces that are brought to bear on a confrontation between a white, non-Jewish, German woman and a group of black, male soldiers from the United States.

As to whether *Opening* explodes a racist premise or reproduces it, I can only answer, yes, it does both. It is perhaps one of those images that women writers must traverse in all its ugly familiarity in order to destroy.[31] Its racist implications challenge the simple appropriation of images of blackness by feminist aesthetics on behalf of a female subjectivity in whose name this text might otherwise be hailed. *Open-*

ing poses an ineluctable confrontation with women's positionality vis-à-vis the dominant order in specific historical contexts. The racist premise that yields this confrontation is cause not for celebration but for self-reflection. It demands, at the very least, that we examine more rigorously the concrete and hence theoretical implications of any alleged universality of *écriture féminine*.

3 | TORKAN's
Tufan: Brief an einen islamischen Bruder
Inscriptions and Positionalities:
Some Particulars

ONE

Recent anthologies attest to the ongoing sense of exciting and often
distasteful challenge with which feminists have taken up the call of
postmodernism. What is generally at stake in these works is the need
to negotiate between the rock of feminist essentialism, which univer-
salizes women's oppression, and the hard places of poststructuralist
undecidability, which tease us with the play of difference while denying us the work—and accountability—of historical agency.[1] While
the craggy issue of essentialism is by no means unique to Women's
Studies,[2] it is primarily in the area staked out by feminist theory that
we encounter what has been termed "a politics of location."[3] Tropes
of place, location, standpoint (and the attendant ones of cartogra-
phy) are conjured up to circumvent the dangers of essentialism and
indeterminacy. Joining in this invocation, the chapter at hand pursues a concept of positionality that would enable us to distinguish,
with a greater degree of refinement, some of the many ways in which
matter and discourse affect the production of embodied subjectivity.
These comments on *Tufan: Brief an einen islamischen Bruder* (Tufan:
Letter to an Islamic Brother) (1983) permit me to indulge in some
mapping of my own.[4]

The term "positionality" (or "positionalities") is of relatively recent vintage in feminist discourse. Perhaps the most influential theoretician to make use of it is Teresa de Lauretis, whose *Technologies of Gender* (1987) has struck many a resonant chord even outside the realm of film theory, where her work finds its most immediate application. Whereas a focal point of *Alice Doesn't* (de Lauretis 1984) was to restore the body of experience to "the subject of semiosis" (182), *Technologies of Gender* has sparked feminist imaginations by conceptualizing the *production* of gender as "*both the product and the process of its representation*" (de Lauretis 1987: 5). We are urged to move beyond the binary fixation on sexual difference (male/female) seen as universal, anterior even to its own construction in either material or discursive terms. The refusal to conflate gender and sex is not peculiar to de Lauretis,[5] but her writings are frequently cited (in a variety of disciplines) to counter the kind of biological or sociological essentialism that results when feminists privilege sexual difference as the already given grounding for all other differences. The type of feminist analysis under fire here does not allow for differences among or within women; indeed, it allows only for "woman as the difference from man, both universalized; or woman as difference *tout court,* and hence equally universalized" (de Lauretis 1987: 2). De Lauretis's feminist critiques of Foucauldian and Althusserian theories of social technologies and ideological apparati lead her to see the "subject of feminism" as "constructed across a multiplicity of discourses, positions, and meanings, which are often in conflict with one another and inherently (historically) contradictory" (1987: x). This yields "a subject constituted in gender, to be sure, though not by sexual difference alone, but rather across language and cultural representations; a subject engendered in the experiencing of race and class, as well as sexual, relations; a subject, therefore, not unified but rather multiple, and not so much divided as contradicted" (1987: 2).[6]

De Lauretis writes toward and with "a view from 'elsewhere,'" characterized as "the elsewhere of discourse here and now, the blind spots, or the space-off, of its representations." These are "the spaces in the margins of hegemonic discourses, social spaces carved in the interstices of institutions and in the chinks and cracks of the power-knowledge apparati" (1987: 25). It is important to note that, in de Lauretis's analysis, these are the blind spots of a simultaneously "discursive and material heterogeneity" (24), in which "women are both inside and outside gender, at once within and without representation" (10). (She distinguishes between being *outside* representation and being *without* representation.) By accounting for the embodied and inscribed positionalities of social experience, de Lauretis is able to treat women conceptually as both construct-ed and construct-ing, that is, as agents in their own construction. (This is not to say that real women are the agents *of* their own construction.) The subject of feminism that de Lauretis explores is "one whose definition or conception is in progress, in this and other feminist critical texts" (10). This subject of feminism emerges as we attend to the historically specific micropolitical practices of discourse, technology, social organization, and everyday life. While de Lauretis insists on "the tension of contradiction, multiplicity, and heteronomy" (1987: 26) inherent in these micropolitical practices, she does not refer her readers to Oskar Negt and Alexander Kluge, whose social theory of subject-object relations and the "proletarian public sphere" bears many striking resemblances to de Lauretis's own (see the discussion of *Geschichte und Eigensinn* above in Chapter One). Whereas their earlier work on the public sphere as micropolitical practice (1972) *is* cited in *Alice Doesn't,* neither it nor their later work is mentioned in *Technologies of Gender.*[7] To be sure, de Lauretis takes us further than Negt and Kluge by scrutinizing the production of gender and processes of semiosis. But the kind of materiality of embodied experience elaborated by Negt and Kluge is no less relevant to de Lauretis's analysis than the discursive practices she so skillfully deconstructs. Not all feminist theorists who cite de Lauretis on the concept of positionality are as careful as she is to delineate the material relations of embodiment in which political acts of signification occur.[8]

Relying heavily on theses presented by de Lauretis in *Alice Doesn't,* Linda Alcoff foregrounds a concept of positionality in her attempt to keep feminist theory from being stuck between the rock and the hard place named at the outset of this chapter. Originally published in *Signs* in 1988 and reprinted the following year in an anthology entitled *Feminist Theory in Practice and Process,* her essay "Cultural Feminism Versus Post-Structuralism: The Identity Crisis in Feminist Theory" is a response to feminist attempts to define woman and poststructuralist attempts to deconstruct the category altogether (1988: 407).[9] Prompted in part by charges initially leveled by feminists "of color" against mainstream (white, heterosexual, middle-class) feminism,[10] Alcoff looks for a way out of the universalist trap by acknowledging the imbrications of gender, class, and race. That is to say, she wants to recognize differences *among* (although not necessarily *within*) women without succumbing to a pluralism of equally valorized differences (or equally valorized experiences of oppression). This is crucial, since what she fears about poststructuralist "undecidability" (420) is the obstacle it poses to discussing either the oppression of real (and different) women or any concept of feminist agency. In order to traverse this difficult terrain, Alcoff tries to combine "a conception of human subjectivity as an emergent property of a historicized experience" (this is where she relies on de Lauretis) with a modified version of the identity politics usually associated with feminists who are women "of color," Jews, and/or lesbians (431). Alcoff urges us "to recognize one's identity as always a construction yet also a necessary point of departure" (432).

The question arises as to why Alcoff would want to retain any notion of identity politics, a brand of feminism that has been soundly criticized for conflating politics, identity, and experience, for assuming that women's experience is by definition authentic and that feminist politics derives directly from women's allegedly equally authentic sense of identity.[11] As Jenny Bourne is often cited for saying: "Identity Politics is all the rage. Exploitation is out (it is extrinsically determinist). Oppression is in (it is intrinsically personal). What is to be done has been replaced by who am I" (Bourne 1987: 1). Alcoff herself is acutely aware of the essentialist pitfalls of identity politics, and it is precisely in order to neutralize this danger that she introduces the concept of positionality. She takes pains to distinguish between essentialist identity politics and something she calls positional identity politics.

> When the concept "woman" is defined not by a particular set of attributes but by a particular position, the internal characteristics of the person thus identified are not denoted so much as the external context within which that person is situated. The external situation determines the person's relative position, just as the position of a pawn on a chessboard is considered safe or

dangerous, powerful or weak, according to its relation to other
chess pieces. The essentialist definition of woman makes her
identity independent of her external situation. . . . The positional definition, on the other hand, makes her identity relative
to a constantly shifting context, to a situation that includes a
network of elements involving others, the objective economic
conditions, cultural and political institutions and ideologies,
and so on. (433)

Alcoff presents these comments as the answer to her question: "What
does position mean here?" (433). Her elucidation makes it necessary
to ask the question again.

Presumably, Alcoff has decided to use a modified concept of identity politics because she sees identity politics as linked to political action. This supports her stated intention of claiming feminist agency
without repeating the mistakes of feminist essentialism. Yet if we look
more closely at the history of this particular margin of feminist theory,[12] we can see that Alcoff has focused on a specific historical turning point in the development of identity politics. The "Combahee
River Collective Statement" marked the moment when African
American feminists began to insist that feminism acknowledge (1) the
simultaneity of different forms of oppression (race, gender, class)
and (2) the differences between the experiences of white heterosexual feminists and those of other kinds of women. The collective argued strongly against the generalized notion of woman as powerless
victim, since this conceptualization obscured white women's complicity in the oppression of other races *and* it also failed to recognize black
women as political agents of survival. To my mind, Alcoff extrapolates from a historical position taken by certain women "of color" to
shore up a definition of identity politics that tendentially—despite
Alcoff's best intentions—obscures any real, political differences
among (or within) women. Ultimately, her characterization of positionality also negates her assertion of feminist agency.

These problems arise when Alcoff underestimates the significance
(and signification) of women's bodies in the construction of experience, [13] an elision that occurs in her reception of de Lauretis (*Alice
Doesn't*) and in her rather puzzling claim that positional identity politics is materialist (433). Identity politics merits this designation, ac-

cording to Alcoff, because it challenges the universalist premise of humanism and hence addresses different relations to power and oppression for different social groups. When Alcoff repeatedly states or implies, however, that identity politics is something that people, especially "people of mixed races and cultures" (432), have to and do "choose," then materiality is reduced to a matter of taking (choosing) a political stand. This should, in my opinion, not be confused with positionality. Although Alcoff does acknowledge that "we are both subjects of and subjected to social construction" (431), the conflation of standpoint and positionality forecloses important conceptual options for evaluating the embodied nature of these material and discursive constructions.[14] While Alcoff's plea for contextual analysis points us in the right direction, we take an unacceptable shortcut if we look only at positions that are constantly shifting in relation to other positions on an unchanging chessboard. And even though the essay stresses the relational shifts of positionality, women are locked into a single and tendentially universalist position when they are seen as occupying a position that "lacks power and mobility and requires radical change" (434). If this position is occupied by all women alike, then we are left unable to account for real differences among women or for contradictory positionalities within women (conflicting relations to power). Furthermore, if "women's position" is always the same with regard to the nexus of power, then we cannot conceptualize historical change as anything other than changes in costume (the chess pieces satisfy the same functions even though individual sets take on different appearances).

As indicated earlier, many of these problems can be traced to an incomplete reception of de Lauretis's concept of experience. This requires some explanation. Alcoff finds *Alice Doesn't* so promising because its author conceptualizes "real practices and events" and hence avoids the overprivileging of language and textuality. She reads de Lauretis as arguing that gender is "a posit or construct, formalizable in a nonarbitrary way through a matrix of habits, practices, and discourses" (Alcoff 1988: 431). This is not exactly wrong, but it is striking that in her discussion of de Lauretis, Alcoff refers to the influence on that scholar by Jacques Lacan, Umberto Eco, and Charles Sanders Peirce only. De Lauretis herself foregrounds these influences. In the background, however, lurks the social theory of Oskar Negt and Alexander Kluge, whose attention to the materiality of subject-object relations lends considerable cogency to the concept of bodily habits of semiosis that de Lauretis adapts from Peirce. Because she does not see the influence of Negt and Kluge at work here, and because she underestimates the role of embodiment in de Lauretis's understanding of semiotic habit, Alcoff stresses "'discursive configurations,'" which she conceives as a "process of political interpretation" (Alcoff 1988: 425, 431). Trying to account for the not-yet and the not-just of real women's "position,"[15] Alcoff pits empirical subjectivity against metaphysical subjectivity (her choice of words) without acknowledging that there are other approaches to materiality (see above, Chapter One) than the neurophysiological or psychoanalytical ones she rejects.

De Lauretis does not need to resort to metaphysics, for her concept of materiality is already imbued with, albeit not confined to, discursivity. To ignore the embodiment of experience reduces the habits of semiosis to *mere* discourse. Again, this makes it unclear *how* "we are both subjects of and subjected to social construction" (Alcoff 1988: 431). When de Lauretis, on the other hand, speaks of the "micropolitical practices of feminism" (*Technologies of Gender*), she means movements by embodied women, in the here and now, across social and discursive spaces that are both within representation and without it (but not outside it). The "margins of hegemonic discourses," "the chinks and cracks" of our social institutions of power and knowledge (de Lauretis 1987: 25), are in fact the "free spaces" (Negt and Kluge) in which some degree of emancipatory agency (micropolitical practice) is possible. Alcoff's arguments suffer then from a fundamental ambivalence. She conceptualizes positionality as "a place from where meaning is constructed, rather than simply the place where a meaning can be *discovered*" (434). But because she does not address either the materiality or the embodiment of these "meaning effects" (de Lauretis 1987: 18), she is left with "the concept of woman *as positionality*" (Alcoff 1988: 434; my emphasis).[16] This relegates women once again to the status of metaphor, effectively denying them both difference (among and within themselves) *and* agency. Positionality does not demarcate a *place*, nor does it consist of choice alone (although it does entail standpoint). Rather, it characterizes a set of specific social and discursive relations in a given historical moment. These relations concern and also produce gender, race, class, sexuality, ethnicity, and other practices through which power is constructed, exercised, and resisted or challenged. How feminists theorize positionality also affects this construction and the relationship of real women to it. Positionality can serve as an analytical as well as a strategic tool with which to explore women's roles as both subjects and objects of construction.[17]

TWO

Given the history of feminist theory, it is not altogether surprising that Alcoff concludes that we are to conceive of "woman" as positionality. From the late 1970s to the late 1980s women's "place" in relation to institutionalized power was discursively located *outside* an allegedly monolithic center of power, on the *margin* of power, or subsequently in an alternative *center* of power. All these conceptions rely on the prioritizing of sexual difference as primary and stable. The tendencies to essentialize women wherever they are "located" and to totalize power have often been accompanied by the slippage whereby "woman's place" becomes a metaphor for women's positions in historical contexts. Place, location, position in turn become metaphors for women themselves (or more precisely, for "woman" itself). The result is not all that different from poststructuralist treatments of "femaleness" as a metaphor for discursive difference per se. Alcoff's concept of "woman as positionality" thus tries to break the mold but succeeds only in cracking it.

The "politics of location" (Rich 1984; Mohanty 1988), especially feminist conceptualizations of the relationship between margins and centers of power, is not just about "place" but also about movement.[18] The danger here is that movement itself (dance and play are popular variations) becomes another metaphor for women's "position." De Lauretis (1987: 26) provides an alternative, positional conceptualization of feminist movements.

> The movement in and out of gender as ideological representation, which I propose characterizes the subject of feminism, is a movement back and forth between the representation of gen-

der (in its male-centered frame of reference) and what that representation leaves out or, more pointedly, makes unrepresentable. It is a movement between the (represented) discursive space of the positions made available by hegemonic discourses and the space-off, the elsewhere, of those discourses: those other spaces both discursive and social that exist, since feminist practices have (re)constructed them, in the margins (or "between the lines," or "against the grain") of hegemonic discourses and in the interstices of institutions, in counter-practices and new forms of community. These two kinds of spaces are neither in opposition to one another nor strung along a chain of signification, but they coexist concurrently and in contradiction. The movement between them, therefore, is not that of a dialectic, of integration, of a combinatory, or of *différance*, but is the tension of contradiction, multiplicity, and heteronomy.

The movements entailed in such micropolitical practices are both material and embodied.[19] That is to say, the embodiment on which feminist movements are predicated cannot be explained by the body as metaphor (an all-too-familiar inscription for "woman").[20] When Adrienne Rich wrote that "a place on the map is also a place in history" (Rich 1984: 212), she emphasized (without naming the term) the positionality of real women's bodies as opposed to purely discursive configurations of these bodies. While attention to processes of embodiment is crucial, it is important not to grant the body an absolute authority that it cannot legitimately claim, given that even real bodies are also subject to social and discursive construction. Neither should the female body, or the margins of power, be conceived as a fixed "place."

Writing against what they call the "all-too-common conflation of experience, identity, and political perspective" (Martin and Mohanty 1986: 192), Biddy Martin and Chandra Talpade Mohanty note that the "search for a secure place is articulated in its ambivalence and complexity through the ambiguous use of the words *place* and *space* in precisely the ways they have become commonplace within feminist discourse" (206). Their keen analysis of Minnie Bruce Pratt's autobiographical essay about growing up as a white lesbian in the southern United States applies the concept of "positionality" and "positionalities" (208) to elaborate "the fundamentally *relational* nature of identity" (196; my emphasis). This is closely akin to Alcoff's position, as is Martin and Mohanty's stance against feminist essentialism and for a notion of feminist agency. In contrast to Alcoff, however, Martin and Mohanty develop an understanding of women's "situatedness in the social" (194) that is based on positionality as historical, material, and experiential. The micropolitical practices they see traced in Pratt's essay are reminiscent of those addressed by Negt and Kluge and de Lauretis.

> The exposure of the arbitrariness and the instability of positions within systems of oppression evidences a conception of power that refuses totalizations, and can therefore account for the possibility of resistance. "The system" is revealed to be not one but multiple, overlapping, intersecting systems or relations that are historically constructed and recreated through everyday practices and interactions, and that implicate the individual in contradictory ways. All of that without denying the operations of actual power differences, overdetermined though they may be. Reconceptualizing power without giving up the possibility of conceiving power. (209–10)

Martin and Mohanty are thus able to conceptualize relations of power and women's experience of and in these relations without totalizing or essentializing either power or experience. This allows for differences among women as well as for the contradictory positionalities of a single woman's experience. Pratt's demographical mapping of specific "race, class, and gender conflicts" (196) shows her living "on the edge" (201) of a particular nexus of power, but Martin and Mohanty do not reduce that edge to a fixed place. By addressing the material configurations of power and experience—which include Pratt's body both as inscribed with, circumscribed by, specific relations of power *and* as the organ of her own feminist agency, her politicized, contextualized movements—Martin and Mohanty also manage to distinguish between standpoint and positionality.

Such a refined concept of positionality, which speaks to the political embodiment of meaning effects, also—and this is important— "refuses the all-too-easy polemic that opposes victims to perpetrators" (Martin and Mohanty, 209). This refusal is germane to debates about feminist essentialism, as is made clear in Mohanty's comparison (1988) of Robin Morgan's introduction to *Sisterhood Is Global* (1984) and Bernice Johnson Reagon's essay "Coalition Politics" (1983). Mohanty's own essay, subtitled "Locating the Politics of Experience," targets a universalist notion of purportedly authentic experience. (Interestingly enough, Mohanty relies on de Lauretis's introduction to *Feminist Studies/Critical Studies* for her critical treatment of feminist experience.) When women are conceived as a homogeneous group by virtue of their supposedly shared *"experience of oppression,"* then the only difference in which they are seen to participate is that between male and female (i.e., sexual difference) (35). This posits women, Mohanty rightly contends, outside history, beyond "material referentiality," free of accountability, and stripped of emancipatory agency (35–38). In this view, she argues, "men *participate* in politics while women can only hope to *transcend* them" (38). Morgan's assumption of universal sisterhood conceives women's experience, as Mohanty puts it, "along two parameters: woman as victim, and woman as truthteller" (34). Mohanty cites this discursive erasure of political differences among women (which is accompanied by an implicit erasure of their embodied positionalities) as an effect of the "logic of imperialism" (34, 41). All this may serve as a rather circuitous route toward discussing a novel written in German by a woman of Third World origin. Born in Iran in 1941, TORKAN emigrated to the Federal Republic of Germany in 1964 and subsequently became a naturalized (!) citizen of that country. *Tufan: Brief an einen islamischen Bruder* (Tufan: Letter to an Islamic Brother) is an autobiographical narrative of her traumatic childhood and adolescence in Iran and her adult attempts to grapple with the ghosts of that past. The text raises questions about universalist conceptualizations of woman as victim and as truthteller. It will come as no surprise that these questions are related to the embodiment of positionality.

THREE

During an interview in October 1989, TORKAN remarked that the only group of German readers to respond to the publication of *Tufan* in

1983 were West German feminists, who applauded the book because it so clearly depicted the female protagonist, in their view, as a victim (in this case, of Islamic patriarchy).[21] Since this reception of the novel cannot be documented (TORKAN was invited by various women's groups to give several readings from the text, but to date there has been only minimal published commentary on it by any critic), this chapter offers an alternative, not to any particular actual reading of *Tufan*, but to a potential kind of reading that the text might seem to invite. After all, the entire first half of the novel, entitled "Erinnerung" [Remembrance], details the brutal victimization of a young Iranian girl by her younger brother, even at an early age a religious fanatic who considers it his duty to police his sister's activities lest she violate the principles of Islam and hence bring dishonor to their family. This entails both physical and verbal abuse perpetrated by Tufan against his sister, Asar. Indeed, the narrator characterizes herself as "das ständige Opfer" [the perpetual victim] (11).

This kind of reading lends itself all too easily to the "production of the 'Third World Woman' as a singular monolithic subject" (Mohanty 1984: 333), a production that, as Mohanty points out in her discussion of colonialist discourses in feminist scholarship, in effect reduces Third World women to the status of objects (Spivak [1987b: 254] speaks of "the continuing subalternization of Third World material"). This happens when Western feminists take as their point of departure a universalist concept of oppression, whereby men are seen as power*ful* and women as power*less*. The sociological dichotomy posited between victim and oppressor replaces the biological one predicated on sexual difference "in order, however, to create the same—a unity of women" (Mohanty 1984: 340). Contextual specificity is ignored in this accounting, Mohanty charges, since it would challenge "the image of an 'average third world woman'" (337). When white Western feminists write about Third World women this way, they implicitly instate themselves as "the true 'subjects'" of feminism (351). All women are understood to be victims, but because many white Western women understand themselves to be better educated, more modern, and *less* oppressed (more free than their Third World "counterparts"), they claim to know better what oppression means and what freedom would or should mean.[22] The self-proclaimed "subjects" of universal feminism thus represent themselves as victims of patriarchy (also universally conceived), at the same time claiming the privileges of alleged superiority that accrue to citizens of the Western world. Mohanty articulates the theoretical and political flaws in this stance. (1) "While feminist writing in the U.S. is still marginalized (except from the point of view of women of color addressing privileged White women), Western feminist writing on women in the third world must be considered in the context of the global hegemony of Western scholarship" (336). (2) The problem with treating contextual specificity as secondary to the presumed anteriority of oppression is that "it assumes men and women are already constituted as sexual-politicial subjects *prior* to their entry into the arena of social relations" (340).

Echoes of de Lauretis and Negt and Kluge: the failure to account for the *production* of power (or of difference or of gender and so on) in specific historical contexts, characterized by material and discursive heterogeneity, allows us (leads us) to totalize, universalize, essentialize concepts of woman/women, man/men, the Third World, and the West. As James Clifford has remarked, "It is less common today than it once was to speak of 'the East,' but we still make casual reference to 'the West,' 'Western culture,' and so on. Even theorists of discontinuity and deconstruction such as Foucault and Derrida continue to set their analyses within and against a Western totality" (Clifford 1988: 272). As Clifford elaborates in his comments on Said's study of Orientalism, "'the West' itself becomes a play of projections, doublings, idealizations, and rejections of a complex, shifting otherness" as Western culture "continuously constitutes itself through its ideological constructs of the exotic" (272). According to Clifford, "the West" is no more a monolithic center of power than "the Third World" is a homogeneous periphery.[23] This is *not* to say that relations of power cease to be an issue.

> When we speak today of the West, we are usually referring to a force—technological, economic, political—no longer radiating in any simple way from a discrete geographical or cultural center. This force, if it may be spoken of in the singular, is disseminated in a diversity of forms from multiple centers—now including Japan, Australia, the Soviet Union, and China—and is

articulated in a variety of "micro-sociological" contexts. (Clifford 1988: 272)

It is these diverse microsociological contexts (Clifford credits the
French anthropologist Jean Duvignaud with the term) in which the
micropolitical practices invoked by de Lauretis, Martin and Mohanty,
and Negt and Kluge are enacted and inscribed.

Innocence, as one can see, is impossible.[24] My own positionality informs the readings I articulate here. I am a white Jewish citizen of the
United States, tenured at a large public university in the American
Midwest; much of my recent research addresses the construction of
minority discourse in contemporary West German culture. The specific implications of my own positionalities (certainly not all of which
have been named here) will undoubtedly be subject to the scrutiny of
others. Yet as I write, I know that within the contexts of German political and cultural history, I write as an "other" (a Jew, an American)[25]
about an other "other" (a woman of Third World origin). The concept of positionality I have sought to develop should allow for us both
as subjects of and as subject to (embodied) construction without ho-
mogenizing the specific manifestations or the political implications of
either subject or object status. Elsewhere I have argued that to categorize TORKAN as an author of "migrants' literature" in Germany
rather than of West German literature of the 1980s is to perpetuate
the ethnocentric notion of an identifiably "German" core (or essence)
of contemporary literature from which difference can be added or
subtracted (Adelson 1990a). Even though I am writing the study at
hand as a scholar and (associate) professor of German literature, I do
not write from or for a purported center of German-ness (how could
I?). The concept of positionality, however, also enables me to acknowledge my complicity as well as my responsibilities in construct-
ing TORKAN as a Third World German woman author of German literature. How to do justice to this task?

FOUR

By virtue of my theoretical elaborations I have already entered into
several discourses. Primary among them in this chapter is the discourse of feminism, where the construction of a monolithic "Third

World" and the homogenized construction of "Third World Women" in particular have been rigorously attacked. One of the reductions to haunt these constructions is the frequent equation between "the Third World" and "the world of Islam." An all-too-familiar string of reductions runs like this: The Third World is monolithic, consisting in its essence of the world of Islam (this reduction has grown increasingly popular since the 1980s, as the Western media have given more coverage to various Islamic fundamentalist movements around the world); the world of Islam is also monolithic, predicated in its essence on an undisputed reading of the Qur'an and Islamic law (this reduction erroneously assumes that there is only one school of Islamic law instead of at least four); the principles of Islam are uniform and rely, in their essence, on the subjugation of Muslim women to Muslim men. Or as Leila Ahmed writes in her discussion of a common American perception of the harem: "Just as Americans 'know' that Arabs are backward, they know also with the same flawless certainty that Muslim women are terribly oppressed and degraded" (Ahmed 1982: 522).[26] Aside from the fact that they fail to account for those parts of the Third World that are not or not primarily Muslim, the reductive equations caricatured here ignore the wide range of diversity that has for centuries characterized the specific historical, political, and cultural manifestations of Islam (see the contributions to *Islam in the Contemporary World* [1980] by its editor Cyriac K. Pullapilly and Seyyed Hossein Nasr for a refreshing contrast to this type of reductionist scholarship).

One could perhaps argue that Western scholars who totalize or essentialize the long history of Islam pursue a "fundamentalist" methodology by treating Islam as natural (or from a Western perspective, "unnatural") and unchanging. This type of ahistoricity contributes to the persistent notion that Muslim women are, by definition, victims, even though, as recent scholarship on women in the diverse worlds of Islam details, there is no "uniform concept of female personhood in Muslim culture" or history (Waines 1982: 653).[27] Whether women in Islam are seen as objects or subjects, weak, sinful, and inferior (to Muslim men) or powerful, venerable, and equal (to Muslim men) depends very much on how one interprets the sacred text of the Qur'an as well as on how one interprets the historical vicissitudes of Muslim

societies. Some feminist scholars have criticized the tendency to privilege not only a *monolithic* concept of Muslim women, but also a *textually codified* one (based on religious and legal documents). This privileging cannot do justice to what Haeri (1989: 149) has called "an
appreciable divergence between the ideal and the actual" (Higgins
[1985: 478–79], Mernissi [1987: viii, x], and Ida Nicolaisen's introduction to Utas 1988 [3] make the point as well). Whether one refers
to this as a split between the actual and the ideal (Haeri) or between
the real and the discursive (Mernissi), we must recall that the concept
of this split can itself be ideological. If we are to avoid the assumption
that the actual/real and the ideal/discursive exist as totally distinct
spheres for Muslim women—in each of which they can function as *either* subject *or* object—then we must somehow account for the multiple positionalities that characterize the material and discursive constructions of their lives. These constructions are produced not in two
discrete spheres but in a process of mutual imbrication. My discussion of the nature of this imbrication addresses a contemporary
arena of West German cultural production only.[28]

Criticizing monolithic constructions of Islam in some anthropological and sociological studies, Chandra Talpade Mohanty identifies five ways in which Third World women have been constructed (in
scholarly discourse) as powerless and homogeneous victims. They
are posited as victims of (1) male violence, (2) the colonial process, (3)
the Arab family, (4) economic development, and/or (5) "*the* Islamic
code" (1984: 338). At least four of these factors could easily be cited as
contributing to Asar's "victimization." The young girl and adolescent
is beaten and harassed by her brother in an Iranian (albeit not, strictly
speaking, Arab) family that condones his behavior; at times the parents actively participate in the beatings. Even though Asar's family—
with the exception of Tufan—is not depicted as being especially religious until the 1970s (her father is a politically "enlightened" man),
we can recognize in their treatment of her the view that a girl on the
threshold of womanhood embodies *fitna* (chaos, disorder), which
threatens to besmirch the *namus* (honor) of the male relatives responsible for safeguarding her moral and sexual integrity. Since Asar's
"transgression" is essentially inevitable (she is a girl, destined to become a sexualized female, a woman), her punishment and humilia-

tion often precede any "real" offense on her part. They are seen as preventive measures; in order to conquer "the witch" in Asar (TORKAN 1983: 11), Tufan must beat his older sister. As the author of *Beyond the Veil* notes, "The Muslim faces two threats: the infidel without and the woman within" (Mernissi 1987: 43).[29] Although Iran was not colonized by the West, one could arguably recognize the influence of Western (particularly U.S. American) imperialism in the political and economic developments represented, either explicitly or implicitly, in TORKAN's novel. The narrator's life spans various phases of the Western-oriented Pahlavi regime and the Islamic Republic (beginning with the fundamentalist revolution of 1979). The educational and employment opportunities available (or not) to Asar as a girl and young woman from a middle-class doctor's family in Iran are determined by a given regime's perceptions of its relationship to American and European economics and ideologies. In this sense, then, we could conclude that the essentialist, ethnocentric traps cited by Mohanty structure the text at hand. This would be the end of our reading. Textual details would not matter. And yet they do.

As Mernissi contends (1987: 13–15), the paradox of a largely Muslim country requiring female labor (and hence a modification of traditional seclusionary practices) in order to compete with Western economies is that the entry of women into spheres of activity previously closed to them can be interpreted as both pro-Western (human rights, individual freedom) and anti-Western (increased relative economic autonomy for the nation). The fact that Asar is allowed to attend school and even pursue teacher training at the university (not, however, without some opposition from her parents) is one small clue that she comes to puberty and then adulthood in an age in which women's rights and roles were especially contested in Iran. Though Resa Shah had banned the veil (1936–41) and made education compulsory for women, the last phase of the Pahlavi period (beginning with the CIA's placing of Muhammed Resa Shah in power in 1953 and ending with the Islamic revolution of 1979) saw the more Western-style attitudes and laws of the government in power contending with the popular anti-Western precepts of Islamic social reform movements. In 1963 Iranian women were granted the right to vote; the Family Protection Laws of 1967 and 1975 gave them some greater freedom in marriage and divorce. These concessions to Westernized concepts of legal rights, however, did not serve to make the oppressive Pahlavi government very popular among Iranians of any sex, and in any case Asar's childhood and adolescence fall before most of the Shah's major reforms in women's rights or the Ayatollah Khomeini's reversals thereof.[30]

The multiplicity of positions ascribed and allotted to Iranian Muslim women during this period is inextricably linked to the contested nature, during the same period, of Islamic identity in Iran. (Mernissi [1987: ix] remarks that Muslim identity is generally disputed in these confusing times.) Although Shi'ism has been the dominant Islamic sect in Iran (see Anne Betteridge in Falk and Gross 1989: 103 and Michael M. J. Fischer in Beck and Keddie 1978: 191), even this branch of Islam should not be understood to be monolithic in either social or religious terms.[31] Not only was the postwar period (until 1979) characterized by ongoing conflicts and shifting negotiations between the government and the Shi'ite clergy, but the leaders of the religious movement(s) were themselves not united or uniform in their positions (Akhavi in Pullapilly 1980: 172–74). Both points are underscored by the role played by Dr. Ali Shari'ati (1933–1977), a popular proponent of Islamic modernism who criticized both the government and the established clergy for corruption and susceptibility to foreign influence (even though Shari'ati himself was educated in France and influenced by Sartre and Marx, among others). Whereas Shi'ism traditionally "disdained political power and kept aloof from it" (Nasr in Pullapilly 1980: 12), Shari'ati favored active intervention in revolutionary social causes for both Muslim men and women. His elaborations on the figure of Fatimeh are held largely responsible for rendering her a role model for educated, socially responsible, politically active women of Islamic faith who reject the Western preoccupations with sexual freedom and materialism *and* traditionalist Islamic notions of female subservience and subordination.[32] Shari'ati, for whom the adult Tufan repeatedly expresses great admiration (albeit not explicitly with regard to the role of Muslim women), was a source of great irritation to the established Shi'ite clergy, as he was to the Shah's regime, which wavered in its political responses to him, seeing perhaps an opportunity to foster divisiveness in the oppositional religious movement. Shari'ati is presumed to have been murdered in London by the Shah's notorious security organization, SAVAK, in 1977 (Akhavi in Pullapilly 1980: 179).

FIVE

Although frequent mention is made in *Tufan* to texts (the Qur'an, Shari'ati's writings, Tufan's unwritten book about Persian history and Arab aggressors), the multiple and contradictory nature of constructions for Iranian women or for Islamic identity is developed not primarily on the basis of textual references, but through the heterogeneous inscriptions of bodily experience that TORKAN's own text enacts.[33] *Tufan* is conceived as an imagined and incomplete exchange between brother and sister. Commencing the letter two months after learning of her brother's imprisonment by the Khomeini regime, the narrator writes for him, "stellvertretend für dich an mich" [in your place, for you, to me] (5). Direct exchange is impossible, and not only because Tufan is first incarcerated and then dead for two months before his sister is informed of his execution. Direct exchange between these two figures is also impossible because they occupy different positions of historical experience; their positions are not interchangeable. This is an important point, since the epithet "perpetual victim," originally applied to Asar, reverts to her brother at the novel's conclusion (161, 174). First jailed and tortured by SAVAK and later accused of being an antirevolutionary by the people he had previously actively supported, Tufan is imprisoned, tortured, and finally shot by the Khomeini regime. No fundamentalist martyr for the revolutionary cause, he would seem to be a victim of the cruel twists of modern Iranian history. One *could* read this transfer to mean that the sister's victimization yields to her brother's, that his victimization is somehow politically more "significant." And yet the text does not support this kind of reading, if for no other reason than that the position of victim is rendered unstable by the first transfer. Furthermore, the brutal treatment suffered by Asar at her brother's hands weighs too heavily to be erased or sublated by Tufan's fate as depicted in the second half of the novel. TORKAN's narrative challenges both the monolithic Eurocentric notion of Muslim woman as victim and the equally monolithic equation of victim and truth-teller. (Mohanty [1988: 34] criticizes this equation in universalist, essentialist feminist discourse.) If this is so, then what is it that validates Asar's own narrative as true? This is precisely not the issue, for TORKAN does not posit her narrator as the medium of "the truth." Asar's is the only narrative voice available to us, and yet this figure admittedly speaks about and for a brother she hardly understands or knows, one she has feared most of her life. By weaving the stories that she consciously constructs from the "fragments" (44) and "splinters of memory" (127) to which she does have access, Asar strives to make sense of her traumatic experiences and her brother's tormented life without filling in the gaps with imagined information, wishful assumptions, or forced meaning. Her narrative reflects the positionalities of her construction as subject and object; these positionalities situate her in and move her through relationships to (1) her brother and the rest of her family, (2) Iranian public life, (3) Islamic religious tenets, and (4) representations of "the West."

In her analysis of engendered space and architecture in Muslim societies Fatima Mernissi notes that the "notion of trespassing is related not so much to physical boundaries as to the identity of the person performing the act" (1987: 143). The inscriptions of Asar's (female) body are predicated either on movements actually undertaken by her or on those merely ascribed to her. In the case of the latter her body is "marked" by confinement (restriction of movement) and/or bruises. No innocent child, Asar responds to her younger brother from the beginning with sibling rivalry, manifested in frequent and furtive pinching attacks on the male intruder. As the narrative unfolds, we can see how Asar's physical aggression is invalidated while Tufan's increasingly aggressive acts of retaliation are sanctioned by family dynamics influenced (but not "determined") by Islamic principles. Once Asar has been caught pinching her brother, he is from then on free to beat "the witch" in her. The young boy who sticks a fork in his sister's cheek (12) finds the legitimation for his behavior in that evidenced by a mullah who beats the nine-year-old Asar for inadvertently revealing too much leg on a rare occasion when she dons a veil to go to the mosque (32). When Tufan laughingly calls Asar a "whore," it is she who gets her lips pricked by their mother, Khak

(33). The young adolescent Tufan then becomes his sister's guardian tormentor. When she is seriously ill, he prays to God to take her before she becomes a whore (81). Things worsen considerably when the family discovers that a lieutenant has had his eye on Asar. This time she is beaten by Tufan and her mother, after which she is confined to her room. It is Tufan who tries to beat her into admitting that she has lost her virginity, and he is the one to demand that she no longer be allowed to attend school (98–99). When she is finally permitted to resume school attendance in order to take her exams, Tufan is assigned the task of watching her every move in the streets. The worst attack comes when Asar's admirer, with whom she has barely had any contact at all, asks her father for her hand in marriage without being accompanied by his own parents. Pandemonium reigns as mother and brother batter Asar into unconsciousness with fists, feet, a coat hanger, an umbrella, and a flower pot. Asar depersonalizes in this instance (107), "leaving" her body in a way common to victims of physical or sexual abuse. This is the last violent incident before the tormented young woman leaves her family home (she is removed to a safe place by a kindly male cousin) and eventually the country. Yet even as an adult in Germany, Asar is haunted by Tufan's threat to disfigure her or worse (7, 28, 112). Indeed, her fear of him is initially what enables her to stay in the Federal Republic (56).

One could cite several passages from the text to support a reading condemning Islamic patriarchy as it is often understood by Westerners.

> Nie habe ich euren Islam gemocht. Ich fürchtete mich gar vor dieser Idee, die euch die Rechte gab, die sie mir nahm. Islam des Mannes: von Gott vergönntes Privileg, all das zu tun, was ich nicht durfte.
>
> Wo ist *mein* Islam? Islam der Frau!: Abfall. Strenge. Vernichtung von Gefühlen. Fanatismus. Elend und Heuchelei.
>
> Ich gestehe: Wenn ich je ein Mosalman gewesen sein sollte, dann nur aus Angst. Angst vor dem Alltag. Angst vor meinen Gedanken. Angst vor meinen Wünschen und Taten. Eine Gläubige aus Angst vor ihrer Umwelt.
>
> [I never liked your (plural) Islam. I was even afraid of this

idea that gave you (plural) rights that it took away from me. Man's Islam: God-granted privilege to do everything that I was not allowed.

Where is *my* Islam? Woman's Islam!: Refuse. Severity. Destruction of feelings. Fanaticism. Misery and hypocrisy.

I confess: If I was ever a Muslim, then only because I was afraid. Afraid of everyday life. Afraid of my thoughts. Afraid of my desires and actions. A woman made pious because she was afraid of her environment.] (25)

The words "Islam" and "man," the narrator informs us, always evoke in her the image of a naked penis (70, 77). Even though Asar is not subjected to sexual abuse, the power over her that accrues to Tufan as a male relative relies on the privileging of sexual difference. (Actual sexuality is not explicitly at issue in the novel. The narrator refers to her own sexual desire only when she rejects her family's ascriptions of a particular, promiscuous heterosexuality to her [170–71]; she refuses to make her own sexuality into an object of representation. In other words, she claims the right to sexual desire that is not circumscribed by a binary fixation of male desire on pious Muslim versus blasphemous whore.)[34] Yet the placement of the narrator's denunciations of "man's Islam" is significant. They directly follow not, as we might expect, descriptions of her mistreatment by her Muslim brother, but discussions of his having been "Islamicized" (24) and tortured (69–70) in a SAVAK prison. (The conversation about his experience of physical and psychological torture takes place during one of the adult Tufan's several surprise visits to his estranged sister in Germany.) This juxtaposition underscores the political heterogeneity of the circumstances in which a specific woman's experience of gender is produced. Tufan's relative power over Asar during childhood and adolescence is not the allegedly absolute power of patriarchy. Neither can we say that Tufan enjoys the fruits of male power in *Islamic* (as opposed to secular) patriarchy, since he is also tortured, horribly disfigured, and finally executed by a fundamentalist Islamic regime. His "maleness" is only one construction among many that shape his life; relative to shifting relations of power, they all are subject to change over the historical time of the text.

Asar's bruised body is then not the only one to bleed on these pages. The narrator's memories of her brother—and both sections of the novel, "Remembrance" and "Return," are based on scenes and experiences recalled—revolve around images of her own abused body and Tufan's bloodied one. Following Tufan's arrest for having participated in an anti-Shah demonstration on the 19th of August (the 28th of Mordad, the anniversary of the putsch against Mossadegh), Asar witnesses her father, a doctor, treating his son on his release. "Ich sah deinen hautlosen Rücken, das rohe Fleisch und das Blut. Sie hatten dich an den Füßen gefesselt, an einen Militärlastwagen gebunden und durch die Straßen bis zum Gefängnis geschleift" [I saw your skinless back, the raw flesh, and the blood. They had bound you by your feet, tied you to a military truck, and dragged you through the streets to the prison] (21). When she hears of his death many years later, she pictures his disfigured face, the left ear torn off, and imagines feeling the bullets in his neck, belly, and lungs. The novel begins and also ends with the image of the narrator's memory of her brother as a bleeding wound inside her that will not heal (5, 116–17, 192). "Da ist etwas, immer wund in mir, das verblutet noch immer und hört nicht auf zu schmerzen. Es ist der Gedanke an dich: die frühe Hoffnung, an die es keine Erinnerung mehr gibt, die Erinnerung an später, die ohne Hoffnung ist" [There is something, always an open wound in me, still bleeding to death and hurting. It is the thought of you: the early hope, of which there is no longer any memory, the memory of later, which is without hope] (5). This notion of memory as a painful physical wound refers not to generic memory but to memories of specific (real) wounds. TORKAN's formulations are not merely a figure of speech signifying that it is painful to remember. Rather, they incorporate, so to speak, the embodiment of experience into the narrative.

This does not, however, lend any authority of anteriority to the bodies of experience, since the physical woundings that abound in *Tufan* are all constructed, politically inscribed, which is also to say that even those taking place in the domestic sphere are not at all private. The physical abuse Asar suffers in her middle-class home, she discovers when she attends teacher training school in Teheran, is comparable to that experienced by her fellow (female) schoolmates from socially less privileged classes (108). Rather than experiencing any political solidarity among these young women, however, Asar elicits only the boredom of her audience when she gives a speech about the exploitation of women (110). She expresses disgust at the hypocrisy of what she calls the real power of women in Iranian society.

> Lügen—Verbergen—Verheimlichen—Schmeicheln—Leid unterdrücken—Liebe vortäuschen—Betrügen—mit Tränen erpressen und Lügen, Verbergen, Verheimlichen . . .
>
> Hier war jedes Mädchen mit seiner Mutter verbündet im verschworenen Kampf gegen den Ehemann, Vater und Bruder.
>
> [Lying—hiding—keeping secret—flattering—suppressing pain—feigning love—deceiving—extorting with tears and lying, hiding, keeping secret . . .
>
> Here every girl was her mother's ally in their sworn battle against husband, father, and brother.] (108)

These "tricks of the powerless" (to borrow from the title of a 1984 anthology edited by Claudia Honegger and Bettina Heintz) are cited by the narrator to stress the positionality of these Muslim women, who are not seen *merely* as objects of construction by Muslim men. This is what permits Asar to see Tufan not only as her tormentor, but also as a product of their mother's machinations. Khak used this son, the narrator concludes, as a "weapon," an "instrument of her will" (147), to bolster her own position in the family.[35] From this perspective Tufan has no self-directed power in the family unit (and we have already seen that he has none outside the family either). Neither does the text support the idea of a "woman's Islam." Despite TORKAN's *designation* of Tufan as "perpetual victim," what emerges from her narrative *production* is the sense of personal accountability for particular men and women who function as both subjects and objects of power in shifting and overlapping political relations. Even the torturous inscriptions of male bodies in the text do not "mark" the persons inhabiting them as homogeneous victims. Tufan is tortured by SAVAK agents and by Khomeini's henchmen. Does his torture "mean" the same thing in both instances? The public display of religious pilgrims' self-inflicted wounds (illegal under the Shah) represents an inscription of yet another sort (for a description of this scene, see TORKAN 1983: 72).[36] Whether Tufan's tortured body is displayed publicly (as in the case of the demonstration mentioned above) or confined to the prison grounds (as in the case of his imprisonment by *both* regimes), the ruling power assigns a public meaning to this wounded body, a meaning that marks but cannot subsume or erase the body of experience (see the discussion of Elaine Scarry's *Body in Pain* in Chapter One, above). In this sense neither Asar nor Tufan is a victim with only object status.

SEVEN

The movements in the narrative back and forth among different phases from Asar's past range from her life in Iran until the early 1960s, when she leaves for Europe, to the last phase, which begins with her first return visit in fifteen years, in 1977, and ends with Tufan's death just after the turn of the decade. These constant shifts in narrative time entail a searching gesture that keeps the narrator from locking herself into one fixed position. The gesture is in this case that of a woman incessantly seeking to position herself in her own history; as she moves through the narration of this search, she constructs herself as a subject of that history.[37] We have already seen that Asar's actual physical movements as a child and young woman are subject to political inscriptions of gender.[38] As her recollection of a military occupation of the university grounds reveals (124), these inscriptions of gender are imbricated in contested inscriptions of national identity. Yet Asar's politically inscribed body is also one organ of her agency. With it she flees to Europe. (Ultimately, this attempt to escape all reminders of her abusive family fails, since Tufan periodically appears on her doorstep.) Her adult female body is also the organ of her movements through public spaces when she returns to Iran as a West German citizen. As the agent of her explorations, she discovers that their medium (her body) is inscribed by a context she does not grasp. An unaccompanied woman moving through public streets, restaurants, stores, and hotels, Asar is identified as a prostitute. Since prostitutes often wear veils (Pakizegi in Beck and Keddie

1978: 224), it is not so much Asar's clothing as the mere fact of her physical movement in public spaces, alone, that invites sexual harassment (128–31, 142–44).[39] Tufan laughs later, explaining to her that she cannot behave as she did, speak Farsi, and *not* be treated as a prostitute (131). She does not comprehend the subtexts of her public exchanges. Similarly, she does not know where to place herself in the public heterogeneity of female bodies at the beach. Confused by the sight of women swimming in skimpy bikinis while others, heavily veiled, dip only their exposed feet in shallow water (138), Asar decides not to swim at all. In time she realizes that the only "position" she can safely occupy in public without incurring harassment (as a single woman) is that of a foreigner. To facilitate the masquerade she decides to speak only broken Farsi (144, 153).

But is this position really only a masquerade? *Tufan* presents us with images of Iranian society and an Islamic culture that are anything but monolithic. And yet, commenting on the many "crass contradictions" she has perceived, the narrator characterizes herself as a "distant spectator" (144). "Ein ferner Betrachter war ich nur, unbeteiligt an dem Treiben und innerlich, wenn auch unbeobachtet, berührt" [I was only a distant spectator, uninvolved in what was happening and internally, even if unobserved, moved]. The notion of not belonging, of being separate, is reinforced by her renunciation of Iran as her country both in legalistic terms of citizenship and in emotional terms of identification (see 119, 162, 167). This renunciation is complete, the narrator would have us believe, after she learns of Tufan's murder.

> Der Schah ist nicht mehr mein Feind und Khomeini nicht mein Führer und der Iran nicht mehr mein Land.
>
> Ich lese die Flugblätter und die Zeitungen aus dem Iran, und ich verstehe diese halb-arabisch gebrochenen Sätze nicht.
>
> Ich sehe Landsleute, die aus Persien neu angekommen sind. Ich kenne sie nicht.
>
> Jeder von ihnen kann dein Mörder gewesen sein.
>
> Ich wende mich von ihnen ab, grau vor Entsetzen.
>
> Ich werde sie nie kennenlernen wollen.
>
> Ich werde nicht mehr Landsmann zu ihnen sagen können.

Ich habe aufgehört, über den Iran, über dieses Land, das einst auch mein Land war, zu urteilen.
[The Shah is no longer my enemy and Khomeini not my leader and Iran no longer my country.

I read the flyers and newspapers from Iran, and I do not understand these broken, half-Arabic sentences.

I see countrymen who have recently arrived from Persia. I do not know them.

Any one of them could have been your murderer.

I turn away from them, gray with horror.

I will never want to get to know them.

I will not be able to call them countryman again.

I have ceased to judge Iran, this country that was once my country, too.] (195)

If we take these statements at face value, then we must conclude that the narrator renounces not only particular historical developments, but any positionality on her own part (other than that of complete renunciation) toward her country of origin. This tendential erasure of positionality reverberates when Asar swears to "erase" herself from her family's memories (157). She claims to have taken the blank spot with her, the blank spot that should have remained as a minimal mark of her having been among them. "Nicht einmal eine leere Stelle hatte ich bei euch hinterlassen! Ich hatte diese Lücke mit mir mitgenommen—diese Leere, sie war in mir, diese Kälte" [I did not leave even a blank spot behind with you! I had taken that hole with me—that emptiness, it was inside me, that coldness] (161). Is such complete erasure possible?

EIGHT

The narrator does not withdraw to no place, to a space of her own free of discursive positionality. While Asar has taken up residence in West Germany, TORKAN produces images of Iran ("the Orient") in a Western European language. The text is, I have argued, a piece of (West) German literature. The narrative voice created by TORKAN often speaks in terms imbued with Orientalist values and categories (Said 1978). While there is much emotion in the text, the style is primarily descriptive, contemplative, and analytical (in marked contrast to the visceral style of Anne Duden or the radically expressive one of Jeannette Lander). The narrator observes and analyzes; the Iranians who are the objects of her observation celebrate, as she puts it, "an endless festival of feelings" (157). Associating progress with the West and Islam with regression, she tends to favor principles of reason and enlightenment (162–63). This could be taken as a stereotypically Western stance, but it is not one that the narrator leaves intact. She acknowledges her failure to understand that reason alone is not the sole motivating factor in religious social movements (163). (Western scholars of German National Socialism have had to make a similar discovery.) The narrator ultimately refuses to claim for herself the (Orientalist) possession of knowledge about Iran; in the end she confesses to "knowing" very little indeed (189). In a related gesture she also rejects the benevolent Orientalism of favorable stereotypes. Her initial appreciation for the "enthusiasm of reciprocal gift-giving" in a record shop (in contrast to the cold exchange of money and commodity in the West [129]) gives way to disillusionment when she realizes that the sales clerk was cheating her blind. Although she finds it ironic that the adult Tufan and the rest of the family praise "the whore" for her successes in the West (170–71), she takes pains not to present *herself* as the stereotyped oppressed Muslim woman who finds success and happiness in the Federal Republic (172). (Such a depiction would be tantamount to the Western feminist imaging of Muslim women discussed earlier in this chapter.) By choosing not to render her everyday life in Germany an object of representation in this novel,[40] TORKAN constructs Asar as the subject of her narrative (it emanates from her as she moves through the social time of history), not some marginal figure palpitating a privileged German "center."[41] The disgust she articulates regarding the hypocrisy of Muslim men and women (111) does not locate her in the place of "Western woman," for she is quite capable of formulating her own critical perceptions of her culture of origin. The obsession of Tufan with photographing "the *other* face of the West," by which he means scenes of ugliness, poverty, and misery in Europe (see 103, 116), is perhaps a subtle textual reference to the many refracting lenses of positionality through which this text is filtered.

Tufan's own wife (from the third marriage his mother has arranged
for him) functions like a cipher for the kind of blank spot Asar refuses to occupy. This is how the narrator describes her nameless sister-in-law:

> Hinter dir stand deine Frau. Ein ruhiges rundes Wesen. Im-
> mer war sie schweigsam, unbeweglich und einfach da. Sie hätte
> auch nicht da sein können—es wäre nicht aufgefallen. Ein
> durchsichtiger Stein neben dir. Ruhig und unberührt von
> deiner verwundeten Seele. Ohne Ohr und ohne Wort gegen
> deine hektische Beredsamkeit. Wie eine weltentrückte Weise
> schien sie sich mit dir und mit sich selbst neben dir abgefunden
> zu haben. Ich hatte nie das Gefühl, daß sie wirklich lebt, daß sie
> neben dir ein lebendiges Wesen hätte sein können. Sie füllte
> den Raum nicht aus. Nie hatte sie gestört, selten kam ein Wort
> aus ihr heraus, das der Erinnerung haften bleiben könnte. Die
> Tränen, die sie manches Mal vergoß, waren ohne Leidenschaft.
> Ihr Lachen war geräuschlos und ohne Freudenstrahlen. Ihr
> Lachen und ihr Weinen lösten keine Erregung aus.

> [Behind you stood your wife. A calm, round being. She was
> always given to silence, immobile, and simply there. She could
> also have been not there—no one would have noticed. A trans-
> parent stone next to you. Calm and untouched by your
> wounded soul. With no ear and no word against your hectic lo-
> quaciousness. Like a wise woman removed from the cares of
> this world she seemed to have accepted you and even herself
> next to you. I never had the feeling that she was really alive, that
> she could have been a living being next to you. She did not oc-
> cupy space. She never disturbed anyone, seldom did she utter a
> word that could stick in one's memory. The tears that she occa-
> sionally shed were without passion. Her laughter was soundless
> and radiated no joy. Her laughter and her tears caused no ex-
> citement.] (169)[42]

This is the Muslim woman without a face whom the essentializing
feminist discourse of "Third World Women" has so often invoked. By

creating her own image—but in relation to this one and several others—the narrator of *Tufan* cannot be said to reproduce the mono-lithic stereotype. For if she, whose experience has been constructed at least in part by the meaning effects of Islam, does not occupy this place, then presumably neither does her sister-in-law. The textual im-age is only a façade, a surface for projections, that marks an unoc-cupied spot of representation while women are busy negotiating the meanings of their own constructed, embodied experiences of multi-ple positionality. In a movement perhaps analogous to that of psycho-logical depersonalization, when a person's spirit leaves his or her abused body to observe it from a place of imagined safety, the narra-tor in *Tufan* strives to negotiate her interpretation of historicized ex-perience around and across images of wounded and tortured bodies recalled, including her own. Unlike the protagonist's body in Anne Duden's *Opening of the Mouth*, these bodies do not function in the text as *cognitive* organs of orientation or sites of repressed historical expe-rience (see above, Chapter Two). They do function as the hetero-geneous loci of the material and discursive inscriptions that the nar-rator's consciousness cannot escape as she writes herself as an embodied (and hence constructed) subject. TORKAN's novel has helped me negotiate my own position on this.

4 | Jeannette Lander's
Ein Sommer in der Woche der Itke K.
Jews and Other "Others":
On Representations and Enactments

The premise of this chapter may be arrogant or foolhardy or both. It is admittedly speculative. For my operative assumption is that some out-of-print novels written in German by a little-known and relatively unsung author of Polish-Jewish-American origins raise some vital questions regarding alternative conceptualizations of contemporary "German" culture[1] as well as feminist models of minority discourse. As will be shown, this has to do with constructs of identity, race, gender, and the embodiment of positionality. Born in New York in 1931 but raised in Atlanta, Jeannette Lander emigrated to West Berlin in 1960. During the 1970s she had three German-language novels published by the well-established presses of Suhrkamp and Insel: *Ein Sommer in der Woche der Itke K.*, 1971 (A Summer in the Week of Itke K.); *Auf dem Boden der Fremde*, 1972 (On Strange Ground); and *Die Töchter*, 1976 (The Daughters). Although they were not marketed as such, these novels could be read as a kind of trilogy in which the traditionally binary constellation of "Jews and Germany" is disrupted and refracted by additional factors of social discourse between Jews and other minorities in a variety of national and political contexts.[2] The tale of one girl's search for identity under conditions of multiple social, historical, cultural, and linguistic displacements, Lander's first novel tracks the coming of age of Itke Kovsky, the fourteen-year-old daughter of Polish Jewish immigrants who operate the local grocery store in a predominantly poor African American neighborhood in Atlanta. Against the more distant background of the war against Nazi Germany, Lander's extensive use of Yiddish, High German, and a Southern Black sociolect rendered into an artificial German dialect underscores the tensions inherent in the three primary spheres of Itke's experience: Jews, African Americans, and white Protestants in early 1940s Georgia.[3] In the second novel a slightly older version of Itke leaves her Jewish home in the United States to follow her non-Jewish German husband, a former soldier for the Third Reich, to Berlin in 1950. When his anti-Semitism surfaces fifteen years later, she returns to visit her parents, only to find that they have become racists and that she herself is an unwelcome outsider in her old black neighborhood.[4] With *The Daughters* Lander has extended her geographic tracing of Jews and their relationships to the Holocaust from 1940s France to West Berlin, Atlanta, Haifa, and Poland in the mid-1960s. The three cities each house one of the adult daughters of a Polish Jew who set out from France in 1941 to seek his own father's grave in Poland. Not surprisingly, he is never seen again. This country of his origin then becomes the site of the daughters' disjointed quest for traces of their own past. In each new setting the history of the Holocaust is displaced (not replaced) by a different constellation of social injustice. In Atlanta Jewish characters are defined in part by their relationship to poor African Americans; in Haifa it is Arabs and Sephardic Jews; in Poland, gypsies of an unspecified clan. Lander's Jewish female protagonists are not merely victims of a traumatic past but are constantly called on to resituate themselves as Jews in their respective presents, in relation to various forms of oppression that affect them and other minorities differently.

The temptation merely to bear witness to the representability of such configurations is great, given their relative rarity in German letters, but such witness is insufficient without an analysis of the ways in which Lander's textual enactment of heterogeneous positionality has far-reaching implications for notions of minority discourse and national cultural identity in the German context. While most reviewers have tended, either in praise or in damnation, to dismiss this writer's

88 Lander's *Ein Sommer in der Woche der Itke K.*

themes as "Jewish American" (and hence deny her contributions to the body of *German* literature), my contention is that these novels attest to the plurivocal and polyvalent nature of what is too frequently posited simply as a relationship between "Jews and Germany."[5] This polylogue has multiple sociohistorical dimensions. For one, Lander's novels explore the construction of Jewishness in settings that are often temporally and/or geographically far removed—or displaced—from the Third Reich but in which the shattering experience of the Holocaust continues to reverberate. Acknowledging the wounds of the German past without being paralyzed by them, these texts pose Jewish identity in West Germany as a topical question, not an archaeological one.[6] This entails an optic that rejects the anti-Semitic determination of the Jew as "Other" to an allegedly intact Aryan "Self" and sees Jews not only as more than mere victims or villains, but as something *other* than mere victims or villains. Given the dominant postwar tendency in German culture and politics to cultivate either philo-Semitic or anti-Semitic stereotypes of Jews, this is no mean challenge on Lander's part.[7] But it would be misleading at this point to say only that Lander allows the paradigmatic "Other" in twentieth-century German history to speak in voices of their own, to speak also as subjects of history. The Jewish figures in her novels do not represent a simple inversion of a purported bipolar "dialogue" between German perpetrators and Jewish victims. Rather, they are engaged in historically determined and mutually imbricated constructions of heterogeneous social identity along with other minorities in and outside German territory.[8] This is not to say that the Jewish-German question becomes solely a matter of how various minority groups—socially and historically marginalized—relate to one another from and on the margins (independent of specific configurations of privilege and power). By temporally and geographically disrupting the binary opposition implied in the "German-Jewish" dialogue, Lander illuminates, as has been said, some of the ways in which historical experience does not disappear but is *refracted* under shifting historical circumstances. The Jewish utopian goal of becoming a *mensch* (not to be confused with the Enlightenment project of attaining majority) is rendered a constant challenge, the conditions of which shift as Jewishness is experienced on the shifting historical ground of different configurations of power.[9]

TWO

The construction of such Jewish "subjects," however, does more than bespeak historical and geographic "displacements" of the Holocaust experience from the subject perspective of some of its victims (intended or actual, depending on how one defines a victim of the Holocaust). Bemoaning the continued prevalence of stereotypes of Jews in German culture, Christiane Schmelzkopf applauds Lander's emphasis on the multidimensionality and open-endedness of her Jewish figures (1985: 292–93). (Lander is in fact the only West German author of the last twenty years to be praised by Schmelzkopf in this regard.) This deviation from stereotypes is in and of itself noteworthy. As Frank Stern has argued, "a selective idealization" of Jews in postwar German culture has been functionalized and monumentalized, in effect placing Jews "unter Denkmalschutz" ("protecting" them as historical monuments [Stern 1991b: 17–23]).[10] While it is certainly true that Lander transgresses traditional stereotypes of good Jews/ bad Jews, what is of particular interest here is the specific manner in which she enacts alternative constructions of "Jewishness." The fact that Lander, in addition to deploying temporal and geographic displacements of the Holocaust experience, *also* displaces the binary component of "Jews and Germany" by peopling her texts with other minorities both in and outside an immediate German context has two particularly striking consequences. Contrary to what one might expect, Lander's representation of other minorities does not serve either to exoticize "otherness" or to essentialize "Germanness" further. This is important, since we know that assumptions of Jewish "exoticism" have not only shored up an array of political and cultural stereotypes (see Gilman's 1985 study, *Difference and Pathology*) but have also influenced both the marketing and reception of contemporary Jewish authors in Germany (Koch 1990), including, perhaps, Lander herself. In a separate essay comparing *On Strange Ground* to a German-language novel by a woman of Jewish Israeli background I have noted that "the relationship between Germans and Jews—however defined—continues to be an essential ingredient in *any* notion of German national identity" (Adelson 1990b: 113).[11] That this is true even after the recent unification of the two German states is evidenced, as just one example, by any discussion of the public ascription of meaning to November 9—1938 or 1989?[12] The point to stress here, however, is this: If the representation of "Jewishness" shifts in some fundamental structural way, then so too does the representation of "Germanness." Rather than introducing a notion of heterogeneity within or among marginalized Jews and other minorities while leaving a notion of a homogeneous German center intact, engaging with Lander's texts as German cultural documents dislodges both poles of the so-called German-Jewish question. The first consequence of Lander's particular representation of Jews and other "Others" is then to unhinge an allegedly homogeneous "German" center against which minorities (in this context) have been defined. If this center no longer holds—this center that has provided the basis for long-standing concepts of German national identity—then neither do the margins to which any number of minorities have been banished. This brings us closer to the second striking consequence I wish to discuss.

"The truth is that the notion of what is German is as much contested on critical and scholarly terrain as is the designation of the Federal Republic as a *Vielvölkerstaat* in the public arena. The debate about what to call literature by non-Germans living in West Germany obscures the point that what is at stake is not the appropriate category of the foreign 'addendum' but the fundamental need to reconceptualize our understanding of an identifiably German core of contemporary literature." Taken from an essay problematizing "migrants' literature" as a critical category (Adelson 1990a: 383), these words could also apply to German literature written by Jewish authors (whether or not these writers are German Jews is immaterial to the argument at hand). The point is not to fail to distinguish historical and cultural particularities affecting the production and reception of various literary texts, but to contemplate the function of difference *in* Germanness rather than outside it. "Not a mask to be tried on or put down at will, to be added to or subtracted from an allegedly essential body of German texts, difference is constitutive of contemporary

West German writing" (Adelson 1990a: 383). *How* specifically difference is constituted remains a crucial question. (And in this sense the categories of both "difference" and "heterogeneity" should be retained precisely because the former is inscribed with the presumption of a white, middle-class, heterosexist norm against which "difference" is recognized as such.)[13]

The second striking consequence of Lander's constant and shifting references to Jews and other minorities in a (broadly defined) "German" context is to preclude a discussion of her work in the still-fashionable terms of "the voice of the Other." That is to say, different constellations of historical oppression and agency do not yield parallel or equivalent manifestations of difference. Itke's immigrant Jewish family and their indigent African American neighbors and customers do not occupy the same sites of positionality in 1940s Atlanta. Neither can Lander's texts be said to support the notion of "woman" as a universal category of otherness. The white Jewish girl in *Itke,* for example, cannot appropriate or even represent the position occupied by Jimmie Lee, her black female confidante, former childhood playmate, and the Kovskys' one-time housekeeper. Since much Anglo-American feminist theory of the 1980s was concerned with dismantling the universalist bias entailed in ethnocentric constructs of "woman" (see above, Chapter Three), the comment that "woman" does not function as a universal category of otherness in Lander's work may seem pedestrian. In the realm of feminist German Studies, however, it marks a relatively unfamiliar and different way of walking. Teresa de Lauretis's *Technologies of Gender* (1987) urged us to move beyond the binary fixation on sexual difference in order to allow for the production of gender and the process of its representation (see above, Chapter Three). Yet even acknowledging that the production of engendered otherness is not necessarily the appropriate paradigm for all other types of socially experienced difference (e.g., race or ethnicity) does not go far enough. As Elizabeth V. Spelman has deftly articulated in her treatise *Inessential Woman* (1988), the relationship between the production of gender and the production of race is not that of the ampersand: "What one learns when one learns one's gender identity is the gender identity appropriate to one's ethnic, class, national, and racial identity" (Spelman

1988: 88). Spelman speaks of "many genders" (176), since not all women share the same gender (nor do all men). What it *means* to be a woman will be different for different women of different races and classes at different historical junctures.[14]

A novel such as *Itke* lends itself well to the study of such historically imbricated constructions. When the narrator designates the protagonist as "Itkeweißjüdisch" [Itkewhitejewish] (14), for example, the latter emerges as a specific female persona who is not first white and then Jewish or first Jewish and then white. Rather, she simultaneously becomes white-Jewish-female at a socially and historically specific juncture, the conditions of which lend equally specific *meaning* to this particular constellation. One of the effects of this is to de-naturalize the concept of whiteness as it de-essentializes the construct of Jewishness.[15] This would be sufficient grounds, I think, to say that if Germanist feminist scholarship merely reproduces the binary construction of "Jews and Germany," it in effect contributes to the misplacement of minority discourse in the realm of German Studies by hypostatizing both "Jews" and "Germans." This cannot account for the historically differentiated production of gender, nor can it adequately account for constructs of race and ethnicity in the postwar era. When Lander unsettles the binary constellation of "Jews and Germany" by peopling her texts with Jews and other minorities in a variety of national and political settings, she effectively challenges Germanist feminist scholarship to conceptualize the production of "gender" as imbricated with the production of "race" and "ethnicity." This may well be a thorny issue for German intellectual historians of recent vintage. In the more particular context of contemporary German feminist criticism, I suspect that the brutally abusive racial ideology and policies promulgated by the Nazis have left in their wake an absolute distaste for even theorizing "race" in a way that would do anything but negate the category altogether.[16] I realize that I am on highly—perhaps even grossly—speculative territory here. I would therefore like to explain at some length my reasons for claiming that Germanist feminist studies should also be addressing questions of racial identity and not just those of gender or even ethnicity. This, I know, is a problematic venture.

THREE

Collaborating for the second time on an interdisciplinary conference, East and West German feminists sponsored a symposium in December 1990 that had as its topic "Jüdische Kultur und Weiblichkeit
in der Moderne" (Jewish Culture and Constructs of Woman in Modernity).[17] Having addressed fellow participants there on the subject
of Jeannette Lander's constructions of Jews and other "Others," I was
asked why I had retained the term "race" rather than speaking, say,
about "discourses of race." The question is a legitimate one, especially
in a national context still scarred by the ideology of a purported "master race." What follows is an attempt to answer the question more adequately than I was able to do at the time it was posed. One way to begin is to cite the concept of positionality that has been elaborated in
the preceding chapters: Positionality *characterizes* the body of social
experience *as well as* the sign-functions of which it partakes, but we
cannot say that positionality *is* the body, since it always implies a complex physical and significatory relationship to structures of power. If
Lander's novels are to be situated in terms of such positionality, however, then we must also allow for the historically variable but nonetheless material effects of racial identity constructs. That is to say, to
the extent that racial discourse is *lived* and not just discursively represented, then we cannot say that race is any more immaterial than gender. This is not by any means to contend that race is a stable property
in either material or discursive terms.[18] In a critical analysis of some
of the 1980s debates on "race" in African American cultural theory
Diana Fuss likewise argues the importance of retaining the category
of race as well as the possibility of doing so without attributing to it
any fixed meaning over time or across discourses (Fuss 1989: 73–
96).[19] Acknowledging the "real material effects in the world" of the
sign "race," she contends that "we can still work with 'race' as a political concept *knowing* it is a biological fiction" (91). Fuss calls for "a closer
look at the production of racial subjects, at what forces organize, ad-
minister, and produce racial identities" (92). This, I submit, is about
the embodiment of positionality. It entails seeing "color" (e.g., black
or yellow or white) not as the actual physical color of a person's skin,
but as a politically inscribed meaning that accrues to a purported
color within specific relations of power.[20] It also necessitates distin-

guishing between "race" and "ethnicity."[21] If Itke were to be seen as "only Jewish" vis-à-vis the German cultural context in which I have proposed to situate Lander's first novel, then there could be no accounting for the simultaneity of her "whiteness" in 1940s Atlanta. And if she were "just white," there could be no accounting for her difference in the German context or for the different kind of difference she occupies in wartime Georgia.[22]

"In American culture, 'race' has been far more an acknowledged component of black identity than white; for good or bad, whites have always seen 'race' as a minority attribute, and blacks have courageously and persistently agitated on behalf of 'the race.' It is easy enough for white poststructuralist critics to place under erasure something they *think* they never had to begin with" (Fuss 1989: 93). This could hardly be said of "white" postwar German intellectuals, who have labored long and hard under the deathly shadow of a supposedly superior racial identity, from which they have distanced themselves in no uncertain terms. Yet to deny the material effects of racial identities in the present is, as Pierre-André Taguieff has shown in the French context, to leave the negotiation of certain kinds of racial identities (usually some form of "white") to the New Right (Taguieff 1990).[23] By failing to examine politically inscribed constructs of race as inextricably intertwined with constructs of gender, feminist German Studies run the risk—as shown in Chapter Two—of sustaining the naturalized invisibility of whiteness. My attitudes toward racial constructs are strongly influenced, however, by U.S. American politics and theory, especially of the last twenty years. In the United States, formations of racial identity have played a very different role than in postwar Germany. In the context of American feminism in particular, identity politics has stressed (among other things) *positive* aspects of racial and ethnic identification for oppressed groups; this has time and again called the ethnocentrism of "mainstream" feminism into question (see Chapter Three for a more detailed discussion of feminist identity politics).[24] While I am certainly not in favor of superimposing a U.S. American notion of identity politics onto the German situation and while I realize that I may be barking up the wrong theoretical tree by digging up this bone of contention at all, I do believe that there is at least a chance that what we know about identity politics in the United States can help elucidate some of the problems involved in representing not only race but also personal, cultural, and national identity in the realm of German Studies. My discussion of Lander's work is an experiment in this vein.

FOUR

Given the Nazi monopoly on a certain kind of German "identity politics," it is no wonder that West German intellectuals tend to see an emphasis on race or ethnicity as evil. Nonetheless, there are some indications that constructs of race are still highly contested phenomena in the realm of things "German." For some time before the recent unification there was much debate about whether Germany was becoming or even had become a multicultural, multiethnic society (*multikulturelle Gesellschaft* and *Vielvölkerstaat* are the most common terms). Yet even in the wake of the generally unexpected "unification," "there was no sign that the new Germany was willing to give up its tradition of racial definition of German nationality" (Brockmann 1991: 12). Since the mid-1980s Afro-Germans and Black Germans have been cultivating their own brand of identity politics.[25] Of those whom Jack Zipes has called the "'new German Jews'" (Zipes 1986) one could say that they cultivate a Jewish identity politics that is not racially or religiously or ethnically determined but founded instead on the politicization of historical experience in the German present.[26] While contested notions of historical and personal identity (both before and since unification) are not predicated on constructs of race alone, representations of race and ethnicity are embroiled in them, even if those representations consist of a blind spot.[27]

In a recent study of mourning and memory in postwar German film Eric Santner has provocatively posited a shift in the conditions for *Vergangenheitsbewältigung* (generally taken to mean "coming to terms with the Nazi past").

> As the perpetrator generation dies out, more properly juridical issues of guilt and complicity yield to more inchoate questions of historical memory and of the mediation and transmittal of cultural traditions and identities. In the next stage the fundamental issue becomes, in a sense, what it means to say "*ich*" and

"*wir*" in a Germany that still finds itself under the shadow of the Final Solution. What are the strategies and procedures by which a cultural identity may be reconstituted in post-Holocaust Germany? (Santner 1990: xii–xiii)

This discursive rendition of a present dilemma raises, for our purposes, an intriguing question. Assuming that it does make sense to say that the residue of actual guilt dies out with the individual perpetrators and survivors of the Holocaust, what transpires in the shift from guilt to memory to identity? What becomes of the notion of responsibility (the *Verantwortung* stressed by Federal President Richard von Weizsäcker in his 1985 speech commemorating the end of World War II in the European theater)? This seems worth contemplating, since identity politics in the United States has at times come under fire for not being political enough. "What is to be done has been replaced by who am I" (Bourne 1987: 1; see also Alcoff 1988 and Butler 1990). How then to foreground the question of German cultural *identity* without reducing it to that of a *Kulturnation,* from which the politics of heterogeneous positionalities have been erased? In the shadows of the "post-Holocaust" modifier for German cultural identity lie, of course, allusions to a racially overwritten history.[28] (The notion of post-Holocaust German identity is never taken to mean, for example, how Germans relate to Communism or trade unionism or homosexuality, just to name a few of the possible options.) I suggest, therefore, that questions of identity and constructions of difference as they are explored in Lander's novels are effectively germane to the broader political issues surrounding competing models of German identity. This has particular relevance for the paradigmatic shift away from literary representations of the body as a metaphor for the nation toward representing the human body as the site of contested identities. Beyond cultural pluralism this type of heterogeneity addresses the politics of making history (past, present, and future). If we ask how literary representations of difference reflect or enact the historical embodiment of contested and conflicted identities, then we bring an awareness of imbricated constructs of race, gender, and ethnicity to our studies of national cultural identity. A discussion of Lander's first novel in German in *this* sense allows for a very different approach to the production of gender than the more familiar feminist discussions of the female body in literature as a site of illness or injury.[29]

FIVE

I have argued in favor of recognizing *Itke* as a piece of German literature. With the German language as its primary medium, this novel was first published by a West German press (to date it has appeared only in German publication). As with TORKAN's *Tufan: Letter to an Islamic Brother,* this theoretical gesture of recognition helps us to renegotiate the "Germanness" of contemporary German culture. In addition, the Third Reich and World War II provide the distant background to the more immediate happenings of the novel. This is of more than purely coincidental interest. Although there is no indication that Itke's Polish Jewish parents fled the Nazi occupation of Poland—presumably, they emigrated to the United States some time before the Johnson Bill of 1924 virtually put an end to the influx of eastern and southern Europeans (Butwin 1973: 80; Gutstein 1988: 153)—Itke comes of age as a Jewish girl in the United States while her counterparts back in Nazi-occupied Europe are being prepared for slaughter. (The family hears Walter Winchell's radio report on this following Joe Louis's victory over Billy Conn [65].) In a sense this story of a very much alive Jewish girl comes back to haunt German culture in 1971 by asserting a place for itself *in* that culture on terms that exceed Nazi ideology. Moreover, traces of yet another era of German history indirectly shape Itke's experience of Jewishness in 1940s Atlanta. Although the heterogeneity of that particular city's Jewish community is not explicitly thematized in the novel, Itke's eastern European heritage and her Yiddish-speaking parents strongly influence her options for and attitudes toward assimilation. As we shall see in our discussion of this young woman's positionality, the text denies her (and us as readers) the illusion of assimilation into white non-Jewish Southernhood.

This illusion was one that had been cultivated by the older, more established German Jewish congregation, which dated back to the mid-nineteenth century (Blumberg 1987). With the 1913 murder trial and subsequent lynching of Leo Frank—an established Jewish industrialist—in 1915, however, this "assimilated" Jewish community was so traumatized that, as one historiographer has noted, "those members who had lived through it still reacted to events occurring more than thirty years later with it in mind" (Blumberg 1985: 33).[30] The fact that a Jew could be and was lynched in the American South meant neither that all tensions and differences *among* Jews in the United States were erased—German Jews consistently saw eastern European Jewish immigrants as a threat to their own status (Lavender 1977: 11; Blumberg 1987: 48)[31] —nor that Jews and African Americans occupied the *same* social position.[32] An additional linkage posited between *German* history and the positionality of both blacks and Jews is directly addressed in the author's afterword. Of the African American soldiers fighting in Europe she writes: "Fighting the oppression of a different minority in a strange country, they put their lives on the line. In armed forces in which they had no equal rights" (263, my translation). The bitter ironies of U.S. American racism also come through in various characters' commentaries when some of the young African American men in the neighborhood enlist in the military. Despite the fact that some of these multidimensional associations between German history and black and Jewish positionalities are only implicitly at play in Lander's representations, they all contribute to the particular way in which she explodes the historically and symbolically reductionistic trope of "Jews and Germany."

SIX

Ein Sommer in der Woche der Itke K. is arguably a kind of German counterpart to Minnie Bruce Pratt's autobiographical essay on growing up as a white Christian lesbian in the American South (Pratt 1984). Published as one of three contributions to *Yours in Struggle: Three Feminist Perspectives on Anti-Semitism and Racism*, the Pratt piece in particular elicited much discussion among U.S. American feminists about what I call positionality. Others have called it "the fundamentally relational nature of identity," noting that different social groups may occupy the same sites but with different functions and experiences (Martin and Mohanty 1986; see Chapter Three of the present study for comments on the significance of this analysis for a feminist concept of positionality). One of the persons to figure prominently in the construction of Pratt's positionality is her father, with whom she shares certain "privileges" while being excluded from others claimed by and ascribed to him. Itke's father, too, is a crucial reference point for her own positioning. In this sense one could easily expand the dimensions of the West German "father books" so much in vogue in the 1970s by including Lander's *Itke* in a discussion of this phenomenon.[33] While most of the texts so labeled deal with a generation of sons and daughters struggling with their fathers' conflicts in National Socialism, Itke's father is, of course, a Jewish man whose personal history does not render him a direct victim of Nazi extermination policies.[34] He—and she—break this particular pattern of paternity, although one of the many poles of Itke's positionality does in fact reside in her relationship to her father. This relationship, however, is both marked by and enacts historically specific, engendered, and racialized constructs of Jewishness.

SEVEN

The narrative of the first chapter begins with a naming of the three circles of Itke's experience.[35]

> Itke.
> Itke with kinky hair, with dark eyes, lives in a circle in a circle in a circle. The innermost circle is Yiddish. The middle one is black American. The outer circle is white-Protestant-American deep in the South. (13)[36]

The designation of the innermost circle as "Yiddish" as opposed to "Jewish" already points to a factor of historical particularity here. For the immigrant family's understanding of "Jewishness" is clearly shaped by the parents' experience as Yiddish-speaking, eastern European, Ashkenazic Jews (as opposed to, say, German- or Hebrew-speaking Ashkenazim or Ladino-speaking Sephardim).[37] Yet even within her immediate family Itke is exposed to engendered constructs of Jewishness as lived by each of her parents (her two sisters are mentioned but scarcely represented in the text).[38] Mamma Kovsky is profoundly invested in honoring the dietary regulations for keeping a kosher household, while Tatte Kovsky is portrayed primarily as a Jewish man trying do what he can toward creating a little more justice in a fundamentally unjust society. (The restrictions he experiences in these attempts characterize his own positionality, about which more will be said momentarily.) This division of labor, so to speak, does not coincide exactly with the dictates of Jewish religious law (*halakhah*), which espouses various ritual obligations for both sexes. To be sure, both Jewish men and women are commanded to observe religious dietary laws, but it is women to whom social tradition, not the sacred Torah, has assigned the task of actually cooking the kosher food and maintaining a kosher home (Berman 1976). According to *halakhic* gender divisions, women are exempt from positive, time-bound commandments, which men are required to perform at specific times in a day, a week, or a year. These include commandments of prayer and the study of sacred text. In Orthodox Judaism women have not been counted in constituting a prayer quorum (*minyan*), which is particularly significant given that communal prayer is the norm in Judaism. During Orthodox religious services attended by both men and women, women are traditionally required to sit separately from the men, ostensibly to preclude the women's distracting the men from their religious fervor.[39] One Jewish feminist sums up these distinctions as follows: "Excluded from the central religious obligations of Judaism and from knowledge of its sources, little else is left to women under *halakhah* other than to act as facilitators for husbands and sons. The result is an identification of women with physical work—childbearing, cooking, cleaning—while men are identified with spiritual activities—prayer, study, rituals" (Heschel 1983: 4).

While Itke's mother could be said to fill the role ascribed to her here (with the exception of the reference to sons), Tatte's brand of piety hardly fits the *halakhic* bill. Not a prayerful man, he neither studies Torah nor performs any of the rituals incumbent on him as a Jewish man. Furthermore, in one scene he eats "treef" (unkosher meat), thereby causing a crisis for his wife, and we are told that he keeps his store open on Friday nights and Saturdays, rather than keeping the Jewish Sabbath day holy. Tatte's "spiritual activities" enact, then, not the codified practice of religious ritual, but a secularized attention to social injustice transposed from his native Poland to the American South. This comes with an element of non-synchronicity. Founded in 1897, the Jewish Labor Bund consisted largely of urban, working-class Jews committed to socialism; their numbers were especially strong in Poland and Russia as the movement grew well into the twentieth century. Differing from both Communists, "who advocated 'normalcy' and assimilation," and Zionists, "who pressed for a Jewish homeland and Hebrew as the national language," the Bundists were committed to both Yiddish and socialism (Klepfisz 1986/5746: 31–40). These are the markers of Itke's parents' Jewishness in the old country. In Atlanta they are no longer members of the working class, even though this history of a shared political consciousness helps make the mortar that holds their sense of Jewish community together in the (for them) new world. This is how Itke's narrative voice describes them:

> Juden aus der alten Heimat, Klumpen im amerikanischen Schmelztiegel, Fremdklumpen, von der brodelnden Masse abgestoßen, sich selbst absondernd, zusammenhaltend mit dem seltsamen Stolz des Fremden, der von Angst kaum zu unterscheiden ist. Kein einziger Arbeiter. Kleine Geschäftsmänner, Händler, Rechtsanwälte, Lebensversicherungsvertreter, ein oder zwei Ärzte, die noch sozialistisch denken wie in alten Zeiten, da die Linke ihre Interessen am besten vertrat.
> [Jews from the old homeland, clumps in the American melting pot, foreign bodies, cast off from the seething mass, keeping themselves separate, holding together with the strange pride of the alien, which can barely be distinguished from fear. Not a single laborer. Small businessmen, traders, lawyers, life insurance salesmen, one or two doctors, who still think socialist like in the old days when the Left represented their interests the best.] (20)

As for his self-image, Max Kovsky takes pride in not owning any property, seeing a world of difference between himself and Mr. Jägel, the deceased Jewish businessman and landlord whose grocery store property he now rents from the dead man's widow. Although Jägel was murdered in his store during a robbery, Kovsky sees no cause to arm himself, for, as he reasons, he is not Jägel. "Ich bezahle meine

Miete wie die Neger, meine Kunden. Sie werden schon nicht schießen auf ein'n Kovsky, nebbich" [I pay my rent like the Negroes, my customers. They won't shoot at Kovsky, the poor things] (16). Offered the opportunity to go into a more lucrative line of business after the riot that leaves his store a shambles, Kovsky declines, still maintaining (in Yiddish) that he is not a good American businessman: he can cut the throats of chickens but not of human beings (256).

Tatte Kovsky's socialist sensibilities also sensitize him to institutionalized racism directed against African Americans. "He screamed wildly that the application forms [for social relief] were required only of Negroes, who got the worst schools, who got the most underpaid jobs, who suck on stones in the land where milk and honey flow" (103). His frequent tirades against U.S. American racism and his various attempts at intervention on behalf of his disenfranchised clientele, however, do not spare him the marks of his own socially inscribed position. As a white man, he stands a better chance of securing the timely release of George, the alcoholic husband of one of Kovsky's African American customers, than any of the blacks. But as a Jewish man with a thick foreign accent, he is also scorned and insulted by the white policeman on duty at the station: "'n gottverdammter Jude bringt sein Geld hierher mitten in der Nacht wegen so'n Scheißdrecknigger. Sag mal, fickt ihr beide die gleiche Niggerhure?'" [a goddamn Jew brings his money down here in the middle of the night because of a shit-filthy nigger. Say, do you both fuck the same nigger whore?] (93). When a white company detective comes to the store looking for Ty Jones, who has purchased a radio on credit obtained under false pretenses, tension thickens in the air as Kovsky closes ranks with Jones and his other black customers against "the Company Man" and denies any knowledge of the man being sought. Even distancing himself from the white authorities, however, he cannot be said to occupy a "black" position. In the narrator's eyes: "Er rückte in das Niemandsland um den Company-Mann, schien kleiner vor dessen Länge, schien runzliger vor dessen Glätte, füllte mit Knoblauchhauch jenes Niemandsland zwischen dem Scotch-und-Soda-Gesicht und den Rüben-und-Schweinsrücken-Gemütern; schickte eine Knoblauchphalanx in den Kampf" [He inched into the no-man's-land around the Company Man, seemed shorter in front of his height, seemed more wrinkled in front of his smoothness, filled with garlic breath that no-man's-land between the scotch-and-soda-face and the turnips-and-fatback-souls; sent a garlic phalanx into battle] (85).

As a white man, Kovsky also does battle with white hospital authorities as the race relations depicted in the novel come to a head. With the broken body of Blue in his arms, the five-year-old black girl whom two policemen in a patrol car have struck and then just as quickly abandoned, he defies the unresponsive maze of separate emergency treatment facilities for blacks and whites and insists that the first doctor he encounters, who is white, attend to the injured child. Kovsky and Blue pay different prices for losing this battle: hers in blood and his in grief. The tendential hazing of economic and racial boundaries that is filtered through Kovsky's only moderately successful attempts at mitigating economic and racial injustice then gives way to a stark indictment of the "whiteness" of his positionality. No property owner, he is nonetheless the white employer to some and the white creditor to virtually all his black neighbors. Their grief and rage over Blue's murder vent themselves along racial and economic lines as the African Americans smash Kovsky's windows and ransack his store.[40] The absence of personalized indictments within this mixed community is evidenced by the fact that individual African Americans warn and protect the Kovsky family against this violent outbreak and that in the light of the next day these Jews and African Americans work together to set things right in the store again. Yet Kovsky's Jewishness is clearly imbricated with his particular immigrant experience of whiteness and maleness in 1940s Atlanta. These latter factors render unto him a position of *relative* social and economic privilege, from which vantage point he has the additional *ethical* privilege of choosing to be generous to those in greater need or not. By closing the novel with a celebration of Kovsky's decision to give away the (safe) food that the white authorities have forbidden him to sell in the wake of the riot (thereby threatening the neighborhood blacks, who have no cash and no credit to buy elsewhere, with a severe food shortage), Lander honors this choice as the more ethical one, while the contours of her text underscore the historicized, engendered, and racialized nature of such privilege.[41]

EIGHT

Itke's own positionality is developed, at least in part, in relation to that of her father, who is both Tatte and Kovsky. When he closes the store at night, he locks and bolts all the doors, securing the boundaries between his Jewish family, which lives above the store, and the rest of the world. From Itke's perspective, he locks out the middle and outer circles of her experience (16); the reader senses that she feels locked in, deprived of these spheres. Mamma Kovsky, too, seems preoccupied with policing Itke's visual perceptions of the more immediate middle circle of the black neighborhood. Any activities beyond what Itke can observe in the store, where she helps out and her African American neighbors function primarily as customers, are triggers for Mamma's impulse to draw the shades before Itke's eager eyes.[42] Although Tatte is much more inclined than Mamma to interact with blacks as heterogeneous, multidimensional human beings who are more than just customers, both parents (as unassimilated eastern European Jews) are imbued with a historically determined sense of Jewish separateness. To them, Itke's inner circle is intact. For her, it is riddled with questions and contradictions, at least some of which stem from a troubled relationship to the engenderment of her Jewish identity. As most feminist critiques of Judaism are wont to point out, traditional religious practice as well as social custom posit the experience and perspective of Jewish males not only as dominant but as normative (Heschel 1983; Lacks 1980; Ozick 1979; Plaskow 1990).[43] Women have been treated "as peripheral Jews" (Adler 1983: 13), not as "full Jews" (S. Schneider 1984: 21).[44] Traditional ritual obligations that accrue to them specifically as women presume certain social functions, notably those of wife, mother, and homemaker. Since none of these apply to the fourteen-year-old Itke, one could say that she occupies a site not yet fully coded in *halakhah*.[45] There is, of course, the assumption on her parents' part that she will both marry and do so within the Jewish faith, but until that point there is not much that religious law demands, specifically, of her. If Itke is never depicted performing any of the rituals associated with Jewish women—monthly purification (*niddah*), candle lighting (*nerot*), and bread consecration (*hallah*)[46]—how can we say that the construction of her Jewish identity is an engendered one?

Feminist theologian Judith Plaskow indicates a direction that would allow us to explore this question further: "Judaism has always been a religion of orthopraxis, assessing spirituality through the manifestation in the deed. The enactment of faith in the world, a central Jewish imperative, has had at least two distinctly different meanings in Jewish theology and practice: social justice and obedience to halakhah" (Plaskow 1990: 214; see also S. Schneider 1984: 35). Although Itke does attend Friday-night services at the synagogue, she does so not out of religious conviction but because she knows her parents are helpless against this particular reason for her absence from the store on a busy night. With the exception of Mamma Kovsky's insistence on keeping a kosher kitchen, virtually all references to *halakhic* observance in *Itke* are tainted with the charge of hypocrisy. (When the Kovsky family attends religious services for the High Holy Days, for example, they drive to the synagogue but park a few blocks away, like most of the other congregants, so that no one will know that they have violated the traditional proscription against riding on a holy day.) This is in fact a common thread in Lander's novels of the 1970s, in which the author tends to associate the purely mechanical cultivation of Jewish rituals and symbols with a failed Jewish spirituality, one that is either oblivious or insensitive to social injustice.[47] Within Judaism there is also a religious-historical tradition that granted to the struggle for social justice the highest priority, over and above the rote performance of *halakhic* ritual. In this sense the prophetic approach to Jewishness differed from the rabbinical one (Plaskow 1990: 214–17).[48] Yet as Plaskow has eloquently proven, the traditions were equally patriarchal in their orientation and imagery (Plaskow 1990: 216).[49] Itke cannot help but position herself as a Jewish woman when she experiences her father as the ultimate arbiter of (Jewish) ethics. This does not mean that she always agrees with him. On the contrary, she is often at odds with his practice of ethics, as, for example, when he violates government regulations for wartime rationing by pooling his customers' coupons so that he can distribute food according to need rather than by the bureaucratic book. But if Judaism posits male experience and perspective as normative, and it likewise ascribes to men the challenge of spiritual activity and ethics, then Itke's character fulfills one of her primary roles as a Jewish woman by gauging her own ethical standards against those of her father. The text reproduces this dynamic to the extent that (with rare exceptions) the only discussions of ethics and politics to which Itke is privy are either those that she has with Tatte or those that she overhears between him and the African American men who frequent his store.[50] These appearances to the contrary, Lander's textual maneuvers succeed in rupturing this dynamic from within, which is to say, on its own terms.

Norms of privilege tend to be insidiously effective when operating invisibly. Initially, Itke's young consciousness (albeit not her personal experience) evidences a naive adherence to absolutes. Seeing herself as "a Jew," she can perceive herself only as being like her father, who in this case embodies a particular kind of normative male prerogative. And yet she is not just like Tatte, for she is both Jewish and female: a Jewish woman in the making (to use Adler's term: a "peripheral" Jew in the making). In a comparable vein Itke wants to and does regard Jews (and blacks and whites) simply as "human beings." Overhearing her parents speak of Jews as a group distinguishable from any other, she accuses Tatte and Mamma of making the same distinctions for which they charge non-Jews with anti-Semitism. "A human being is a human being" (62), she insists with a degree of self-righteousness.

Zwei Bärenaugkreise sahen rabbinisch auf Itkeabtrünnerin, während zwei Bärenlippen rund verkündeten, sie hätten niemals behauptet, ein Jude wäre kein Jude. Ein Jude sei nicht ein Nicht-Jude. Ein Jude wäre *erst* ein Jude. "*Aber:*" ründeten sich verkündende Lippen, er muß die gleichen Rechte haben wie Nicht-Juden. Erst sei er Jude, aber dann sei er Mensch.

Mamma sah eulisch aus der Ecke.

"Es wäre besser, wenn er erst ein Mensch wäre, und dann Jude. Eventuell käme dann keiner auf die Idee, ihm irgendwelche Rechte zu verweigern", trünnte Itke weiter ab.

[Two bear-eye-circles looked rabbinically at Itke-renegade, while two bear-lips roundly pronounced they had never claimed that a Jew was not a Jew. A Jew is not a non-Jew. A Jew is *first* a Jew. "*But,*" the pronouncing lips rounded, he must have the same rights as non-Jews. First he's a Jew, then he's a human being.

Mamma looked owlishly out of the corner.

"It would be better if he were a human being first and then a Jew. Maybe then it would not occur to anyone to deny him his rights," renegaded Itke further.] (62)

The argument continues with Itke tenaciously defending her views. What she fails to see here is that her father speaks from his experience and perception of Jewishness in a world highly politicized around constructs of racial and ethnic identity. This is all the more striking given that the scene in which Itke makes this stand is dominated by various accounts of Joe Louis's boxing victory over Billy Conn, Tatte's commentary on how even a black world heavyweight champion will be cheated by white society, and Tatte and Mamma's discussion about Jews being carted off to concentration camps in Europe (61–63). In a sense Itke's blindness to the engendered nature of her Jewishness also makes her blind to the experiential differences that distinguish her father's particular humanity from that of other men. Her experience, as the novel unfolds, teaches her differently. The novel's narrative voice reflects this experience from a politically more seasoned perspective, which accounts for the narrator's alternately first-, second-, and third-person references to and epithets for the young girl.

"I—Itkescholar—put on my imaginary glasses, immediately became irrevocably superior to them all" (103). "Them all" in this case refers to Itke's Jewish immigrant parents and her poor African American neighbors. As a first-generation, white American she has been educated in white schools all her life (in addition to the Yiddish school she attends a few times a week). Her accent-free speech and English literacy are signs of white privilege that also distinguish her Jewishness as well as her whiteness from those of her parents. In her father's eyes these linguistic assets make her a perfect accomplice in this scheme of righting social wrongs. Before he goes down to the jail to get the local drunk released, he has Itke call first, with her perfect English, to determine if George is being held there (88). The passage that began with Tatte's ranting and raving about bureaucratic night-mares of paperwork for blacks, forced to suck on stones in the land of milk and honey, ends thus: "and gave the forms, naturally, to me" (103). Itke becomes entwined in her father's double legacy of social responsibility and white privilege, even as her privilege begins to outstrip his in linguistically and educationally circumscribed ways. The fact that she is not yet of an age to run her own business in early 1940s Georgia and hence lacks the economic status that falls to her father as a "white" businessman hardly restores her to innocence. Hearing the chilling tale that her black neighbor, Mrs. Stevens, has to tell comes with a painful reckoning for Itke.

Wresting an evening of independence from her reluctant parents, she receives her father's chain of keys so that she can lock all the doors the following night while home alone. She sleeps "comfortably, cozily, happilyboughtbetrayed" (43) into the day of her anticipated freedom. When Mrs. Stevens comes by later that night to make sure that "Miss Itke" is all right, the girl invites the nervous woman into her family's residential quarters to show her that the screams that had aroused her concern had come from the Kovskys' radio. Hesitant at first to enter a white home lest someone think she does not know the difference between right and wrong, the elderly neighbor finally agrees. Engaging with Itke in cautious conversation, Mrs. Stevens gradually relaxes into the story of her son, known to the community as the hunter, an independent loner who tried to live in simple dignity, away from people, whom he had reason to trust less than animals (53). On a vacant plot of land owned by Mrs. Jägel (the widow of Kovsky's predecessor) the hunter had built a shed for shelter. Refusing to pay the rent she demanded, he offered to raze the building if she ever wanted to build something else on the site. The impasse gave way to catastrophe when a group of black men, despising the hunter for his independent ways, managed to put the Ku Klux Klan on his trail—only ostensibly on behalf of the property owner. Mrs. Stevens's son and his girlfriend perish in the fire of the burning cross. Thoroughly engrossed in this tale of horrors, narrator (Mrs. Stevens) and listener (Itke) are jolted out of their momentary symbiosis by Mamma Kovsky's worried Yiddish voice. Having returned home to find her elderly neighbor and young daughter both in tears, she wants an ex-

planation. This leaves "Mrs. Stevens fromm und schlechtgewis-
sentlich weinend erklärend sich beschuldigend unschuldig im Hause
der Weißen" [Mrs. Stevens devout and with a bad conscience crying
explaining blaming herself innocent in the house of the whites] (59).
Mrs. Stevens's internalized perception of herself as a black intruder
on white territory is too deeply ingrained to allow her to accept
Mamma and Tatte Kovsky's invitation to cross the threshold into the
white living room where they could all listen to the "Brown Bomber's"
big boxing match together. She suddenly remembers she has something cooking on her stove. Itke is the one to let her out. "Itke with the
new Itkekeys let out Mrs. Stevens, for whom doors were locked that
stood open. Locked myself in again" (60). Itke's anticipated evening
of adolescent independence marks her as the keeper of her white father's keys. As she comes of age, they become her keys as well, the
two-sided instruments of her own imprisonment. A short time later
her mother tells her in Yiddish that learning will be her "key to all the
doors of the world" (66), but what this daughter learns is that her
"personhood" is not just Jewish and female but also ineluctably white.

What it means for Itke to be a white Jewish girl in 1940s Atlanta is
something she experiences and constructs with her body, the material vehicle of her presence in the world. Every time she fills out application forms for social relief for her African American neighbors,
uses her perfectly assimilated voice to speak with the authorities, or
turns the keys that lock Mrs. Stevens out and herself in, Itke's body is
complicitous in the construction of her own whiteness. Moving
through the public spaces of Peachtree Street in downtown Atlanta,
she is conscious of the ethnic and religious difference that sets her
and the other eleven members of her Jewish girls' club apart from the
other (white) southern girls walking the same street. For Itke, this
particular difference is one of cultivated consciousness; physically,
the B'nai B'rith Girls are indistinguishable from their white, non-
Jewish counterparts (43–44). It is primarily her whiteness, rather
than her Jewishness or even her femaleness, that Itke experiences
through the phenomenology of her body use (rather than the mere
color of her skin).[51] This disturbing realization is brought home to
her on her fifteenth birthday, which falls in September after the summer of her maturation that began in May.[52] Having chosen to spend

this entire day helping with the cotton harvest, Itke finds herself toiling in the hot sun with other white schoolmates as well as black field laborers whose skill in picking cotton comes from having to make a living at it. Her back sore and head pounding, fingers rubbed raw, Itke has comparatively little cotton to show for hours of sweat.

> Die Neger hatten mehr, pflückten schnell, gewandt. Sie kannten die Mittagsonne. Einer pflückte hinter mir her die Baumwolle, die ich übersehen hatte, kam rasch bis zu mir heran: "Ihr verpaßt mehr, als ihr holt, Missy. Die Baumwolle, die wächst ganz bis auf die Erde nieder, so hat sie Gott gemacht. Sieht aus, wie wenn er wollte, man muß sich ganz bis auf die Erde niederbeugen, um sie zu holen, die Baumwolle. Weiße und Schwarze gleich."

> So ist das. Und ich hab' das von oben geholt, und dir das gelassen, wonach man sich bücken muß, wie der Heuchler, der ich bin—und das, ohne zu wissen, zu wollen—ganz natürlicher Heuchler.

> [The Negroes had more, picked fast, skilled. They knew what the midday sun was like. One of them behind me picked the cotton that I had overlooked, hurried up to me: "You're missing more than you're getting, Missy. Cotton, it grows all the way down to the ground. That's how God made it. Looks like he wanted folks to have to bend down all the way to the ground in order to get it, the cotton. Whites and blacks the same."

> That's how it is. And I picked it from the top and left you the cotton that you have to bend over for, like the hypocrite that I am—without wanting to, without knowing it—a completely natural hypocrite.] (225)

This loss of innocence regarding her whiteness in a social context where whiteness connotes power and privilege follows shortly after her personal initiation into heterosexual lovemaking. The textual function of Itke's physicality as reflected in her sensuality and sexuality cannot, however, be understood only in relation to her male lover, Sonny, a relative visiting from the North while on leave from the U.S. army.

Unlike Anne Duden and TORKAN (see above, Chapters Two and Three), Lander highlights the erotic sensibilities of her central female character. In the postwar German context this could perhaps be considered a gesture toward reclaiming the materiality of a Jewish body from the realm of abstraction, representing it as an organ of experience not limited to the experience of victimization. (This might, for example, explain why early German reviewers of Lander's work so often seemed to respond with intense irritation to her unabashed mixing of Holocaust-related themes with questions of Jewish female sexuality.[53]) Long before her Jewish cousin arrives on the scene, however, Itke's erotic fascination is with Jimmie Lee, the Kovskys' eighteen-year-old African American housekeeper and the younger girl's model for boundless female sensuality. On the one hand this manifests itself in Itke's desire for Jimmie Lee to teach her how to dance sensually and freely with men, how to think and move with her belly instead of her head (134). On the other hand it also manifests itself in what might be seen as Itke's desire for Jimmie Lee herself. Cleaning the Kovskys' quarters in blue rubber gloves, red high-heeled sandals, and a black skirt with a slit up the back and nothing underneath, Jimmie Lee peppers her recounting of the weekend's dancing with the affective phrase "Hoo!" She claims that she can't be bothered with all the elastic bands on women's underclothes, always cutting into her and slipping out of place: "Hoo!" (131). Itke then sees: "A golden-yellow satin-jersey-blouse that swayed along with Jimmie Lee with hoo" (131). Trying to talk to Jimmie Lee while the latter cleans the inside of the oven, Itke addresses herself to "the rear end in the black skirt with the slit that used to be between the knees now almost up to the hoo" (131). Once she has persuaded Jimmie Lee to teach her to dance the high step, Itke is dizzied by the actual experience.

High step in blue rubber gloves, pulling me close, pushing me away, holding me tight, throwing me off, pulling me 'round, glove high and backside to backside, glove out and belly to belly and thigh to thigh and knee to knee with Jimmie Lee.

Hoo. (133)

The dance lesson is as close as the text comes to erotic physical contact between the two women. Yet even during Itke's lovemaking session with Sonny outside a room in which Jimmie Lee is making passionate love with her black male lover, Brother Wilson, Itke's eyes are all on the other woman, whom she can see through the window. Taking her nonverbal cues from the more experienced female sexual partner, Itke perceives sex with Sonny as a kind of fusion with Jimmie Lee. "Sonny kissed my Jimmie Lee lips" (244); "Sonnybrotherarm reaches around our waist from the back" (245). The names of the two women are joined in reverse order—"Jimmieleeitke" and "Itkejimmielee"— until they become one at the moment of simultaneous orgasm: "Jimmieleeitkeone" (244–45). It is *as if* they were the same woman.

This would, of course, be a troubling reading, at least to someone concerned with differentiated constructs of female identity. Valerie Smith has addressed some of the problematic ways in which representations of black women often function in feminist writing. For one, she cautions that the "association of black women with reembodiment" can resemble racist philosophical and historical associations between women of color and "animal passions" (V. Smith 1989: 45). Such associations in literature also cause us to wonder if stereotypes are being substituted for characters (see Christian 1985: 1–30). Furthermore, black female figures can be misused when they serve "to humanize their white superordinates, to teach them something about the content of their own subject positions" (V. Smith 1989: 46; see also Lorde 1984: 115). One could reasonably argue that within Jewish tradition there is already a certain linkage posited between *Jewish* women and gross matter or physicality (Adler 1983: 15–16; Lacks 1980: 1–2; Plaskow 1983: 225),[54] but this could scarcely account for the *relational* nature of Itke's orientation toward Jimmie Lee. To say that this orientation is relational is by no means to say that it is reciprocal, for there is no indication that Jimmie Lee regards Itke with anything remotely resembling erotic fascination. While there may be an element of homoeroticism in the way the younger girl sees the older one, it is less likely that Itke desires *her* and more likely that Itke desires to be *like* her. Lander's text, however, consistently undermines the assumption that this is possible. One indication of this (I shall elaborate on others shortly) is the African American woman's response to the Jewish girl's claim that they are both "human beings," closer than sisters. "'We live like sisters is right, here at your place. Here at your place. Come on! You can't live like we do. You don't know how" (152). The purported sisterhood is a bogus one, since it appears intact only as long as the differences between the two women are denied.[55] Jimmie Lee knows better, and in this sense she cannot be said to "humanize" her white employers' daughter. On the contrary, she puts another chink in Itke's faith that people are *just* human beings, all the same. Although Jimmie Lee does teach Itke some things, she is hardly the only character, black or white, to function in this capacity. And given that Jimmie Lee is only one of ten highly individuated African American female characters in this particular novel (with Itke and her mother being the only fully developed white female characters of any religious or ethnic background), it seems unlikely that Jimmie Lee's sensuality could be classified as stereotypical.[56]

Earlier I said that Itke desires to be *like* Jimmie Lee and that the text illuminates the impossibility of this project. What we might read as Itke's homoerotic attraction to her African American confidante *in any event* functions to show that the construction of Itke's gender as a Jewish woman does not proceed solely along the normative vector of maleness. Whereas she is positioned (and situates herself) as a Jewish woman vis-à-vis her father, as I have shown, she also situates herself as a Jewish woman in her heterosexual activities with Sonny (another Jewish male) by orienting herself, as the text clearly reveals, toward another woman. This disrupts the normative code of traditional Judaism in a way that is at once radical and fundamental—*more* radical and fundamental than merely allowing for the occasional deviation from the norm (whereby a Jewish woman might cultivate her sexuality outside the prescribed confines of a heterosexual marriage within the Jewish faith).[57] A more radical disruption occurs when Itke's relationship to Jewish maleness is not only predicated on that norm but also constructed along vectors that exceed it.

While it is not necessarily very radical to say (in the 1990s) that relationships between or among women are often determined by relationships between women and men—this is the standard feminist criticism of a dominant heterosexist perspective—something has to shift in our perception of the two "women" under discussion if we begin to allow for the particularity of their respective experiences of gender. In postexilic formative Judaism, Leonard Swidler details, the increased need to hold the Jewish community together by more stringent policing of the boundaries between it and surrounding cultures meant tighter control over Jewish women within the community as well as increased hostility toward non-Jewish women outside it.[58] Non-Jewish women, in this view, are constructed as being even more alien than the "otherness" of Jewish women. The specific historical conditions for this development have shifted over and over again in the sands of time, but the ideology of Jewish separateness remains part and parcel of the religious culture (despite its various manifestations).[59] When Itke constructs herself as a sexualized Jewish female—in part—through her orientation to Jimmie Lee, she effectively says: I am not merely Jewish (like Tatte *or* Mamma); I am also *like her*, a woman who lives and breathes outside the normative Jewish construct of womanhood.

We have already seen that Itke's relationship to her father engenders her Jewishness as female; yet it would be misleading to conclude from this that she and Jimmie Lee are both engendered in the same way. For Itke to say "I am also like her" is to say that they are both more than and different from what normative Judaism would have them be. Furthermore, by transgressing the boundaries of that normative vision, Itke points to the existence of a broader social and discursive reality to which constructs of her Jewishness and her femaleness (and her whiteness) are also inextricably tied. The "excess" of Itke's vision as developed in the novel draws attention then to the understanding that Itke and Jimmie Lee do not in fact occupy the same sites of womanhood. The Jewish girl becomes a woman, but she does not experience her Jewishness merely "as a woman." This phrase, which Elizabeth V. Spelman debunks as "the Trojan horse of feminist ethnocentrism" (Spelman 1988: x, 13), tendentially erases the multivalent social embeddedness of constructions of female identity. Their identities "as women" cannot be surgically isolated from the simultaneously operative and differing factors of race, class, and ethnicity. To call Itke's (partial) orientation toward Jimmie Lee "homoerotic" would thus reproduce the blind spots of ethnocentric feminism. For, in Spelman's terms, the two "women" do not share the same gender.[60]

TEN

If the concept of positionality is useful for exploring configurations of embodiment that are not only construct-ed but also construct-ing, then it behooves us to examine in greater detail the textual function of Itke's physicality. To be sure, her sexual activities explode some of the parameters demarcated for her by *halakhah*. Yet while Jewish female sexuality is traditionally seen as something to be controlled and contained within heterosexual Jewish marriage,[61] Mamma and Tatte Kovsky are not exactly rigorous in policing their daughter's *movements*. Itke herself, contemplating the possibility of being caught pregnant and unmarried, feels that she would be abandoned by white society but not by her parents (151).[62] Her sexual encounters with Sonny are in effect only one manifestation of a more broadly conceived sensuality that transgresses boundaries. The first time that Itke and Sonny engage in sexual intercourse, they are in her room upstairs, above the family store, a scene that carries far less textual weight than a subsequent encounter, one that places Itke outside the inner circle of her Yiddish-speaking family. Lander has prepared us for such transgressions throughout the text by cultivating sensory indications of Itke's yearning to cross the line that seeks to define and contain her.

The central female figure is often pictured at a window. The chapter that includes Mrs. Stevens's story, the boxing championship match, and Itke's argument with her parents about people being just people ends with her sitting at the window, from where her parents allow her to watch their African American neighbors rejoice in the streets over Joe Louis's victory. "Itke jenseits des Kreises, diesseits des Umkreises; Itke in der Zone, die ein Fenster bildet, von dem aus man alles sieht, woran man nicht teilhat" [Itke beyond the inner circle, this side of the middle circle; Itke in the zone that forms a window from which one sees everything in which one has no part] (67).[63] Teresa de Lauretis's comments about borders seem appropriate here: "Borders stand for the potentially conflictual copresence of different cultures, desires, contradictions, which they articulate or simply delineate." They "mark difference itself; a difference that is not just in one or the other, but between them and in both. Radical difference cannot perhaps be represented except as an experiencing of borders" (de Lauretis 1984: 99).[64] As often as Mamma Kovsky tries to pull the shades on Itke's window of perception, she is doomed to fail, for Itke's eyes refuse containment. She raises the blinds herself and sees Biggs-Mamma do her voodoo conjuring (24–25), Beatrice running for help for her injured child (26), a drunken George raping his wife (36).

Bearing witness to a world not immediately her own, Itke violates her own culture's injunction against women serving as witness (Greenberg 1981/5742: 7; S. Schneider 1984: 34; Swidler 1976: 115). But her vision is not the only sense to take her where her whole body has not yet been allowed to go. She hears a secret pair of lovers whispering in the family garden; the air she smells from the window is "blumenschwanger, gardenien- und magnolienschwer, pfirsichherb und rosenstaubig, zikadenlaut, libellenflüglig" [pregnant with flowers, heavy with gardenias and magnolias, peach potent and dusted with rose pollen, loud with cicadas, whirling with dragonfly wings] (175). When she finally takes her entire body with her, she sneaks out the back door and crawls through a hole in the fence. "Came for the first time directly into the Saturday evening, which belonged to the Negroes" (236). This escape from the enclosure of her Jewish identity tainted with white privilege comes shortly after Tatte Kovsky has returned from the hospital with the devastating news of Blue's death. It is, predictably, a short one.

Excluded from full participation in religious rituals of communal prayer and Torah study, Jewish women were sometimes categorized in rabbinic terminology as "inside" persons (Plaskow 1990: 84–85; Greenberg 1981/5742: 85). Plaskow explains that this inside/outside split is not the same as the dichotomy often posited in the modern secular sense of public versus private spheres (Plaskow 1990: 84). Having literally crawled across the imagined line between the inner and middle circles of her world, Itke attempts to walk with an "upright gait" (Ernst Bloch). Neither the religious category of inside/outside nor the civic one of private/public adequately conveys the divisions she tries to bridge, for neither accounts for constructs of racial identity. Her escape garners her a new epithet: "Itke-Outside" (239). For the first time she stands outside her inner circle looking back in at her parents, who look small and defeated (239). From this vantage point she sees Brother Wilson enter her world to warn the Kovskys that it might be better to close shop early: "'there's something in the air'" (241). Left behind by Brother Wilson, this world is wrapped by the narrator in biblical allusions: "against it, raging from all sides, the sand blows" (241). Itke stands what she takes to be her ground far, far away from the ghetto pathways of her Jewish immigrant parents' tales. "Ich bin auch gegangen. Stehe außen. Habe euch verlassen. Den Schritt getan, den trennenden" [I left, too. Am standing outside. Abandoned you. Took the step, the one that separates us] (241).

But how free is she to carve out a path entirely of her own making? She follows in Brother Wilson's footsteps, which lead them both to Jimmie Lee's house. Brother enters, while Itke remains on the outside, watching the lovers through an open window: "entirely without shades" (243). Nevertheless, her temporary location outside her inner circle in no way places her inside the middle circle. The entire scene in which Itke-Outside perceives her sexuality as "fusing" with that of Jimmie Lee-Inside is structured (literally: framed) by the window that separates them. It remains a window, not an open door for Itke to walk through, and she remains on the outside with her white Jewish male lover. By the time the riot actually breaks out, she is back inside the store trying to comfort her tearful mother. The chapter concludes with the image of Itke herself closing the door, "shades down" (252). There are apparently limits to the boundaries that can be crossed. But to say that Itke is back inside the family store is not to say that she is back inside the inner circle in the same way as before. Her movements *outside* the inner circle have changed the nature of her being *in* it. Her sexual coming of age is not equivalent to her political coming of age, but the two processes coincide in Lander's text. The structure of the narrative and the tenor of the narrative voice both detail and foreground the various elements imbricated in the construction of Itke's positionality. The theatrical heading that introduces the chapter in which Itke loses her virginity reads, in part: "a stranger blurs the boundaries between the circles of Itke's surroundings" (193). Her initiation into sex with Sonny shifts her relationship to her parents' world as well as her *awareness* of her relationship to Jimmie Lee's inner circle. By the same token, as the narrative stance insists, her sexuality is also inscribed with her positionality as white, Jewish, and female in early 1940s Georgia.

ELEVEN

The novel itself is framed by additional commentary on the part of the author. In her preface Lander gives a very brief historical account of two variations of folk theater, allusions to which structure the staging for each subsequent chapter: nineteenth-century American minstrel shows and a Yiddish play called *The Dybbuk,* which premiered in Poland in 1920 but draws on a medieval tradition of Jewish mysticism.[65] Lander links the origins of the minstrel show to the institution of American slavery, to a time when white masters of cotton and peach plantations made their black slaves perform for them. Later performers, she notes, were whites who appeared in blackface.[66] In Lander's description *The Dybbuk* portrays a young man who dies of a broken heart when his beloved is forced to marry another; on her wedding day his spirit takes possession of her body, thereby "freeing" her (from being tied to a man she does not love). "In a summer in the week of Itke K.," Lander writes, "a strange union takes place between these two pieces of folk art" (9). Two pages of "afterthoughts" by the author complete the framing of the novel. Here she explicitly addresses some of the historical conditions for social unrest among African Americans, positing World War II as a turning point on a path that eventually led to the civil rights movement. In order to grasp the aggression felt by black Americans in response to a long history of economic and political injustice, she contends, one has to become acquainted with these people "as they thought, felt, acted, lived" (264). This she sees as one of the objectives of her novel.

One might conclude from such comments that the author manages to combine (*vereinigen*) two radically different traditions of folk theater and provide her readers with an authentic rendition of African American life in 1940s Georgia. It would be foolish to do so. For every turn of the novel's staging is designed to counter any assumption of authentic representation or naturalized identity. We have already seen that Itke's positionality is constructed along vectors of difference. These vectors are themselves subject to material and discursive construction. Even the novel's sense of historical time toys with readerly assumptions of chronological authenticity. While the title refers to "a summer in the week of Itke K.," the text actually represents a full-blown summer (May to September) in terms of a week. The year is specifically cited as 1942, but Joe Louis fought Billy Conn and Abe Simon in 1941 (see note 3), and even that dating is unsettled by conflicting references to dates and locations for Louis's various boxing matches.[67] Such detailed subterfuge is relatively minor compared with the repeated shifts in perspective that undo the childish naiveté of Itke as experiential subject by privileging the political astuteness of Itke as narrative agent. Complementing this process of estrangement (from assumptions of authenticity) is the staging to which I have alluded above. This refers to both the theoretical framing of the protagonist's perceptions and the novel's plot, as well as to Lander's use of language.

The first paragraph describing Itke places her living "in a circle in a circle in a circle" (13). Unlike the metaphors of centers and margins common to feminist rhetoric of the 1980s (see above, Chapter Three), these circles set the stage for Itke's maturation without positioning her either at a purportedly monolithic center of power or on a supposedly fixed margin of oppression. She is located at the center of her own experience, in that her perceptions emanate from them, but her experiences are not construed as the center of her world. And as we have seen, she moves across boundaries in ways that make perceptions shift. Although Lander draws only loosely on the formal components of minstrel shows and Yiddish theater, she has selected two forms in which circles comprise part of the staging. Minstrel shows took place in what was known as "the burnt cork circle," with performers arranged in semicircular fashion (Wittke 1976: 136). In *The Dybbuk* a wronged dead man calls the living to trial, which necessitates drawing a circle to partition the living from the spirits of the dead. Tellingly, the original title of Ansky's famous play was "Between Two Worlds" (Lifson 1965: 103). Whereas *The Dybbuk* enacts an encounter between the living and the dead, the minstrel shows staged a certain kind of relationship between "black" and "white" Americans. Not surprisingly, then, Lander deploys these elements not to unify Itke's experiences, but to clarify the multidimensional nature of their construction. Although we are told that the first four chapters are minstrel shows and that the subsequent four are dybbuk scenes, each chapter draws its stage personnel from both the inner and middle circles of Itke's experience. Indeed, the first chapter is introduced as a minstrel show "in which Itke describes the circles of her environment in order to ascertain what boundaries they have" (11). The second part of the ninth chapter is "simultaneously an act of *The Dybbuk* and a *minstrel show,* in which Itke and the Negroes simultaneously break out" (237). The staged exploration and transgression of boundaries point to the constructedness of the borders themselves. But to say, as the heading for the final chapter does, that "everyone takes a stand true to himself" (253) is not to say that the characters reach a place of authentic identity free of staging. It is to say that the characters' actions are inscribed by their positionality as they also contribute to its production.

Since both minstrel shows and Yiddish theater in the United States relied on singing and dancing (Wittke 1976; Tuerk 1983: 143), Lander can draw on this additional vehicle for estranging the events of the novel from our perspectives as readers. This element of "performance" is, moreover, linked to the theme of authentic (natural) versus staged (constructed) identity. In minstrel parlance the common term for performing was "faking," and a performer was known as a "faker."[68] This seems all too modest a nod toward acknowledging that these "fakers" only claimed to be representing "authentic" black culture. Although *The Dybbuk* is not a play by non-Jews about Jewish culture, its drama derives from a dead man, whose lifelong obsession with his magical powers led him to evil excess, taking possession of a young woman, from whose body his spirit must be exorcised. Such repeated allusions to the constructed nature of Itke's embodied positionality also mean, however, that her perceptions of the African Americans in her "middle circle" elude her appropriation of their experience. We see the figures in all the circles as Itke sees them, which does not mean that we see them *as they are.* By the same token, Lander's use of language makes it clear that Itke does not speak *for* the African Americans around her. And yet while they speak their own language in the novel, Lander carefully debunks any notion of "authentic" black speech. In my view this is a pivotal marker of Lander's brilliance. As Sander L. Gilman has determined, there is in German society "a strong tradition of the myth of a homogeneous language that defines the Other as possessing a different tongue" (Gilman 1986: 20). At times this "special language of the Other" has been considered "a sign of the innate, biological difference inherent in the very concept of race" (213). The constructedness of racial identity in *Itke* is underscored by the startling constructedness of Lander's language.

As noted earlier, Lander's first novel is written in German, Yiddish, and a Southern Black sociolect rendered into an artificial German dialect. This can only come as a shock to a German reading public. Although a knowledge of German may go a long way toward understanding some Yiddish, there is enough of a gap between the two languages to call for a glossary of Yiddish words, which the publishers have appended to the novel. Even Lander's use of German is sometimes idiosyncratic (as some of the passages cited have already shown): broken, sensual, phenomenological, musical, poetic.[69] Lander's rendition of a 1940s Southern Black sociolect as an artificial German dialect, replete with double negatives, effects a particular quality of estrangement in the German context, since the words evoke a sense of familiarity that the syntax shatters. (One wonders how Lander could have created such linguistic estrangement if she had written the novel in American English. Presumably, the temptation to identify the speech patterns of the African American characters as "authentic" would be too great. Anyone attempting to translate this novel into English would have to resolve this dilemma.) The rich, inauthentic contours of this text also challenge any tendency to *categorize* language too readily. Itke, who initially seeks to cling to an absolute faith that people are "just" human beings, also demands absolute consistency and integrity of speech. If her father mixes English words with Yiddish ones, she chastises him or pretends not to understand (91). And yet as she herself comes to realize, the boundaries of the three circles' speech-worlds are no more secure than any of the other boundaries she has transgressed. "In meine Sprachwelt rissen die Grenzen der anderen Sprachwelten ein" [The boundaries

of the other speech-worlds ripped into my own] (90). Her father's
Yiddish is punctuated with "new world" words. Several of his African
American customers use an occasional Yiddish or even Hebrew
phrase that they have learned from him. Having just joined the U.S.
army, Brother Wilson attacks the ironies of American racism with bitter eloquence in a High German that the white policeman who insulted Jews and blacks could never hope to reproduce (198–200).
Itke fails in policing the borders of her own speech, as she mixes
"white" English and Yiddish or uses a "black" expression (90). She
feels defenseless against the double negatives cultivated by both minorities as well as the poor Protestant "trash" that is 150 percent white
(91). It seems that there is no "purity" of linguistic or racial identity
here, as the different speech-worlds in the novel are not only highly
stylized but also subject to reciprocal incursions.

TWELVE

If the stylistic function of the theatrical and linguistic elements in this
novel is to effect its readers' estrangement from what we are allowed
to experience, quite vicariously, then to what extent can we say that
Itke's various codes constitute a true heteroglossia? Tobe Levin has
suggested a Bakhtinian reading, since the two forms of folk art
staged in the text "represent masquerades or multiple transgressions
of the self" (Levin 1990). David Carroll characterizes the Bakhtinian
carnival as "the repeated affirmation of the possibility of alternative
relations in the midst of order and control" (Carroll 1987: 91). And
yet this is precisely what Lander's various codes of estrangement do
not effect. The author presents us instead with a text that tracks the
highly specific and fundamentally embodied multiplicity of the protagonist's positioning in the worlds of her life. The lives and "masks"
of the other characters are all filtered through her eyes, interpreted
in relation to the construction of her heterogeneous identity. In this
sense none of the "faking" in the novel attains the status even of an
authentic masquerade. None of it is "free" from order and control.
The multilingualism enacted here is as much about the work of
agency as it is about the play of subterfuge. Pertaining neither to the
female subversion of the bilingual heroine (Yaeger 1988) nor to car-

nivalistic interventions à la Bakhtin, *A Summer in the Week of Itke K.* represents and refracts the mutually imbricated poles of a heterogeneous positionality that characterizes the discursive and material constructions of one figure's particular experience. To speak with Elaine Scarry (1988: vii–xxvii), the multiplicity of speech invokes the heterogeneity of the human body's presence in the material world.[70] Even bodies "matter" in discourse.

I have tried to delineate the ways in which Jeannette Lander makes Itke's body "matter" to us. Intervening in the production of contemporary German literature, the author represents not good Jews or bad Jews, but a particular Jew, her positionality no longer predicated on the *centrality* of the Holocaust in the construction of her "Jewishness" vis-à-vis "Germanness."[71] On the shores of feminist literary theory Lander breathes life into a *particularly* embodied construct of "female" identity, a precious gift indeed. For as we have seen, a woman conceived without the burden and boon of specific, positional embodiment is "all and only woman" (Spelman 1988: 187) and can lay no claim to a particular place in history. To repeat: "Historical and cultural identity is not constituted by having a body with particular identifying features" such as "black" or "white" skin, "but it is impossible without such features and the significance attached to them" (Spelman 1982a: 54). In this sense I suggest that the "double focus" (Weigel 1985) of much of 1980s Germanist feminist criticism— the utterly crucial attention to how women are both privy to power and not—yields nonetheless a kind of blurred vision. In order to account for constructs of "difference" in a German field of cultural and political heterogeneity, we will need more than doubled vision that allows us to see only in terms of either male-female, German-Jewish, white-black, or then-now. Even in the contemporary German context, race—though not by any means a universal or biological category—"matters."[72] Indeed, all the particular vectors of positionality matter in mutually imbricated ways as the making of human bodies in recent postwar (West) German literature sets about making and unmaking configurations of German history.

Conclusion

This book has sought to reformulate questions of subjective agency and historical determination that have both provoked and propelled German Studies as well as Women's Studies for twenty-odd years. Deploying the premises of one area of study to interrogate the other leaves neither field intact. And yet neither field exists outside a broader international context in which contemporary theories of power and signification vie for our attention. Here we are compelled to recast the Gordian knot that binds us to the worlds of matter and of discourse even as it posits an absolute split between them. We live in this knot, in countless variations, for we are at once subject to and subjects of material and discursive construction.

In order to explore the specific nature of this configuration in contemporary West German prose and culture, it has been necessary to consider the imbricated production of history and the human body as socioaesthetic constructs. A refined concept of embodied positionality compels us to recognize some of the decisive ways in which human bodies, real as well as imagined, engage in material and discursive sociality. In contrast to more familiar tropes of place or location, the notion of positionality elaborated here enables us, furthermore, to pursue the production of gender as simultaneously and inextricably intertwined with the production of race, nationality, class, religion, ethnicity, and other signifying social practices through which power is manifested, resisted, or challenged. As feminist scholars have had no monopoly on attempts to negotiate the complex interplay of materiality, embodiment, and signification, this treatise on making bodies making history also asks how it is that other critical theories do or do not account for the positionality of embodied relationships to power and discourse.

With particular regard to the West German context before 1989, Chapter One examines representative efforts to reinstate the body to German critical theory (Sloterdijk; Negt and Kluge) or to address bodily functions in postmodernism (Kamper and Wulf). While Oskar Negt and Alexander Kluge's unconventional social theory does address contradictions of multiple and unstable subject-object relations—and hence the contradictory production of human agency in social process—it does not explicitly acknowledge the constitutive influence of signification. On the other hand, feminist scholarship has shown social theories to be profoundly lacking if they do not or cannot attend to the intricate and often contradictory signification of embodied relations to power. This is made abundantly clear by de Lauretis's sophisticated approach to the production of gender, but it is likewise apparent in Turner's assessment of social bodies, which we both have and are, and Scarry's insights into the structuration of torture. Agnes Heller's theory of semiotic processes of historical interpretation indicates, further, that historical relationships are rooted in concrete, sentient experience, while narratives of history constitute interpretations of bodily experience. De Lauretis, Turner, and Scarry illuminate processes of signification whereby political meaning is inscribed both on and by embodied agents of social change. History is a construct of our making, with which, according to Heller, we not only seek to understand our present but also are capable of choosing and creating change, which can manifest itself as our future.

These interdisciplinary excursions into the realms of sociology, semiotics, history, literature, and feminism are intended to sharpen a focus on what we could call, in Heller's terms, the present-present age of West German culture. If the questions we ask of the past are in effect prompted by present needs, then literary representations of any past-present age can be seen to articulate present dilemmas. In this sense Judith Ryan's discussion of individual responsibility in postwar German literature is no longer adequate to the changed circumstances of the more recent postwar era (roughly 1968 to 1989). Specifically, in the West German arena of the last twenty years, one ascertains that bodies in literature function no longer as victims of history or as allegories for the nation but as heterogeneous sites of contested identities. We must account for the *construction* of subjects from whom we demand moral choices or political acts or from whom, alternatively and deterministically, no such choices are deemed possible. The particular nature of some of these multivalent identities is the subject of the three chapters of applied textual analysis offered here. Although all human bodies partake of materiality and discursivity, they do not do so uniformly. A rigorous discussion of feminist positionalities—and of the function of positionality in contemporary feminist discourse—reveals historicized and racialized constructions of gender as well as engendered and racialized constructs of German history and national identity. Tracking the embodiment of positionality in literary representations of heterogeneous identity, we are able to unravel some of what we know about the production of subjective agency in our time.

How does a racist image become the pivot on which a text that aspires to feminist aesthetics comes to turn? Chapter Two's positional analysis of *Opening of the Mouth* reveals the culturally and historically specific tensions structuring Anne Duden's production of white German women, African Americans, and Jews in postwar Germany. This serves to undermine any alleged universality of either writing or suffering held to be "woman-centered." Chapter Three's discussion of *Tufan* begins with a critique of feminist scholarship that cites a concept of positionality as the answer to feminist essentialism and poststructuralist undecidability but ignores the requisite embodiment of positionality. This elision leaves us, once again, unable to negotiate difference, contradiction, or agency. The productive movements of TORKAN's narrative enact not a Western stereotype of "Third World Woman," but a positional subject imbricated in contested constructions of Iranian, Muslim, female, and German identity. As with the textual performance of Jews and other "Others" in *Itke*, recognition of such imbricated identities highlights the need to rethink our understanding of contemporary West German culture and feminist models of minority discourse. Jeannette Lander's first novel explodes the binary constellation of "Jews and Germany" that has plagued German representations of Jews since World War II. This poses a challenge to German Studies and Germanist feminist scholarship as well, since both could be said to have "mis-placed" minority discourse. Chapter Four's insistence on discussing racialized constructs of Jewishness, Germanness, and gender should remain a source of provocative discomfort. But if, having read Chapter Four, we can return to the other chapters of textual analysis and not be equally provoked by the reference to race in Chapter Two or the absence of such references in Chapter Three, the point will have been lost. For to assume that constructs of racial identity "naturally" play a role in representations of African Americans or just as "naturally" fail to play a role in representations of Iranians is to reproduce blind spots of historically circumscribed perceptions. Constructs of racial identity do not become problematic in the realm of German Studies only when they are applied to Jews. Rather, they become problematic—which is to say, politically charged—whenever relations of power are contested and constructed along vectors to which racial identity is ascribed. Nothing is immediately given. Even to say that this study explores imbricated socioaesthetic constructs of engendered, racialized, and historicized bodies of experience is not to say that any chapter merely replicates the terms of any other. Historically specific representations of cultural heterogeneity and subjective agency merit equally particular theoretical analyses of embodied positionality.

To those who have felt, as I have, trapped between the much-touted dominion of discourse and the uneasy feeling that even in the age of postmodernism people and things do continue "to matter," this book addresses a need that has been voiced by but is not confined to feminist scholarship. Alluding to Simone de Beauvoir's often cited pronouncement that one is not born but rather becomes a woman, Judith Butler characterizes the construct of "woman" as "a term in process, a becoming, a constructing that cannot rightfully be said to originate or to end. As an ongoing discursive practice, it is open to interventions and resignification" (Butler 1990: 33). (*Gender Trouble* also entails a critique of de Beauvoir's adherence to a Cartesian model of embodiment.) Butler's phrasing beckons tantalizingly, since it could easily apply to certain aspects of the construct of positionality that has been traced, enacted, deployed in these pages: "a term in process, a becoming, a constructing that cannot rightfully be said to originate or to end." What better way to conclude an exploration of complex positionalities than to determine that no "conclusion" is possible, that the process is an ongoing one, and that there is always more to be known? And yet to say that positionality cannot properly be understood as originating or ending is decidedly not to say that its production occurs outside any delimited sociohistorical matrix. Even if only for split seconds at a given moment, positionality characterizes and engenders embodied agents of history, who are at once subjects of and subject to material, discursive, historical construction. The specific dimensions of these constructions call forth equally particular questions regarding accountability and innovation in historical process. Like a river that rages or gently flows, even a state of flux manifests itself in material ways, and every political agenda selectively responds to critical junctures of its own transitions. For its reading of contemporary (West) German culture, this study has argued that constructs of gender and race are crucial analytical coordinates for tracing the production of German cultural identity since 1945 *and* that gender and race constructs, taken individually or together, are insufficient to account fully either for what it means to be a "German" or for what it means to be a "woman" in the 1970s and 1980s. While works by Anne Duden, TORKAN, and Jeannette Lander lend themselves especially well to this articulation, countless other German-language cultural texts may be profitably mined for insights into the embodied signification of German history. Since all literary prose of the last two decades relies on some configuration of human bodies, there are many positionalities that remain to be explored, illuminated, and mobilized. The ongoing process of German "unification" will undoubtedly shift the ground of figuring identity in a German context many times over as we turn toward a new marking of time. Once again, this is and will presumably continue to be history in and of our making.

Notes

CHAPTER ONE: OF BODIES, SECRETS,
AND THE MAKING OF HISTORIES

1 Horkheimer and Adorno 1972: 231. Cumming translates the original "Nachtseite" as "dark side."

2 Nägele (1986: 94) calls this shared concern "the common family romance of a struggle with the history of the bourgeois European Enlightenment."

3 Dews (1987) demonstrates that the Enlightenment subject was never as monolithic or "self-identical" as is fashionably assumed today, a position also taken by Manfred Frank in Frank et al. 1988 (7–28). For some other alternatives to the poststructuralist debunking of history and its traditional subject, see Dallmayr 1981, Frank 1984, Huyssen 1981 and 1984, Jameson 1981, Sangari 1987, and the essays in Foster 1984.

   The Dews book provides a remarkably rigorous, comprehensive critique of the philosophical underpinnings and political implications of the poststructuralist theories advanced by Derrida, Lacan, Foucault, and Lyotard. This detailed comparison of poststructuralism and modern German philosophy is not to be overlooked.

4 Butler (1990: 71) describes *social* bodies in much the same way. This is perhaps misleading, since it does not fully account for the materiality of socially constructed experience.

5 In her introduction to *Literature and the Body* (1988) Elaine Scarry cites "the fact that the human body is at the present moment a special site of attention and concern," a phenomenon she explains as follows: "The

very extremity of the scepticism about the referential capacities of language in the past decade made it almost inevitable that at the moment when language was finally reconnected to the world, the primary site of reconnection would be not just this or that piece of material ground but the most extreme locus of materialization, the live body" (xx–xxi). This makes sense, however, only if we regard live bodies as the precondition for the making of histories, which is *not* to say that these bodies exist anterior to historical experience or social construction. The "attempt to restore the material world to literature," as Scarry puts it, can be attributed not to "a kind of collective regret at the very weightlessness, the inconsequentiality of conversations about literature" (Scarry 1988: xxi) alone, but rather to a variety of technological, political, economic, social, and ideological assaults on possibilities for subjective agency. What is at stake is less the question as to whether the institution of literature continues to "matter" than the concern as to *how* those broader social issues to which literary texts refer (however nonmimetically) persist in "mattering" in the last decades of the twentieth century. (I am grateful for Scarry's insightful comments on the verb "to matter" [xxii–xxiii].)

6 In his introduction to *Historical Studies and Literary Criticism* (1985) Jerome J. McGann tries to salvage some sense of referentiality for critical studies of literature without resorting to a supposed anteriority of meaning. Whereas Said's differentiation between filiation and affiliation (1983: 16) underscores the location of critical consciousness both in and outside a given culture, my emphasis here is on the body and its images in literature. Said, however, is one of the few critics even to make specific mention of the body in the context of what he calls "making sense of textual experience" (27).

7 See Klaus Theweleit's *Male Fantasies* (1987: 416) and Peter Sloterdijk's *Critique of Cynical Reason* (1987). The German originals were first published in 1980 and 1983, respectively.

8 The reference to Auerbach is from "Engorging the Patriarchy" (McGann 1985: 229). For critical commentaries on Foucauldian theory, see de Lauretis 1984, Dews 1987, Said 1983, and Turner 1984. Tracing the progression of Foucault's intellectual concerns, Dews notes in the 1970s a shift in emphasis from "the disenchanted nature of modern consciousness" to "the processes of corporeal regulation and control by means of which a stable self is produced." As Dews goes on to point out, "despite this verbal insistence, the notion of the body remains little more than a cipher in Foucault's work of this period." This renders Foucault's account of the body "curiously anodyne," according to Dews. "Without

some evocation of the intrinsic forces of the body, without some theory which makes the corporeal more than a malleable *tabula rasa,* it is impossible to reckon the costs imposed by an 'infinitesimal power over the active body,' or the sacrifice involved in the 'individualizing fragmentation of labour power'" (163–64). Dews is citing here from *Discipline and Punish* (1977).

9 Judith Butler's otherwise rigorous critique of ontologizing tendencies in feminist conceptualizations of sex and gender leaves unclarified the question of materiality. If we agree that all bodies are subject to discursive construction and that no body exists anterior to such construction, as Butler cogently argues, must we necessarily conclude that materiality is solely an issue of signification? See especially Butler's comments on agency (1990: 142–49). Laqueur 1990 also grapples with related issues concerning the contextual, historical making of sex and sexual difference.

10 Arguing in a related context against the deconstructionist erasure of the human subject, Frank (1988: 28) calls for a hermeneutic of personal identity "'over time.'" In section 3 of this chapter some aspects of the poststructuralist position on the body are explored in somewhat more detail.

Elisabeth Lenk (1983) has written a lengthy German study against the assertion of a disembodied "subject." Her focus is on dream structures.

11 I would translate the title of the Negt and Kluge study as "History and Something with a Mind of Its Own." This is not entirely satisfactory, since the word *Eigensinn* (stubbornness, wilfullness, arbitrariness) defies smooth translation just as that which it is intended to connote here defies easy categorization.

12 For a comparison of how the bomb functions in the construction of subjectivity in texts by Sloterdijk, Botho Strauss, and Christa Wolf, see Adelson 1986.

The first English translations of Sloterdijk's *Critique* were limited to the first two chapters (Sloterdijk 1984). Since then the entire two volumes have appeared in English in the Theory and History of Literature series of the Univerity of Minnesota Press (Sloterdijk 1987).

13 For a more detailed review of Sloterdijk's *Critique*, see Adelson 1984. As the review points out, Sloterdijk's kynic is implicitly *male*. A lengthy, sometimes too generally unsympathetic review by Klaus Laermann (1988) focuses on Sloterdijk's book as symptomatic of the narcissistic 1980s. For an astute discussion of *Critique of Cynical Reason* in the postmodern context, see Andreas Huyssen's foreword to the English translation of Sloterdijk's study.

14 For an insightful English-language review of *Geschichte und Eigensinn,* see Bowie 1985–86.

15 To the extent that they maintain the category of identity but conceive it in terms of nonidentities, Negt and Kluge show an affinity with Dews (1987), for whom neither the Enlightenment subject nor today's subject is the agent of oppressive totalization that some proponents of post-structuralism see in them. For their expanded understanding of the term "proletarian," see Negt and Kluge 1972.

16 On this point compare Frank (1984; 1988: 7–28). Dews (1987: 231) cites as one of the central failings of poststructuralism "the lack of any concept of individuation as an identity which is developed and sustained through the awareness of non-identity. Post-structuralism does indeed seek for difference, but it does so through an immersion in fragments and perspectives, not perceiving that this splintering is itself the effect of an overbearing totality, rather than a means of escape from it." Neither can Lacan, to whom alone among prominent poststructuralists Dews attributes insight into the split nature of subjective identity (235), account for the specificity of political and social oppression, since for Lacan, "primal repression is a function of the entry into language as such, and not into a particular symbolic order which, because it bears the stamp of a specific power structure, fails to provide adequate resources for an expressive articulation of the self" (239). Negt and Kluge's notion of "subjective splinters" is thus distinct from any celebratory poststructuralist "splintering" of the subject.

For a critical, lucid examination of Fredric Jameson's (1981) intriguing but not altogether cogent attempt to reconcile a poststructuralist notion of a decentered subject with a Marxist theory of cultural production, see Hohendahl 1988.

17 An alternative translation of this passage might read: "The historical falls into the categories of that which has been done with and that which is past but not over—unfinished business, imperfection, inherited defects (*Erbübel*), the historical *hangover*." Sloterdijk uses the English *hangover* in the German original (539).

18 On the subject of the body, two additional West German studies merit mention. With his long essay on the 1970s, appropriately entitled *Erfahrungshunger* (Hunger for Experience, 1980), Michael Rutschky was one of the first to note the growing emphasis on the body in West German society and culture. But in contrast to Kamper and Wulf, he stresses again and again the leitmotifs of the decade: horror and pain. He comments furthermore on their significance in the culturally and politically

specific contexts of the disillusioned student movement, the Red Army Faction's terrorist campaign, and the government's often traumatizing counterinsurgency measures. In another vein altogether, Mattenklott (1982) offers philosophical explorations on the metaphysics of the body. Kreuzer (1987: 309, 319 n. 46) makes passing reference to a "trendy" scholarly interest in the body.

19 Gert Mattenklott's recent essay "Körperpolitik oder Das Schwinden der Sinne" (1988) begins by noting the current popularity of and seemingly ubiquitous interest in "body fitness (*Körperertüchtigung*), body image and body therapy, bodily identity and body politics, body language and body awareness" (231), tracing this phenomenon to the early 1960s and to the West German reception of Herbert Marcuse and Norman O. Brown's theories of eros and civilization. In rather desultory fashion Mattenklott goes on to point out that the political implications of the contemporary fascination with the body are ambiguous. His examples are taken primarily from the realms of hair and clothing styles and Venetian carnival.

Kroker and Cook (1988) go so far as to dispute the very materiality of the human body in their "panic theory" of postmodern culture: "Once the veil of materiality/subjectivity has been transgressed (and abandoned), then the body as something real vanishes into the spectre of hyperrealism" (v). Strongly influenced by Baudrillard's "conception of experience as a *simulacrum*" (120), they see late capitalism moving "from the commodity relation based on wage/labour exploitation to the simulated economy of excess" (159). In this account nothing is real (especially not sociality or discourse), and the self of the 1980s is at best "a blip with a lifestyle" (279). For more essays on the body as the "missing matter" of postmodernism, see *Body Invaders: Sexuality and the Postmodern Condition* (Kroker and Kroker 1988).

20 For insights into some of the significations of the "embodiment" or "disembodiment" of women in contemporary feminist literary theories, see Susan Bordo, "Feminism, Postmodernism, and Gender-Scepticism" (Nicholson 1990: 133–56); Carrol Smith-Rosenberg, "The Body Politic" (Weed 1989: 101–21); and Valerie Smith, "Black Feminist Theory and the Representation of the 'Other'" (Wall 1989: 38–57). See also the essays gathered in *Gender/Body/Knowledge: Feminist Reconstructions of Being and Knowing* (Jaggar and Bordo 1989).

21 For an insightful study of the ways in which mind/body dualisms have affected both the traditional philosophical treatment of women as well as some earlier feminist theories of emancipation, see Elizabeth V. Spelman, "Woman as Body: Ancient and Contemporary Views" (1982).

Interestingly, Spelman singles out Adrienne Rich as one major white feminist whose work does not practice the kind of dualism that devalues bodily experience. She notes further "that not only does Rich challenge an assumption about the nature of the bodily that has been used to oppress women, but, unlike other feminists who do not challenge this assumption, she takes on the question of the ways in which sexism and racism interlock" (128).

22 The quotation marks around "human" serve as a reminder that cultural constructions determine what classifies as such and that "human" is often deployed as the equivalent of universal man (see Butler 1990).

23 Turner discusses the sensualist materialism of Feuerbach's theses on digestion ("man is what he eats") as an ultimately inadequate attempt to resolve this shortcoming in Marxian thought (inadequate because it treats eating as an individualistic rather than a socially conditioned act [189]).

24 Anthony Giddens's essay, "Action, Subjectivity, and the Constitution of Meaning" (Krieger 1987: 159–74), problematizes the traditions of subjectivism versus objectivism in sociology and presents his alternative "structuration theory" to account for the simultaneous construction of social agents as subjects and objects.

25 George Mosse, *Nationalism and Sexuality: Respectability and Abnormal Sexuality in Modern Europe* (1985), provides a good example of Turner's thesis that the government of societies functions through the regulation of bodies. For another example, see Jeffrey Weeks, *Sex, Politics and Society: The Regulation of Sexuality Since 1800* (1981).

26 Turner explicitly states that any analysis of the regulation of bodies in society must derive from the *fundamental* analysis of the regulation of women's bodies by men. But his contention that patriarchy has been replaced by what he calls "patrism" is, to my mind, less than cogent. He essentially argues that widespread institutionalized patriarchy has been eradicated in the industrialized West, leaving in its wake a "culture of discriminatory, prejudicial and paternalistic beliefs about the inferiority of women" (156). "Patrism" is thus a kind of subjective afterimage following the alleged collapse of the economic, political, and legal structures that comprise patriarchy. Turner's perception that patriarchy has already collapsed in the West is based on the notion that "patriarchal power cannot be uncoupled from the existence of the patriarchal household and that the development of capitalist society, by destroying the traditional household, undermines traditional patriarchy" (3). While I agree that social theorists must account for radical changes in the traditional household, I am far from convinced that all vestiges of patriarchy

have disappeared from Western laws, markets, and political institutions. Since Turner's "patrism" argument is peripheral to his reading of bodies in society, my criticism of the former in no way calls the latter into question.

27 For additional comments on the interiority of sexed bodies, see Butler 1990: 134–41.

28 As Adolf Muschg points out, Fritz Zorn regards the cancer that eventually killed him as a "cognitive organ" (*Erkenntnisorgan*) (Zorn 1977: 18). Such an approach seems to have hinted at alternative ways of understanding the modern body.

29 In this context it is worth noting that Dews (1987: 41) locates a crucial difference between Derrida and Adorno in their respective stances on "concrete experience." "Derrida fails to question the transcendental and speculative interpretations of experience which he inherits from Husserl and Hegel, and is therefore obliged to jettison the concept altogether as tainted with presence. For Adorno, by contrast, it is necessary to maintain both that there is something *given* in experience, and that there is nothing given *immediately*." Dews, however, does not discuss the body of experience here.

On the subject of Lacan, Dews disputes the charges of linguistic idealism leveled against this French psychoanalyst, pointing out that the latter does allow for "the real" outside signification. Looking more closely at how Lacan posits the relationship between the discursive and the nondiscursive, however, Dews concludes that that for which this theory *cannot* allow is social content, since for Lacan "the incompatibility between desire and speech . . . follows simply from the nature of language as such" (104–8).

30 In her contribution to the Center for Twentieth Century Studies conference "Displacements: Cultural Identities in Question," held in Milwaukee in April 1991, Karen Remmler similarly explored certain parallels between postmodernist discourses about bodies and actual forms of torture (e.g., fragmentation, disruption, laceration, rupture). Her thoughtfully provocative comments are slated for publication as "Sheltering Battered Bodies in Language: Imprisonment Once More?" in an anthology on cultural displacements edited by Angelika Bammer, forthcoming from Indiana University Press.

31 Although Turner speaks of *living* bodies, I am reminded here that even dead bodies are not always so easily erased from history by the discourse of power. See, for example, Paul Virilio's article on the bodies of the disappeared in Argentina (Kamper and Wulf 1982: 363–79).

32 Scarry cites the collusion of the civilian public with torturers when it shows disdain for persons who have "confessed" under torture, for, she argues, the outside world loses all content for the person being tortured and one cannot betray something that has ceased to exist (29–30, 330 n. 10).

33 Elie Wiesel's novels (1972) characterize concentration camp experiences in comparable fashion. The narrator, imprisoned at Buna, feels reduced to a single organ, his hungry stomach (78). On the evacuation march, however, he experiences his self as distinct from his body, the latter an object of hatred for the former (118). Once liberated from Buchenwald, he looks into a mirror for the first time since his days in the ghetto of Sighet and sees a corpse looking back at him (153). Of course, the literary text poses additional complications for the understanding of the role of the body in constituting subjective agency, for in literature the body can never be reduced to sheer pain, as in actual torture, nor can the self be posited as wholly disembodied, as it is constructed (and narrated) in relation to various images of the body.

Reading Russell A. Berman's scathing assessment of deconstruction as a critical method, one cannot help but recall Scarry's analysis of the structuration of bodies in torturous pain: "Far from trying to change the world, deconstruction does not even want to interpret it but smugly abolishes it instead, writing it off as a figment of the imagination of language. Wars and revolutions are, if noticed at all, regarded as just so many texts and documents: fine enough, unless you get in the way of a bullet" (Berman 1990: 5).

34 For more detailed theoretical investigations into the relationship between historical and literary discourse, see White 1973, 1978, 1987; Jameson 1981; Koselleck and Stempel 1973; and Stierle 1979. The essays edited by Kocka and Nipperdey (1979) explore the disputed status of theory and narrativity in the writing of history. Lützeler (1986, 1987) and Schulze and Wetzels (1983) discuss the imbrications of history and literature in a variety of literary texts. A volume edited by Hartmut Eggert et al. (1990) address history as literature.

Although he does address the tensions between facticity and fictionality in historical discourse, Koselleck (1979) stresses semantics rather than narrativity per se. At the heart of his anthology is a concern for the ways in which concepts of historical time are constructed and the meanings they thereby acquire. To the extent that he posits experience of the past and expectations of the future as constitutive, albeit in different ways, for a variety of historical presents, Koselleck pursues an analytical agenda comparable to that of Agnes Heller, whose theory of history I am about to discuss. Without elaborating at any length on the *body* of historical experience, Koselleck does note that there are levels of experience that elude language (300). In this regard I discern an affinity between his account of history and Turner's of the body.

35 This number is cited here only for the symbolic status to which it has generally attained. Jews were not the only group victimized by the heinous Nazi policies, and the actual number of those murdered in the Third Reich far exceeded six million.

36 This calls for further refinement of Peter Szondi's distinction between Walter Benjamin, who sought the future in the past, and Marcel Proust, who sought to escape the present into the past (1986: 153), and of Hans Ulrich Gumbrecht's comparable criticism of the contemporary tendency to flee the present into the past rather than seeking to orient the present between past and future (1985: 41). Heller makes us realize that both responses to the past are, however contradictory (one utopian and the other regressive), responses to problems of the present. Since the past exists only in the images of it sustained or cultivated by the present, it is not a real place or time to which one *can* flee.

See La Capra (1987) and Cowart (1989) for diverse accounts of the structural and ethical relationship between past and present in a variety of novels. Neither set of analyses reflects, in my opinion, the theoretical refinements of Heller's model. La Capra treats the relationship between past and present as a metaphorical dialogue; Cowart speaks of "historical actuality" (32) as if it were something that could be attained if an author were sufficiently talented.

37 Since, according to Heller, the preconceptions underlying the historian's reading of symbols from the past-present age become "co-constitutive in the testimony itself" (140), the Rankean dictum that historiography should reveal "how something really happened" becomes a norm that can never be satisfied but retains its normative status nonetheless: "All theories are committed to reconstruct how an event really happened and no theory can accomplish this. More precisely, we shall never know whether any of them did, which amounts to the same thing" (145).

38 In May 1985 West German Chancellor Helmut Kohl and American President Ronald Reagan jointly visited a cemetery where members of the German Wehrmacht and the Waffen SS are buried. This—and not a concentration camp site—was originally supposed to be the scene of the official U.S.-West German commemoration of the end of the Second World War. Targeted by much public protest, Reagan and Kohl made

the token concession of also visiting the former concentration camp site at Bergen-Belsen. See Hartman (1986) for a chronology of events and a variety of public commentaries as well as the texts of the official speeches given both at Bitburg and at Bergen-Belsen.

Prinz-Albrecht-Straße 8 was the location of the Gestapo headquarters in what is now West Berlin. A small exhibit over the extant foundation of the kitchen facilities documents the Gestapo organization and its torturous activities while the remaining expanse of the property has been left empty as a haunting memorial to those who were murdered there (see Rürup 1987 and Tuchel and Schattenfroh 1987).

As Erenz (1986) clearly delineates with the example of Berlin, many localities must decide what to build or what not to build on those properties that housed Nazi terror. In some instances buildings have been razed, street names changed, and new buildings erected. In others (as in the case of the Gestapo headquarters in Berlin) ruins have been uncovered and left as they have been found.

The fact that the mere *presence* of historical artifacts does not in itself guarantee critical historical understanding motivates Erenz's (1987) criticism of one of the main exhibits commemorating seven hundred fifty years of Berlin history. "The visitors are meant to experience and empathize—they do not get the chance to *think*." Erenz deplores this commodification of history (*Geschichte konsumgerecht*).

The numerous essays comprising the *Historikerstreit* have been collected in Augstein et al. 1987. On the heels of this volume followed Eike Henning, *Zum Historikerstreit: Was heißt und zu welchem Ende studiert man Faschismus?* (1988). For insightful English-language essays on the *Historikerstreit* and related issues, see *New German Critique* 44 (Spring/Summer 1988) and Charles S. Maier, *The Unmasterable Past: History, Holocaust, and German National Identity* (1988). Included in the former is an English translation of the remarkable correspondence between Martin Broszat and Saul Friedländer on the subject of "historicizing" National Socialism. Readers may also wish to consult Friedländer 1986, Diner 1987, and Santner 1990: 46–54. Halverson (1989) refers to additional publications on the subject in German and in English.

39 One can conceivably argue that the neoconservatives evidence some of the empathy Heller demands of historiography, but certainly not the partiality for "those who suffered the most" demanded by the theory of history Heller proposes.

40 Habermas (1987: 138) cites Saul Friedländer on this point.

41 What reconstructions and permutations of German history will ensue from the process of German unification remains to be seen.

42 Seeba (1980: 202) notes that history in literature is accessible only through images of history (see also Ryan 1983: 16, 137), but it follows from Heller (and Benjamin, I would add) that this is also true of history in any other kind of narrative as well (and we can know history, indirectly, only through the narrative of testimony). We need then to bear in mind that any analysis of specifically aesthetic modes of historical image-making also tells us more about the needs of the present than about those of the past.

43 By this I do not mean to imply either that the bodies of concentration camp prisoners were not also subject to certain forms of commodification or that there is no brutalization of real or discursive bodies in contemporary society. I am merely highlighting the *dominant* modes of bodily experience associated with each era.

44 The official English translation reads: "'the same one he used to walk on'" (270).

45 Analyzing trends in the European novel since the 1970s, Judith Ryan also cites a paradigmatic shift in conceptions of history. Her focus on silt as a "new metaphor for the historic process" (1991: 55) does not, however, account for the construction of human bodies in the texts that she considers representative in this regard. This is perhaps most obvious in the case of Süskind's *Perfume,* a narrative strewn with female bodies victimized by a genial parfumeur whose own body exudes no human smell. Although Ryan notes that the silting paradigm is not the dominant one in contemporary German literature (56), she does attribute to its appearance "the entrance of postmodern ideology into the German arena" (60). For further thoughts along these postmodern lines, see Ryan's (1990) discussion of pastiche in Süskind's bestselling novel.

  Lengthier treatises by Hoesterey (1988), Santner (1990), and McCormick (1991) also entail various readings of recent West German culture vis-à-vis theories of postmodernism. McCormick's second chapter, entitled "The Body, the Self," deals primarily with Peter Schneider's *Lenz* and Karin Struck's *Class Love.* Interested readers may also wish to consult Huyssen 1986, Huyssen and Scherpe 1986, and Kaes 1990.

46 I am unfortunately unable to include a contemporary novel written in German by an Afro-German author, since to my knowledge no such text yet exists. I look forward to the day when I can be apprised otherwise.

47 The field is rich in opportunities to explore related questions in other prose texts as well, including many written by men. Some of the other authors I hope to include in a project currently under way are Botho Strauss, Patrick Süskind, Bodo Kirchhoff, Edgar Hilsenrath, and Alexander Kluge.

1 The original German title of the text is *Häutungen* (Stefan 1975). For the English translation, see Stefan 1978. Schmidt (1982: 120) cites the sale, by 1980 alone, of two hundred thousand copies of Stefan's book. Jeanette Clausen provides an early English-language essay on *Shedding* in "Our Language, Our Selves: Verena Stefan's Critique of Patriarchal Language" (Cocalis and Goodman 1982: 381–400). Silvia Bovenschen's essay on female aesthetics prompted much theoretical debate on women's writing. See Bovenschen 1976 for the German original and Bovenschen 1977 for the English translation, which was also reprinted in Ecker 1985 (23–50).

2 The German title of the original publication is *Übergang* (Duden 1982). Further references to this work, cited in parentheses in the text by page number, are to the English translation (Duden 1985b). The story from which the German text takes its title bears in English a title different from the book title: "Transition."

3 I should emphasize at the outset that my comments do not provide a comprehensive picture of racist elements in contemporary German women's writing or in West German society. Rather, I explore the issue of racism, which is, of course, not primarily textual, by examining its structural function in the text. I wish to draw critical attention to the much-too-muffled issue of racism against persons of color in the German tradition of women's writing, obviously a complex tradition, for which neither Stefan's book nor Duden's work alone can stand as exemplary. What I hope other scholars will help provide is a more systematic investigation of the different ways in which writing by German women has or has not appropriated the racism of the culture at large. I hope, further, that my elaborations on the problems and challenges of *Opening of the Mouth* will also provoke fruitful discussion among feminist theorists who do not necessarily concern themselves with German feminism or German literature per se. For a critical survey of the image of blackness in German culture generally from the eighteenth century to the mid-twentieth century, see Gilman 1982. Weiner (1991) cites some additional bibliographical references with regard to images of blacks in twentieth-century German literature before 1945 (see esp. 486 nn. 12 and 14). One important article that examines the issue of race in a piece by Ingeborg Bachmann is Lennox 1984.

4 A German text may lend itself particularly well to this provocation, given that West German discussions of feminist theory have until very recently been more influenced by dialectical materialism than by the An-

glo-French terms of poststructuralist feminist discourse. Sigrid Weigel's work (cited in the discussion to follow) is especially notable for its intelligent attempts to integrate these two strains of critical analysis. Inasmuch as a useful discussion of the particularities of German feminist theory would lead us well beyond the confines of this work, I refer interested readers to the collection of diverse essays gathered by Gisela Ecker and published, in English, as *Feminist Aesthetics* (1985). For those readers fluent in German, I recommend Brügmann 1985.

5 The same can be said of Duden's second book, *Das Judasschaf,* published in 1985 by Rotbuch in Berlin.

6 This tendency to color-blindness was echoed at the May 1986 annual meeting "Frauen in der Literaturwissenschaft" (Women in Literary Studies) at the University of Hamburg (West Germany), where I presented a shorter version of this chapter. One of the some four hundred participants asked if we could not just as easily consider the race of the GIs irrelevant to our reading of the text. My impression was that Duden had become a kind of cult favorite for a large percentage of the German women attending the conference. They seemed noticeably unsettled and quite surprised by my critical reading of her text.

7 Duden actually uses the word in the chapter entitled "Heart and Mouth." The English translation of *Opening of the Mouth* lacks the double entendre: "I was without my right of say—it had been taken away" (43).

8 I am retaining my phrasing as originally published in *Signs* (1988), since to change it now would be to rewrite a phase of the history of feminist theory. For a rigorous philosophical discussion of ways in which the feminist distinction between sex and gender can be seen to reproduce compulsory heterosexuality (and not predate it), see Judith Butler, *Gender Trouble* (1990).

9 See Cixous (1976: 145; 1980: 256). The original French text of the 1976 publication in German can be found in *La jeune née* (Cixous 1975: 115ff.). For an English translation, see the "Sorties" chapter of Cixous and Clement 1986. See Rich 1977: 62 and Reinig 1976: 120. American readers unfamiliar with Reinig may wish to read Bammer 1986.

10 See also Kristeva (1976: 168). The 1976 text is translated from the French: *Les cahiers du Grif* (Brussels: Transédition, 1975).

11 Moi 1985 was intended to address this need for a feminist notion of historical agency if the subject (as phallocentric) is to be deconstructed. Weigel's essay, "Double Focus" (1985), may also be read in this context.

12 Martin is of the same mind. See her 1983 essay, pp. 213–14.

13 Weigel's review of *Opening* in fact claims the following: "Anne Duden's book deals with what precedes a utopia in now-time, a utopia which is

not projected onto a matriarchal prehistory or an unattainable future: the book deals with a radical opening to the world" (Weigel 1983b: 47).

14 Ernst Bloch's phrase, taken from his treatise *Das Prinzip Hoffnung* (The Principle of Hope), which was written between 1938 and 1947 but not published until 1959, implies that utopia is more oriented to real possibilities for an unalienated present than to an eternally distant future.

15 I wish to stress that my analysis addresses the aesthetic function of blackness in the text *as Duden has chosen to structure it.* Interestingly enough, class affiliations make up one social specification that recedes from the text. One may *surmise* that the black GIs and female protagonist do not belong to the same economic class, but the text provides no real corroboration for this, an omission that further foregrounds the question of race.

16 Here I cannot refrain from adding a note to draw attention to the obvious datedness of this sentence, which both takes the deployment of U.S. soldiers on West German soil as a given and fails to mention the presence in West Germany of asylum seekers from any number of countries ascribed to the so-called Third World.

17 On woman's relation to space and time, see Herrmann 1980 and Kristeva 1982b.

18 Recall Martin's comments on Foucault's relevance for feminists: "Foucault's work does not negate the possibility of concrete political struggle and resistance. It does insist that we understand and take account of the ways in which we are implicated in power relations and the fact that we are never outside of power. He does not advocate *a* position; however, he is obviously aware of the possibilities for new pleasures and new forms of resistance created in every confrontation" (Martin 1982: 12).

19 See the review of *Opening* by Weigel (1983b: 46).

20 Contrast this with the analysis found in Gubar 1982.

21 Cixous argues against the homogenized understanding of woman as historical subject that would deny that she occupies multiple sites simultaneously (see 1980: 252–53; 1976: 138; Cixous and Clement 1986: 88).

22 This question has its counterpart in the final "But where to?" of "The Country Cottage" (39), where the woman has succumbed to the erasure of boundaries between inner and outer space.

23 This distinction is important if we are to avoid the sexist assumption that women "like" the violence to which they are often subjected.

24 Since this particular passage is omitted from Harriet Anderson's translation, "Double Focus" (Weigel 1985), I cite here, in my own translation,

the German original, "Der schielende Blick," which can be found in Stephan and Weigel 1983.

25 Cixous's admonishment to "hurry: the continent is not impenetrably dark" (1980: 255) is similarly problematic.

26 Consider, for example, the analyses of dark spaces in Gilbert and Gubar 1980.

27 Trying to deflect the charge of racism against Duden's text, Sigrid Weigel (1987b: 128–29) claims that Duden counters the Eurocentric structures of the Enlightenment tradition by restoring multidimensionality to "the dark." While this is certainly true of Duden's treatment of darkness, it is decidedly not true of her treatment of dark-skinned persons. She does not portray, as Weigel contends, "concrete" blacks. Contrary to Weigel's assumption, my intention is not to prescribe any particular treatment of blacks, but to analyze the specific textual functions of Duden's abstractions. Neither do I share Weigel's view that the perpetrator-victim relationship *necessitates* such abstractions (as the analysis of TORKAN's novel in Chapter Three shows). It strikes me as significant that Weigel develops her discussion of *Opening* (and her criticisms of my analysis) by citing theoreticians such as Cixous, Irigaray, Kristeva, Lacan, and finally Derrida. According to Derrida, she notes, "the genesis of writing corresponds to the universal image-function of female-ness and the absence of the real woman." She sees Duden's text as taking up *this* "place of female-ness" (127). The theoretical slant evident in *Die Stimme der Medusa* (The Voice of Medusa), Weigel's major study of contemporary German women's literature (in many ways a remarkable and valuable undertaking), allows only for abstract, universal schemes of difference, thereby precluding a rigorous analysis of the concrete historical and textual complexities affecting cultural constructions of race and gender. (For some additional comments on *Opening* in this regard, see Frederiksen 1989: esp. 103–5).

Along similar lines Biddy Martin's "Zwischenbilanz feministischer Debatten" faults Weigel for privileging sexual difference such that other kinds of difference cannot adequately be accounted for (Martin 1989b: esp. 184–86). Martin's criticisms are based on a reading of Weigel's often cited essay from 1983, "Der schielende Blick," most of which was reprinted in 1985 in the English translation, "Double Focus." My opinion is that Weigel's earlier works are not unequivocally locked into the position that Martin ascribes to her here, but the repeated references to "the perspective of woman" that are scattered throughout *Die Stimme der Medusa* do lend some credence to Martin's objections. One finds in other works by Weigel, however, analyses that are far more richly differentiated withregard to historical productions of gender and other paradigms of cultural difference. See, for example, Weigel 1987a and 1991.

Hubert Winkels (1988: 42–58) evidences a similar blind spot when he discusses Duden's work as exemplifying Kristeva's and Lacan's assessments of the relationship of the body, semiosis, and signification. By highlighting the violence inherent in language per se, however, he fails to account for the sociopolitical implications of specific historical contexts in which differences are constructed. (See above, Chapter One, note 16, for a synopsis of Peter Dews's related critique of Lacan.) Winkels's exclusionary abstractions are, of course, much more severe than Weigel's, since Winkels treats Duden's "semiotics of the body" without accounting in any way for the fact that the body under construction is in this instance that of a woman. For a comparable account of *Opening* as a postmodern text, see T. Menke 1986.

28 See the passage from Toni Morrison's *Sula* cited in Lanser 1981 (234–35).

29 The "double existence" cited by Weigel and Martin for women in general is doubly true in the context of white women's role in the oppression of other races. See Adrienne Rich's essay "Disloyal to Civilization: Feminism, Racism, Gynephobia" (1978) in Rich 1979.

30 The pastoral allusion is to Hegel 1971: 79.

31 I am alluding here to Weigel's critique of Cixous and Irigaray, in which she calls for women writers "to traverse" the regressive images we have internalized (Weigel 1984a: 112; 1985: 79–80). Weigel makes brief references to some of the many similarities between *Opening* and "Der Fall Franza" by Ingeborg Bachmann in her review of the former (Weigel 1983b: 47). One significant difference, however, is that Franza is ill, whereas the woman in Duden's text is injured in an attack. Franza internalizes the attacks on her person in a way that Duden's protagonist does not. By smashing her head against the wall, Franza fails to make the most crucial distinction between her self and the image that inadequately represents her. In other words, Franza destroys herself *along with* the image.

CHAPTER THREE: TORKAN'S *TUFAN*

1 My phrasing of the problem undoubtedly obscures important nuances of the many diverse and highly sophisticated approaches to this issue. For selective elaborations, see *Coming to Terms: Feminism, Theory, Politics* (Weed 1989) and *Feminism/Postmodernism* (Nicholson 1990). An earlier

anthology that speaks to the debates on essentialism is *Feminist Studies/ Critical Studies* (de Lauretis 1986). See also later essays by de Lauretis (1989; 1990). Fuss (1989) tackles this problem from a variety of angles. Some elucidating contributions from the perspective of African American feminist critical theories can be found in *Changing Our Own Words* (Wall 1989).

2 In his discussion of Edward Said's study of Orientalism (1978) James Clifford (1988) argues against essentialism in culture studies. For different responses to humanist essentialism, see the 1984 special issue of *boundary 2*, especially the articles by Abdul R. JanMohamed and William V. Spanos.

3 Adrienne Rich's famous essay (1984) has been both influential and symptomatic in this regard.

4 To date this novel has been published only in the German original (TORKAN 1983). All English translations are my own. The author's nom de plume is taken from her actual first name; her full name is Torkan Daneshfar-Pätzoldt.

5 See, for example, any number of articles by Biddy Martin, Chandra Talpade Mohanty, and Gayatri Chakravorty Spivak, some of which are cited in this chapter. See also Butler 1990 and de Lauretis 1990.

6 Mae Gwendolyn Henderson offers this expansion of de Lauretis's characterization of the "subject of feminism": "*a subject 'racialized' in the experiencing of gender*" (Wall 1989: 19).

7 Negt and Kluge's unconventional concept of a "proletarian" public sphere, it should be noted, challenges the public/private dichotomy of the bourgeois public sphere.

8 Two scholars who seem to do justice to the complexity of de Lauretis's concerns and whose own equally sophisticated arguments are relevant to this chapter are Biddy Martin (1989b) and Chandra Talpade Mohanty (1988). I would also like to mention Mae Gwendolyn Henderson's pertinent analyses of constructions of race and gender in novels by Sherley Anne Williams and Toni Morrison; see "Speaking in Tongues: Dialogics, Dialectics, and the Black Woman Writer's Literary Tradition" (Wall 1989: 16–37).

Although I consider Negt and Kluge's ruminations extremely important in any discussion of materiality, it is not my intention to downplay the significance of the many fine feminist theorists whom de Lauretis cites. She has already recounted and critiqued their analyses with great perspicacity, however, and her efforts need not be duplicated here. Furthermore, because of the sometimes quirky nature of their work and insufficient accessibility to translations of it, Negt and Kluge tend not to be taken very seriously in the United States. Though I hardly wish to posit them as "saviors" of feminist theory, I do think that their discussion of subject-object relations is relevant to feminist concerns of the 1990s.

9 Page references are to the original publication.

10 Alcoff refers to the pivotal "Combahee River Collective Statement" of 1977. (This was also the year in which Barbara Smith's influential essay "Toward a Black Feminist Criticism" first appeared.) In *Technologies of Gender* (1987: 10) de Lauretis dates this "shift in feminist consciousness" back to 1981 and 1982, when *This Bridge Called My Back: Writings by Radical Women of Color* (Moraga and Anzaldúa) and *All the Women Are White, All the Blacks Are Men, but Some of Us Are Brave* (Hull et al.) were published, respectively. These texts were authored by women from a variety of racial and ethnic backgrounds. It should be noted that Cheryl A. Wall, in her introduction to an anthology of essays on writings by black women, cites a 1970 publication by Toni Cade as the beginning of a renewed "effort by black women to define themselves" (Wall 1989: 2). See note 19 in Alcoff (1988: 412) and note 14 in Wall (1989: 214) for more extensive bibliographical references.

I have put "of color" in quotation marks because of the colonialist assumptions inherent in what Spivak (1987a: 333) has termed feminist "chromatism." In her introductory essay in Mohanty et al. 1991, however, Chandra Talpade Mohanty retains "women of color" as a *political* term connoting a "*common context of struggle* rather than color or racial identifications" (7). In the same volume Barbara Smith provides an extensive list of additional bibliographical references on this issue (102).

11 See Biddy Martin, "Lesbian Identity and Autobiographical Difference[s]" (1989a); Chandra Talpade Mohanty, "Feminist Encounters: Locating the Politics of Experience" (1988); and Martin and Mohanty, "Feminist Politics: What's Home Got to Do with It?" (1986) for especially astute critiques of these assumptions.

12 Spivak (1990: 156) speaks of the need to consider "the history of margins: the place for the argument, the place for the critical moment, the place of interests for assertions rather than a shifting of the center" [as she suggested in an earlier essay]. The earlier essay to which Spivak refers is "Explanation and Culture: Marginalia" (Spivak 1987b: 103–17).

13 Elizabeth Weed's introduction to *Coming to Terms* (Weed 1989: ix–xxxi) points out just how problematic the notion of "experience" has been for feminist theory. See also Fuss 1989 (113–19) for a discussion of essentialism in the feminist classroom.

14 I have similar objections to feminist standpoint theory, an overview of which is included in Sandra Harding's article "Feminism, Science, and the Anti-Enlightenment Critiques" (Nicholson 1990: 94–99). Nancy Hartsock, a major proponent of "the feminist standpoint," proceeds from the sexual division of labor to a feminist epistemology based on a supposed ground of sexual difference (see Hartsock 1985: esp. 231–51). She relegates race and discourse to secondary issues by privileging a conventional understanding of materiality (as labor). This is done to stress the alleged commonalities among women, which she sees as necessary for the adoption of a feminist (political) standpoint (231–32). The call to marginalize ourselves as a matter of political choice or standpoint (Hartsock 1987: 201) is not unique to feminist theory—compare Jeffrey Peck's and Henry J. Schmidt's contributions to current debates on German Studies (Peck 1989; Schmidt 1987)—but in either context it fails to appreciate the extent to which the construction of our social beings (material and discursive) and the range of political choices available to us are not *simply* matters of individual free will.

Although Judith Butler does not specifically deploy a concept of positionality in *Gender Trouble* (1990), she does argue convincingly against foundationalist feminist identity politics. Avoiding the pitfalls to which Alcoff falls prey, she rejects the notion of free will versus determinism and insists that we acknowledge agency as always constructed. Butler's emphasis on agency as a practice of "signification and resignification" (144), however, begs the question as to what constitutes her operative understanding of materiality.

In yet another context Caren Kaplan (1987) foregrounds the issue of positionality in her adaptation of Deleuze and Guattari's concept of a minor literature (1986), but she does so in such a way that deterritorialization and exile are generalized to a condition of the postmodern world, and feminists are encouraged to make themselves minor. How materiality fits into this approach to positionality is not at all clear. For a more lucid discussion of some political positions of postmodernism (but only by implication of materiality), see Sangari 1987.

Reading the finely honed analyses presented in *Changing Our Own Words: Essays on Criticism, Theory, and Writing by Black Women* (Wall 1989), I am struck by the frequency with which reference is made to a complex concept of embodied positionality. Of black feminist critics Wall writes: "We bring to our work a critical self-consciousness about our positionality, defined as it is by race, gender, class, and ideology. The position or place we are assigned on the margins of the academy informs but does not determine the positions or stances we take" (1–2). This formulation accounts for black women as both construct-ed and construct-ing. Wall (10) and Valerie Smith, "Black Feminist Theory and the Representation of the 'Other'" (Wall 1989: 42), cite the same passage from de Lauretis's introduction to *Feminist Studies/Critical Studies* regarding multiple, heterogeneous, and self-contradictory identities constructed across representations of race, class, and gender.

Smith, however, is disturbed by what happens "when Anglo-American feminists and male Afro-Americanists begin to *rematerialize* their discourse" (44; my emphasis). Acknowledging the contextualized pressures coming to bear on recent developments in literary theory (notably the provocation of deconstructionist methodologies), Smith nonetheless finds the linkage between black women and rematerialized theory "conceptually problematic" (45). For "this association of black women with reembodiment resembles rather closely the association, in classic Western philosophy and in nineteenth-century cultural constructions of womanhood, of women of color with the body and therefore with animal passions and slave labor" (45). Hooks (1990: 23) argues against reproducing a dichotomy that can conceive of black experience only in opposition to abstract thinking or critical theory. (Sander L. Gilman's study, *Difference and Pathology: Stereotypes of Sexuality, Race, and Madness* [1985], notes a similar nineteenth-century association established for prostitutes as white women seen as both *working* and *sexualized*.) What this underscores for me is how important it is to scrutinize social and discursive *constructions* of race, which under no historical circumstances is a ground unto itself.

15 Compare this to Sigrid Weigel's concept of women's "double focus" on the oppressive configurations of patriarchy and feminist visions of utopia (Weigel 1985). Note that this is very different from Joan Kelly's often cited "doubled vision" of the imbrication of sexuality and economics (Kelly 1984).

16 Even though de Lauretis notes in passing that her 1989 essay on essentialism is "in a sense a dialogue" with Alcoff and with herself (1989: 33), she does not address the blind spots in Alcoff's arguments that I have sought to delineate here. Since the point of departure for this particular piece by de Lauretis is the author's impatience with self-righteous feminists accusing other feminists of essentialism, she polemically argues in favor of a certain kind of essentialism. It is predicated not on a presumed difference between male and female but on "an essential difference between a feminist and a non-feminist understanding of the subject and its relation to institutions; between feminist and non-feminist

knowledges, discourses, and practices of cultural forms, social relations, and subjective processes; between a feminist and a non-feminist historical consciousness" (1989: 3–4). She bases her arguments in large part on the development of Italian feminism and the challenge it poses, in her estimation, to Anglo-American feminist theory. Readers interested in pursuing this should consult de Lauretis's essays from 1989 and 1990, as well as *Sexual Difference* by the Milan Women's Bookstore Collective, which de Lauretis's 1990 essay serves to introduce. This later article argues both against "biological or metaphysical essentialism" and for "the notion of essential and originary difference" (18–19). This attempt, which I find provocative but not consistently convincing, will presumably fuel continued debate among feminists in the 1990s.

17 Mohanty (1984: 336) stresses the strategic and analytical aspects of productions of the category "women."

18 See, for example, *Feminist Theory: From Margin to Center* (hooks 1984) as well as hooks's essay "Choosing the Margin as a Space of Radical Openness" (hooks 1990: 145–53). For a feminist commentary on the instability of marginality, see Trinh T. Minh-ha, *Woman, Native, Other: Writing Postcoloniality and Feminism* (1989), whose third chapter is in large part a reprint of "Difference: 'A Special Third World Women Issue,'" which appeared in *Discourse* 8 (1986–87).

19 When Hélène Cixous claims in "Laugh of the Medusa" that women occupy multiple sites simultaneously (Cixous 1980: 252–53), she does not allow for embodied materiality (in spite of repeated references to woman's body). For an excellent critical discussion of conceptualizations of margins, centers, and micropolitics in the arena of feminist Germanistics, see Martin, "Zwischenbilanz der feministischen Debatten" (1989).

20 Discussing the issue of embodiment versus disembodiment in feminist and deconstructionist analyses, Susan Bordo (Nicholson 1990: 133–56) argues that the human body is in fact not protean but inescapably embodied, that is to say, limited in its range of available "movements" and accountable for its "locatedness in space and time" (esp. 140–45).

   In her essay "The Body Politic" (Weed 1989: 101–21) Carroll Smith-Rosenberg offers some brief but insightful comments on "the simultaneous separateness and inseparability of material and discursive practices, of 'actions in the world' and symbolic gestures" (101). Whereas she addresses female bodies in relation to power, her focus here is on the issue of sexuality and abortion.

   In her extensive study of contemporary German women's literature Sigrid Weigel (1987b: 94–97) discusses the historical role of the body in some feminist theories of subjectivity, but what she highlights is the female body as the place where "femaleness" is inscribed and female desire articulated. She does not address the female body specifically as an organ of experience.

21 Within the context of German Studies the conceptualization of woman as victim has only recently begun to be debated. The publication of Claudia Koonz's controversial study of women in the Third Reich (Koonz 1987) was influential in prompting this debate. (Comments in Chapter Two, above, on the reception of Anne Duden's *Opening of the Mouth* are also relevant to this issue.)

The especially polemical writings by Christina Thürmer-Rohr (1987, 1989) attack a feminist blind spot that precludes acknowledging women's historical role as anything other than pure victim. Although she rejects the category of "victim" as too general and depoliticizing, and although she criticizes the feminist tendency to erase differences among women, her own arguments seem to rely on a monolithic notion of sexual difference ("women" versus "men"). She speaks of women as being *outside* power and yet accuses them of being accomplices in maintaining the patriarchal status quo, which Thürmer-Rohr sees as assigning to women the labor of hope, meaning, and faith. By focusing on the alleged complicity of "women" in historical developments toward the potential liquidation of the human race by nuclear, military, and technological means, however, Thürmer-Rohr implicitly reveals her own Eurocentric bias. The conscious preoccupation with an imminent nuclear threat is clearly rooted in the Western European context of the 1980s, when the deployment of additional nuclear missiles on West German territory (and elsewhere, in keeping with NATO's "double-track resolution" of 1979), prompted a revitalization of Western European peace movements. I do not by any means intend to minimize these concerns, but I do think that the historical and political context of Thürmer-Rohr's arguments limits their usefulness for my discussion of the category of "victim" in *Tufan*. Her terminology derives from feminist theory, to be sure, but her analysis neither addresses nor allows for the simultaneous material and discursive production of categories of gender, race, ethnicity, class, or sexuality. For an English translation of the 1987 volume, see Thürmer-Rohr 1991.

22 Mohanty (1984: 337) explicitly argues against just this kind of feminist "othering" in which Third World women are homogenized in order to bolster the (relative) hegemonic standard of white Western feminism. In the context of West German minority literature and culture Heidrun

Suhr (1989: 92–94) similarly laments the tendency to reproduce Western stereotypes by assuming "the white German woman" as the "unquestioned standard of comparison."

23 Criticizing him for omitting "German Orientalisms" from his own particular definition of Orientalism (circumscribed by British, French, and later U.S. imperialism), Clifford charges Said with "Occidentalism" (see 267, 271).

Martin and Mohanty (1986) also dispute, in the realm of feminist scholarship, "the feigned homogeneity of the West and what seems to be a discursive and political stability of the hierarchical West/East divide" (193).

24 I am reminded of Virgil Lokke's pointed subtitle for his introduction to a 1987 anthology of essays on literary theory: "Taxonomies Are Never Innocent" (Lokke 1987).

25 See Sander L. Gilman's contribution to a 1988 symposium on interdisciplinarity and German Studies (Gilman 1989) as well as my response to it (Adelson 1989).

26 Ahmed goes on to comment that the alleged degradation of Muslim women by Muslim men has been propagated by Western Christian males "from the time they began writing about Islam." Given that these Christian men "were also the guardians and advocates of the natural superiority of the male and his rightful control over the female," Ahmed queries, why should they have been troubled by the gender relations they perceived in Muslim societies (524)? Another question that comes to mind here is why, if these white Christian men—"the guardians and advocates of the natural superiority of the male and his rightful control over the female"—were the authors of the alleged Western superiority over Islamic cultures (built, as it were, on the oppression of Muslim women), should Western feminists trust this posture in the first place?

27 For an alternative view (to Muslim women as "victim") in the Iranian context, see Guity Nashat, "Women in Pre-Revolutionary Iran: A Historical Overview" (Nashat 1983: 5–35). For a variety of detailed studies of the heterogeneity characterizing the real lives and cultural representations of Muslim women, see the relevant articles in *Women and Revolution in Iran* (Nashat 1983), *Women in the Muslim World* (Beck and Keddie 1978), *Islam in the Contemporary World* (Pullapilly 1980), *Unspoken Worlds* (Falk and Gross 1989), *Women in Islamic Societies* (Utas 1988), *Women in the World* (Iglitzin and Ross 1976), and *Women and the Family in the Middle East* (Fernea 1985). See also Nashat 1980, Tabari 1980, Higgins 1985, Tohidi 1991, Schick 1990, and the following extremely interesting book-length studies: Haeri 1989, El Saadawi 1983, and Mernissi 1987.

28 For a recent study of gender and discourse in Arabo-Islamic culture, see Malti-Douglas 1991. See also Ahmed 1989.

29 Mernissi's and El Saadawi's somewhat unconventional position is that Muslim practices of secluding, restraining, and controlling women are founded not on the belief that females are weak, passive, and inferior, but on the assumption that they are powerful, active, and destructive. For some additional comments on the concepts of *fitna* and *namus,* see El Saadawi (136), Mernissi (xxviii, 31, 161), and Nicolaisen (Utas 1988: 6). In "On Changing the Concept and Position of Persian Women," Michael M. J. Fischer observes that although the concept of *namus* was not formalized in Iran, there was nonetheless a general consciousness of it (Beck and Keddie 1978: 197). Regarding the policing of female relatives by fathers, brothers, and husbands, see Nicolaisen (Utas 1988: 6), Mernissi (82), Nashat (1980: 179), Behnaz Pakizegi (Beck and Keddie 1978: 217), Erika Friedl (Beck and Keddie 1978: 647), and Hamideh Sedghi (Iglitzin and Ross 1976: 220–24). In their introduction to *Women in the Muslim World* Beck and Keddie ascertain that the onset of puberty usually brings increased restrictions for Muslim girls (24). In the same volume Pakizegi writes about female adolescence: "This period is characterized by a gradual definition and limitation of her activities and position. From a young age her physical activity is limited"; brothers tell their sisters what is and what is not allowed (217).

30 See Nashat 1980 for an especially useful overview of the many shifts in Iranian women's rights from 1936 to 1980. For some discussion of what followed the 1979 revolution, see Tohidi 1991.

31 See Shahrough Akhavi's essay "Shi'i Social Thought and Praxis in Recent Iranian History" (Pullapilly 1980: 171–98) for an excellent study of the diverse developments affecting the Shi'ite resurgence in Iran. For an interesting analysis that highlights the contested nature of Islamic identity in an older period, see Leila Ahmed, "Feminism and Cross-Cultural Inquiry: The Terms of the Discourse in Islam" (Weed 1989: 143–51).

32 For more detailed discussions of Shari'ati's philosophy, see Marcia K. Hermansen, "Fatimeh as a Role Model in the Works of Ali Shari'ati" (Nashat 1983: 87–96); Fischer (Beck and Keddie 1978: 189–215); Guity Nashat, "Women in the Ideology of the Islamic Republic" (Nashat 1983: 195–216); Nashat 1980; and especially Akhavi (Pullapilly 1980: 171–98). For a concise discussion of the primary distinctions among traditionalist, modernist, secularist, and fundamentalist concepts of Islam, see Jan Hjärpe, "The Attitude of Islamic Fundamentalism Towards the Question of Women in Islam" (Utas 1988: 12–25).

33 I am reminded of Judith Butler's characterization of gender as "performatively produced" rather than "expressive" (1990: 24).

34 This is the adult Asar speaking. As a teenager with a "boyish" figure, she suffers from not being acknowledged as a woman. This acknowledgment comes, even in her own eyes, only once a boy professes his love for her.

35 Mernissi (1987: 125) makes reference to the pattern of older Muslim women seeking power through their sons.

36 Even Asar burns her own hand to commemorate the renunciation of her first fantasy of love (96).

37 In an altogether different historical context Mae Gwendolyn Henderson (Wall 1989: 31) deftly traces the double-edged "tracking" of a female slave's body in the narrative of *Dessa Rose* by Sherley Anne Williams. As the man who claims to own her (having inscribed his ownership on her body) tries to track the runaway slave, he is forced to read tracks "authored" by her. "If the pursuit/flight pattern emblematizes a strategic engagement for discursive control, Dessa's tracks also mark her emergence as narrator of her own story."

38 This also applies to the proscription against her climbing cherry trees (50).

39 Pakizegi observes that in Iran "the mere physical movement of women in the city is highly restricted" and that a woman alone in the streets is harassed whether she is veiled or not (224). Pakizegi's comments predate the 1979 revolution, as does Asar's return visit to Teheran.

40 It is very much an object of representation in TORKAN's second novel, *Kaltland: Wah'schate Ssard* (Cold Land: Cold Fear) (1984). In *Tufan* there are only vague references to life in Germany as "cold" (128, 172) and one reference to the racist attitudes that contribute to European nations' refusal to grant asylum to Iranian refugees (182).

41 See Adelson 1990a on this point as well. Credit is due Sangari 1987 (183) for the "palpitating" figure of speech.

42 Compare also the scenes in which she is described, learning how to swim in the ocean in her full dress, as a blimp on the horizon (140) or sitting on a suitcase in the airport, patiently waiting to be found eventually, oblivious to all about her (184).

CHAPTER FOUR: JEANNETTE LANDER'S
EIN SOMMER IN DER WOCHE DER ITKE K.

1 This corresponds to Jeannette Lander's perception of herself as a "Ger-

man author of Jewish-American-Polish origins," as stated in a discussion following a reading given by Lander and Barbara Honigmann in Essen on December 13, 1990.

2 In addition to the three novels cited here Lander authored some English-language texts in the 1950s as well as some German short stories in the 1970s. A fourth novel, *Ich, allein* (I, Alone), was published in 1980 by AutorenEdition of Munich. Lander is currently working on a new novel set in Sri Lanka (private conversations with author in Essen, December 15, 1990).

3 It is difficult to date the events of this novel precisely. Although one of the characters cites the year as 1942 (200), textual references to boxing matches between Joe Louis and Billy Conn and Abe Simon (59–63) would have to situate the present of the novel in the summer of 1941 (see F. Menke 1969: 267).

4 I have written more extensively on this novel in an article entitled "There's No Place Like Home: Jeannette Lander and Ronnith Neumann's Utopian Quests for Jewish Identity in the Contemporary West German Context" (Adelson 1990b). My comments in this chapter are therefore confined to *Itke* and, more peripherally, *The Daughters*.

5 Even within the context of German national history this relationship has never been as simplistic or as static as the catch-phrase might imply. For a smattering of critical reflections and bibliographic references regarding this problem, see Scholem 1976, Rabinbach and Zipes 1986, Brumlik et al. 1988, Zipes 1990–91, and virtually any issue of *Babylon* (Diner et al. 1986ff.).

6 Although Jack Zipes argues for the centrality of the Holocaust in postwar relations between Jews and Germans, he shares Saul Friedländer's reluctance to mythologize and thereby abuse it (Zipes 1991: 36–37; Friedländer 1984). I propose that Lander does much to demythologize both Jews and the Holocaust in contemporary German culture.

7 Elsewhere I have decried the absence of "a vital notion of the multidimensionality and heterogeneity of Jewish life in the Federal Republic" (Adelson 1990b: 116). For a discussion of stereotypes of Jews reflected in postwar German literature, see Müller 1984, Angress 1985, Schmelzkopf 1985, Röll and Bayerdörfer 1986, and Gilman 1986–87. The outcry prompted in 1985 by the attempted staging of Fassbinder's play *Trash, City, and Death* attests to the ongoing controversy over public representations of Jews in Germany. See *New German Critique* 38 (1986) for critical comments in this regard. Lichtenstein (1986) provides the German documentation.

8 The fact that the consequences of National Socialism exceed the borders of German statehood is discussed by Anson Rabinbach in his introduction to Rabinbach and Zipes 1986 (5).

9 For an excellent discussion of "the Jewish question in the German question" from 1945 through the *Historikerstreit* of 1986, see Rabinbach 1988.

10 The functionalization of a purported homogeneity of Jews and Jewishness has even been noted in one critical analysis of institutionalized Jewish Studies in West Germany (Oswald 1991).

11 For critical insights into the post-1945 history of this phenomenon, see Rabinbach 1988.

12 See, for example, Stern 1991a and Gilman 1991, both in *New German Critique*'s special issue on German unification. As enlightening analyses by Dan Diner and Daniel Krochmalnik demonstrate, the meaning of November 9 was highly contested in German history even before November 1989 (Diner 1989; Krochmalnik 1989). For readers who may be unfamiliar with these dates in German history, November 9, 1938, is the date of the Nazis' infamous pogrom against German Jews, often euphemistically referred to in English as the "Night of Broken Glass." November 9, 1989, refers to the demise of the Berlin Wall, which was a major step toward the subsequent unification of the two postwar German states.

13 In her insightful analysis of the simultaneous yet nonsynchronous constructions of race, class, and gender Elizabeth V. Spelman suggests avoiding the term "difference" in favor of "heterogeneity" because the former wields normative implications (Spelman 1988: 174). For *analytical* purposes, however, I think that "difference" is useful in that it calls on us to address configurations of power and privilege rather than mere variety.

14 Spelman 1988: 81. While this study highlights the simultaneous constructions of race, gender, and class identities, Spelman's analysis also *allows for* but does not explicitly examine other historically determined factors of identity formation (e.g., sexuality or nationality). Butler (1990), on the other hand, specifically addresses constructions of compulsory heterosexuality in feminist discourse. Although her study states at the outset that "gender is not always constituted coherently or consistently in different historical contexts" and that "gender intersects with racial, class, ethnic, sexual, and regional modalities of discursively constituted identities" (3), Butler does not examine these imbrications in any further detail. From different perspectives Spelman and Butler both insist on the constructed multiplicity of gender, always historically constituted.

As early as the late 1970s, African American feminists were proposing something other than merely additive analyses of oppression (B. Smith 1979), since such analyses had a way of rendering black women invisible. (As "women," black women were presumed to suffer oppression like white women, and as "blacks," they were presumed to suffer oppression like black men; no allowance was made for their specific positionalities, which were neither merely "black" nor simply "female.") See also hooks 1984 in this regard.

Barbara Smith and Elizabeth V. Spelman's caveats have both been cited in support of Valerie Smith's analysis of the problematic function of "black women" in both Anglo-American feminist and male African American literary theories (V. Smith 1989: 47).

15 Citing Coco Fusco's arguments against "naturalizing" white ethnicity, bell hooks gives us "Representing Whiteness," an insightful essay about the construction of race/gender in Wim Wenders's 1988 film *Himmel über Berlin* (English title: *Wings of Desire*). See hooks 1990: 165–71. See also Spelman 1988: 134 on the dangers of taking "whiteness" as a given.

16 Christina von Braun's work is one stunning and challenging exception to this rule (which I may well have overstated). Compare her historically trenchant analyses of German identity formations along racially engendered lines (von Braun 1989). She also notes both that "the image of the Jew becomes a constitutive element in the German symbiosis, the German homeland, the German identity" and that German identity is itself an unstable construct (103, 105). See also Weigel 1991 for a discussion of racial discourse in Heinrich von Kleist's "Verlobung in St. Domingo."

17 The institutional sponsor for this international conference was the Kulturwissenschaftliches Institut (Essen) im Wissenschaftszentrum Nordrhein-Westfalen. With Sabine Schilling, Inge Stephan, and Sigrid Weigel as editors, partial proceedings of the conference are scheduled for publication in 1993 with the Cologne publishing house of Böhlau.

18 On some of the ways in which race is an unstable yet nonetheless material effect of social constructs see, for example, Susan S. Lanser's rereading of "The Yellow Wallpaper" (Lanser 1989) and Chandra Talpade Mohanty's introduction to *Third World Women and the Politics of Feminism* (Mohanty et al. 1991: 1–47, esp. 24). Michael Omi and Howard Winant's pivotal study, *Racial Formation in the United States* (1986), is often cited in this regard as well.

19 Fuss concentrates her analysis on works by male theorists, notably Henry Louis Gates, Jr., Houston A. Baker, Jr., and Anthony Appiah. She limits her discussion of black feminist criticism to the charge that with

the exception of Hazel Carby and Hortense Spillers most black feminist critics rely heavily on essentialist assumptions. I am not convinced that this account of black feminist criticism is either adequate or accurate. Compare my comments on this branch of criticism above in Chapter Three, note 14.

20 This is in effect what the editors of *Third World Women and the Politics of Feminism* (Mohanty et al. 1991) do when they use the term "feminists of color" to designate not feminists of nonwhite races, but feminists who occupy, however variably in historical terms, oppositional positionalities vis-à-vis colonialism. While this goes a long way to avoid Spivak's charge of feminist "chromatism" (Spivak 1987a: 333), I am not convinced that it allows, say, for historically specific constructs of *Jewish* female identity in historical periods in which Jews were neither colonized nor colonizers.

21 Fuss notes how the conflation of race and ethnicity has posited "'Blackness' as an ethnic marker (equivalent to Germanness or Jewishness)" and "historically worked to homogenize black identity, to de-particularize the black subject" (Fuss 1989: 92).

22 It is important to note that even in the German context racial categories of "color" have a history of instability. Sander Gilman discusses a long tradition of German associations between Jews and blackness (Gilman 1985; 1986: 1–21); in Otto von Bismarck's circle, he points out, Jews were called "white Negroes" (1986: 7). Nazis later referred to Aryans who were "receptive to Jewish thought" as "white Jews" (Engelmann 1988: 434). Perhaps the best-known treatise on images of blacks in Germany before 1945 is Gilman's 1982 study, *On Blackness without Blacks*. In his recent article on jazz and literature in the Weimar Republic Marc A. Weiner includes some additional references to studies of blacks in German literature through the end of World War II (Weiner 1991: 486).

23 Taguieff distinguishes between "discriminatory racism" and "differentialist racism," the latter of which relies on *praise* of difference to justify keeping "other" cultures and races separate and stripped of power.

24 Fuss highlights the positive effects of identity politics in a broader context: "The politics of identity has operated as a vital political strategem in virtually all of the social movements of the 20th Century, including the Civil Rights Movement in the U.S. and the many struggles for national liberation throughout the world" (Fuss 1989: 96). In a separate chapter she discusses identity politics in reference to "Lesbian and Gay Theory" (97–112).

25 The main organization in this movement is the ISD, "Initiative Schwarze Deutsche" (Initiative Black Germans). An affiliated women's group is

ADEFRA. Katharina Oguntoye explains that the terms "Afro-Germans" and "Black Germans" are used as equivalents, since "black" is an internationally political referent and not all Black Germans are of African descent. They would include, for example, Black Germans of American descent as well as Asian Germans (see Oguntoye 1989: 37). Note the similarity between the signification of the color "black" here and that deployed in the phrase "feminists of color" as used by Mohanty et al. 1991 (compare note 20 of this chapter).

Oguntoye (1989) offers a brief, informative history and overview of the Black German and Afro-German women's movements. She also discusses the genesis of the pathbreaking book *Farbe bekennen: Afro-Deutsche Frauen auf den Spuren Ihrer Geschichte* (Oguntoye et al. 1986). An English translation has only recently been published (Opitz et al. 1991).

In her introduction to *Third World Women and the Politics of Feminism* (Mohanty et al. 1991: 8) Mohanty cites studies of "Blackness" in the British context that might be compared with the German situation in that "blackness" denotes not a racial identity so much as a premise for building political coalitions against dominant forms of oppression marked by imperialist or colonialist histories.

26 The articles in *Babylon: Beiträge zur jüdischen Gegenwart* (Babylon: Contributions to the Jewish Present) demonstrate this (Diner et al. 1986ff.).

27 These developments have also affected institutional studies of German literature. Jeffrey M. Peck, for example, has noted in the growing internationalization of the IVG (International Association of Germanists) a "process of dislodging *Germanistik* from its base in one national identity" (Peck 1987: 317).

28 Santner discusses other possible modifiers as well in his first chapter, "Postwar/Post-Holocaust/Postmodern: Some Reflections on the Discourse of Mourning" (Santner 1990: 1–30).

29 See Weigel 1987b (111–15) and Berger et al. 1985 (130–70) for some feminist analyses of the female body and/as illness in the German context. I do not by any means intend to downplay the significance of such studies, merely to draw attention to a different way of approaching women's bodies in literature. Weigel is sensitive to some of the ambiguities in the relationship between women's writing and constructs of the female body (112) and also discusses images of female bodies in terms of radical subjectivity (116–29). This latter section includes Weigel's comments on the Anne Duden text discussed here in Chapter Two. See note 27, Chapter Two, for some thoughts on my disagreement with Weigel regarding the deployment of blackness in the Duden piece.

30 For a more detailed account of the Leo Frank case, see Golden 1965, Dinnerstein 1973, and Samuels and Samuels 1956. Gutstein's one-page entry on this case (1988: 152) contains several factual errors but does refer to eyewitness testimony that did not surface until 1982 and was hence not available to earlier researchers.

31 One hardly accounts adequately for differences among Jews in the United States by referring only to the tensions between German Jews and eastern European Jews in the American "melting pot." For some articles on various Jewish communities and experiences in the American South and the U.S. as a whole, see Dinnerstein and Palsson 1973 and Lavender 1977. The latter also contains some information on black Jewish communities in the United States.

32 Whereas the lynching of one of their members came as an unfamiliar shock to Atlanta's Jewish community, Golden points out that alone in the week of Leo Frank's arrest three African Americans were lynched in the state of Georgia; that in 1913 (some) white southerners often saw no need to try African Americans before lynching them; and that for every month during the year of the Frank trial an average of four African Americans were lynched (Golden 1965: 39, 312). According to Blumberg (1985: 60), the first year in which no lynchings were officially reported in the United States was 1952. The legacy of the Frank case takes some odd twists. As recently as 1961 a white supremacist organization in Atlanta focused on the Leo Frank case and the threat to (white, non-Jewish) southern womanhood it supposedly symbolized, claiming that the 1954 Warren Court decision in favor of racial integration was an act of revenge for the Frank lynching (Golden 1965: 220 n. 2).

See "'Is the Jew a White Man?' Press Reaction to the Leo Frank Case, 1913–1915" (Levy 1974) for a detailed discussion of some of the complex ways in which southern racism and anti-Semitism were reflected in public discourse about this case. Levy's study revolves around the fact that the state's star witness against Frank was an African American, a circumstance that was as anomalous for the time as it was exploited in the press. As Levy puts it: "Who was to be believed: Leo Frank, the Jew, or James Conley, the black man? Did Frank, a Jew, kill a Christian girl, or did Conley, a black man, kill a white girl? When such questions were raised in one fashion or another in 1914 and 1915 they were likely to mean one thing to Jews, another thing to blacks, and yet something else to other Americans" (213). Levy notes further that, whereas national press sentiment tended to regard Leo Frank as a white man, "such national, essentially elitist, sentiment counted for little among Southern white 'plain folk,' and in the end Frank died" (222).

33 One could likewise benefit from addressing Lander's third German novel, *The Daughters* (1976), in such a discussion.

34 The father in *Daughters,* in contrast, disappears and is presumed dead in Nazi-occupied Poland. For some insights into the more commonly discussed "father books," see Michael Schneider 1984 and Santner 1990: 36–46. Weigel (1987b: 160–67) specifically discusses father-daughter books, as does Gättens (1989). Peter Schneider's *Vati* (Daddy), published in 1987 as an account of Rolf Mengele's relationship to his notorious father, was a relatively late and highly controversial addition to this body of texts.

35 Each chapter actually begins with a synopsis of the events to follow in terms of a musical and/or dramatic staging. I return to the effects of this staging element later.

36 Since Lander's use of language is extremely expressive, often idiosyncratic, I provide the original text plus my English translations, except in the case of passages where the translation seems sufficient.

37 For some succinct comments on the historically divergent experiences of Ashkenazic and Sephardic Judaism, see Lavender 1977: 305–14, esp. 311. Ashkenazim are usually defined as Jews of German or eastern European descent; Sephardim descend from Spanish or Portuguese Jews; Mizrahim descend from Jews in Africa, Asia, and the Middle East (Plaskow 1990: 112). Plaskow is only one of several scholars to point out that Ashkenazic Judaism often functions as the spoken or unspoken normative standard for "Jewishness."

38 At the December 1990 conference in Essen (see note 17) someone commented that we were discussing biographies of real Jewish women on the one hand and imaginary configurations of Jewishness on the other. This led me to suggest that it might be useful to introduce a concept such as "das Jude" in order to remind ourselves that in both spheres positional constructs of Jewishness are at play. (In German the grammatically neuter article could modify "Jewish" to yield "that which is Jewish," but not any of the nouns for Jewish persons, which would require either the masculine or feminine article.) The problem with a term such as "das Jude" is, however, that it might appear to be gender-neutral. This is not the case.

39 While the religious dictates sketched here derive from Orthodox Judaism, they are familiar to other branches of Judaism as well. In more modern times (especially since the mid-nineteenth century) one notes growing differences between Orthodox Judaism and the Reform, Reconstructionist, and Conservative movements in Judaism. This is partic-

ularly noticeable with regard to the status of women in religious life. For historically oriented accounts of women and/in Judaism, see Swidler 1976 and Lacks 1980. For a variety of feminist positions on this relationship, see Beck 1982, Heschel 1983, Kaye/Kantrowitz and Klepfisz 1986/5746, Koltun 1976, Ozick 1979/5740, Plaskow 1990, and S. Schneider 1984. Greenberg (1981/5742) seeks to combine feminism and religious Orthodoxy. Appleman (1979) and Ghatan (1986) take the position that Orthodox Judaism has always held women in nothing but high regard. Levinson (1989) provides, in German, encyclopedic accounts of Jewish women who played important roles in biblical as well as postbiblical times. For a collection of essays on Jewish notions of masculinity, see Brod 1988.

40 The economically privileged black Dr. Kelsey also has his windows smashed during the riot, indicating that even the term "race riot" is misleading.

41 In a presentation delivered to the German Society for American Studies Annual Convention held in June 1990 at the University of Bonn, Tobe Levin also noted the "structural inequality" inherent in Kovsky's acts of generosity, no matter how humanely motivated they may be. This is a crucial point. I disagree with Levin, however, when she goes on to argue that *Itke* "tries, unsuccessfully, to privilege the similarities between the inner and the middle rings, representing two peoples of Zion, in the diaspora, who are indeed metaphorical kin." As I intend to show, Lander's consistent focus on conflicting constructs of positionality provides an effective counterweight to the purported privileging of supposed affinities between the blacks and Jews in *Itke*. I am grateful to Levin for sharing her unpublished manuscript with me and allowing me to cite from it.

42 The ultimate ineffectiveness of Mamma's attempts to police Itke's perceptions of the middle sphere is a subject to which we shall return, as is the function of Itke's role as witness.

43 Whereas Ozick (1979) argues that the issue of women's status in Judaism is primarily sociological and not theological, Plaskow (1990) counters that the problem is indeed theological as well. In this view a Jewish feminist project sells itself short if it demands only equal rights of participation in religious ritual. Plaskow reasons that the fundamental theological bias against women will be adequately addressed only once Jewish (religious) communities are conceived, articulated, and represented in radically different, nonsexist, nonhierarchical ways.

44 Adler (1983: 13) notes that in contrast to children and Canaanite slaves, "only women can never grow up, be freed, or otherwise leave the cate-

gory." Plaskow (1983: 226) draws yet another comparison: "The Gentile projection of the Jew as Other—the stranger, the demon, the human-non[sic]-quite-human—is repeated in—or should one say partly *modelled on?*—the Jewish understanding of the Jewish woman. She too is the stranger whose life is lived parallel to man's, the demoness who stirs him, the partner whose humanity is different from his own." Plaskow borrows the "human-not-quite-human" phrase from Dorothy Sayers's book *Are Women Human?* (1971).

45 Neither is she depicted as a harlot, which would be the biblical alternative (Lacks 1980: 88). Itke's budding sexuality does figure significantly, however, in a different context addressed later in this chapter.

46 As an Orthodox Jewish woman who also tries to wrestle with feminist issues, Blu Greenberg (1981/5742) provides a rare firsthand account of these rituals.

47 For my assessment of the function of this issue in *On Strange Ground* (1972), see Adelson 1990b: 127–28.

48 The Jewish notion of *tikkun olam* (Hebrew for "the right or just ordering of society") is nonetheless a rabbinic concept (Plaskow 1990: 217).

49 To say that the rabbinic tradition was patriarchal is not to say that the rabbis shared homogeneous attitudes toward women. See Swidler 1976: 72. Lacks (1980: 9) dates the rabbinic period from 200 B.C.E. to 500 C.E.

50 On a few occasions her white Yankee cousin, a soldier on leave, also becomes involved in these discussions with the other men. In a different kind of political vein Itke also espouses her views on hypocrisy in conversations with Jimmie Lee.

51 And yet it should be noted that Itke's brand of white southern womanhood is decidedly not intended in the Ku Klux Klan's long-standing call to defend "Southern womanhood," understood to be white *and* Christian. See Golden 1965 for repeated references to the Klan's deployment of this rhetoric.

52 The events depicted in the novel actually span several months, not just a week of chronological time.

53 This juxtaposition is especially striking in *The Daughters* (1976).

54 "As in the Christian tradition, in which the Otherness of women is expressed in the language of mind/body dualism, Judaism tenders a similar distinction between *ruhniut* [spirituality] and *gashmiut* [physicality], men and women" (Plaskow 1983: 225). Plaskow notes, however, that this dichotomy does not carry the same weight in Judaism as it has in Christianity (Plaskow 1983: 232 n. 7).

55 When Jimmie Lee shatters Itke's perceptions of togetherness by announcing her plans to quit her job with the Kovskys—in order to earn

more money at the new airplane factory so that she can put her auto-
didactic lover through medical school—the narrative voice draws on
Old Testament allusions to the inseparable Ruth and Naomi: "Your people are my people" and "Where you go, there I too shall go" (159). But
Itke's people are not Jimmie Lee's people, and Itke learns that Jimmie
Lee will be leaving without her. By the time Jimmie Lee loses her factory
job, the Kovskys have already hired another housekeeper to replace her.

56 Neither would I say that *Itke* represents "the black male" as a stereotype.
George, the possible exception, seems stereotyped as a male alcoholic.
While there are fewer male African American characters in this novel
than female African American figures, they too seem highly individuated. The tendential stereotyping of minorities poses somewhat more of
a problem, I suspect, in *The Daughters,* partly because so few minority individuals are represented.

57 Sonny is Jewish and male, to be sure, but without the bonds of marriage
Itke's lovemaking with him is illicit (Plaskow 1990: 189; Eisenberg 1979:
141).

58 Tracing historical developments, Swidler (1976: 55) refers specifically to
the perceived threat posed by Hellenistic culture, which granted women
higher status than did Jewish culture of the time. In this sense the religious bonding against non-Jewish women served to keep Jewish men
within the faith as well as to keep Jewish women in their place, that is, un-
tainted by "other" notions of women's rights and responsibilities.

59 Swidler (1976) discusses a variety of Jewish sects in the formative period
of Judaism. Plaskow (1990: xvi) notes that different manifestations of
rabbinic Judaism have coexisted with equally "various and changing
forms of popular Judaism."

60 One is likewise reminded of Judith Butler's elaborations on the multiplicity of "female" genders (1990). Lanser's analysis of the politics of
color in feminist readings of Charlotte Perkins Gilman's "The Yellow
Wallpaper" provides an excellent example of how a blindness to hetero-
geneously constructed positionality allowed a feminist text to pass for a
universal one (Lanser 1989: 434). Given Lander's explicit focus on historical constructs of racial and ethnic identity, it seems inconceivable that
Itke could pass for a universal woman's text.

In the postwar German-Austrian context Dagmar Lorenz criticizes
the universalizing posture adopted by the non-Jewish Brigitte Schwaiger in telling and marketing the story of Eva Deutsch, a Jewish survivor
of the Holocaust. By privileging the supposed commonality of a shared
"woman's perspective," Lorenz argues, Schwaiger trivializes the Nazi

atrocities and denies her own historical positioning as a woman who is also non-Jewish and Austrian (Lorenz 1991: 14–15).

61 Discussing divergent Jewish associations between female sexuality and evil, Plaskow (1990: 189) notes that even in the more sensuous mystical tradition of the Kabbalah, heterosexual marriage was still the prescribed norm.

62 This is a far cry from the constant surveillance and harassment to which TORKAN's female protagonist is subjected in *Tufan* (see above, Chapter Three).

63 It should be noted that Itke is also the object of her African American neighbors' visual observations as she moves in and through the public spaces of the store, the street outside, and the streetcar.

64 Referring to Gloria Anzaldúa's conceptualization of being "on the border," as presented in her 1987 study *Borderlands/La Frontera*, Chandra Talpade Mohanty points out that not just any border is being theorized here "but a historically specific one: the U.S./Mexican border. Thus, unlike a Western, postmodernist notion of agency and consciousness which often announces the splintering of the subject, and privileges multiplicity in the abstract, this is a notion of agency born of history and geography. It is a theorization of the materiality and politics of the everyday struggles of Chicanas" (Mohanty et al. 1991: 37).

65 An English translation of *The Dybbuk,* along with background information, is available in Ansky 1974. A detailed history of American minstrel theater is provided by Wittke 1976. Readers should be warned that the latter makes for painful reading, since Wittke's language and perspective evidence the racist bias peculiar to Wittke's historical "white" perspective (the book was copyrighted in 1930).

66 We know from other sources that blacks who performed in minstrel shows also used blackface (see Wittke 1976: 129).

67 Compare the details of Lander's "staging" (60–61) with the information recorded in the *Encyclopedia of Sports* (F. Menke 1969: 246, 266–67).

68 I have this from an anonymous, undated, and unpaginated article written for the *Boston Commercial Bulletin* by "An Ex-Manager and Performer." A photostatic copy of the article, entitled "Negro Minstrelsy: The Old Fashioned Troupes," can be found in the Main Library of The Ohio State University under the call number PN3195B75.

69 Compare Adelson 1990b: 131 for some comments on stylistic elements in Lander's second novel.

70 In addition to the linguistic codes that I have discussed, Lander cites others, including those of a Yiddish fairy tale, Midrashic story, and reli-

gious testimony at a revival meeting with a black Sanctified Church group.

71 Note that the present time of *Itke* is set prior to both the end of the Third Reich and the founding of the state of Israel, while the novel was written long after these historical events had begun to function as the sole hinges on which German public discourse about "Jews" could imagine turning.

72 In the other chapters of textual analysis I have identified some of the ways in which my own Jewishness has influenced my readings of the texts under discussion. In the case of *Itke* I have been challenged *not* to assume that I speak in an unconstructed, "natural," or "authentically Jewish" voice either about the Jewish characters or for any other Jewish person. As a Jew, I do feel certain qualms about saying that race does and should "matter" in the context of contemporary German Studies. I can only reiterate that I do not use "race" to mean a stable, universal, or biological category. I say that "race matters" in order to draw attention to the ways in which constructs of racial identity are also imbricated in varying constructs of other types of identity and experience, even if these are articulated primarily in terms of gender, class, ethnicity, culture, nation. This is what reading Lander has taught me.

Works Cited

Adelson, Leslie A. (1984). "Against the Enlightenment: A Theory with Teeth for the 1980s." *German Quarterly* 57: 625–31.

———(1986). "The Bomb and I: Peter Sloterdijk, Botho Strauß, and Christa Wolf." *Monatshefte* 78: 500–513.

——— (1989). "Der, die oder das Holocaust? A Response to Sander L. Gilman's Paper." *German Quarterly* 62: 205–9.

———(1990a). "Migrants' Literature or German Literature? TORKAN's *Tufan: Brief an einen islamischen Bruder* (1983)." *German Quarterly* 63: 382–89.

——— (1990b). "There's No Place Like Home: Jeannette Lander and Ronnith Neumann's Utopian Quests for Jewish Identity in the Contemporary West German Context." *New German Critique* 50: 113–34.

Adler, Rachel (1983). "The Jew Who Wasn't There: *Halakhah* and the Jewish Woman." In *On Being a Jewish Feminist: A Reader,* ed. Susannah Heschel, 12–18. New York: Schocken. Originally published in *Response* 7 (1973): 77–82.

Ahmed, Leila (1982). "Western Ethnocentrism and Perceptions of the Harem." *Feminist Studies* 8: 521–34.

——— (1989). "Arab Culture and Writing Women's Bodies." *Feminist Issues* 9: 41–55.

Alcoff, Linda (1988). "Cultural Feminism Versus Post-Structuralism: The Identity Crisis in Feminist Theory." *Signs* 13: 405–36. Rpt. in *Feminist Theory in Practice and Process,* ed. Micheline R. Malson, Jean F. O'Barr, Sarah

Westphal-Wihl, and Mary Wyer, 295–326. Chicago: University of Chicago Press, 1989.

Angress, Ruth (1985). "A 'Jewish Problem' in German Postwar Fiction." *Modern Judaism* 5: 215–33.

Ansky, S. (1974). *The Dybbuk: Between Two Worlds.* Trans. S. Morris Engel. Los Angeles: Nash.

Anzaldúa, Gloria (1987). *Borderlands/La Frontera: The New Mestiza.* San Francisco: Spinsters/Aunt Lute.

Appleman, Rabbi Solomon (1979). *The Jewish Woman in Judaism: The Significance of Woman's Status in Religious Culture.* Hicksville, N.Y.: Exposition Press.

Augstein, Rudolf, Karl Dietrich Bracher, Martin Broszat, Micha Brumlik, et al. (1987). *"Historikerstreit": Die Dokumentation der Kontroverse um die Einzigartigkeit der nationalsozialistischen Judenvernichtung.* Munich: Piper.

Bammer, Angelika (1986). "Testing the Limits: Christa Reinig's Radical Vision." *Women in German Yearbook: Feminist Studies and German Culture* 2, ed. Marianne Burkhard and Edith Waldstein, 107–27. Lanham, Md.: University Press of America.

Beck, Evelyn Torton (Ed.) (1982). *Nice Jewish Girls: A Lesbian Anthology.* Trumansberg, N.Y.: Crossing Press.

Beck, Lois, and Nikki Keddie (Eds.) (1978). *Women in the Muslim World.* Cambridge, Mass.: Harvard University Press.

Benjamin, Walter (1980). *Illuminationen: Ausgewählte Schriften.* 2d ed. Frankfurt am Main: Suhrkamp.

Berger, Renate, Monika Hengsbach, Maria Kublitz, Inge Stephan, and Sigrid Weigel. (Eds.) (1985). *Frauen/Weiblichkeit/Schrift.* Berlin: Argument.

Berman, Russell A. (1990). "Troping to Pretoria: The Rise and Fall of Deconstruction." *Telos* 85: 4–16.

Berman, Saul (1976). "The Status of Women in Halakhic Judaism." In *The Jewish Woman: New Perspectives*, ed. Elizabeth Koltun, 114–28. New York: Schocken.

Bettelheim, Bruno (1960). *The Informed Heart: Autonomy in a Mass Age.* Glencoe, N.Y.: Free Press.

Bloch, Ernst (1959). *Das Prinzip Hoffnung.* Frankfurt am Main: Suhrkamp.

Blumberg, Janice Rothschild (1985). *One Voice: Rabbi Jacob M. Rothschild and the Troubled South.* Macon, Ga.: Mercer University Press.

——— (1987). *As But a Day: To a Hundred and Twenty, 1867–1987.* Rev. ed. Atlanta: Hebrew Benevolent Congregation.

——— (1991). "Miss Daisy and I: Memories of Jewish Atlanta." *Reform Judaism* 19: 10–13.

Böll, Heinrich (1962). *Billiards at Half-Past Nine.* No translator cited. New York: McGraw-Hill.

Bordo, Susan (1990). "Feminism, Postmodernism, and Gender-Scepticism." *Feminism/Postmodernism,* ed. Linda J. Nicholson, 133–56. New York: Routledge.

Bourne, Jenny (1987). "Homelands of the Mind: Jewish Feminism and Identity Politics." *Race and Class* 29: 1–24.

Bovenschen, Silvia (1976). "Über die Frage: Gibt es eine weibliche Ästhetik?" *Ästhetik und Kommunikation* 25: 60–75.

——— (1977). "Is There a Feminine Aesthetic?" Trans. Beth Weckmueller. *New German Critique* 10: 111–37.

Bowie, Andrew (1985–86). Review of *Geschichte und Eigensinn. Telos* 66: 183–90.

Brockmann, Stephen (1991). "Introduction: The Reunification Debate." *New German Critique* 52: 3–30.

Brod, Harry (Ed.) (1988). *A Mensch among Men: Explorations in Jewish Masculinity.* Freedom, Calif.: Crossing Press.

Brügmann, Margret (1985). "Weiblichkeit im Spiel der Sprache: Über das Verhältnis von Psychoanalyse und 'écriture féminine.'" In *Frauen Literatur Geschichte: Schreibende Frauen vom Mittelalter bis zur Gegenwart,* ed. Hiltrud Gnüg and Renate Möhrmann, 395–415. Stuttgart: Metzler.

Brumlik, Micha (1987). "Neuer Staatsmythos Ostfront." In *"Historikerstreit,"* by Rudolf Augstein et al., 77–83. Munich: Piper.

Brumlik, Micha, Doron Kiesel, Cilly Kugelmann, and Julius H. Schoeps (Eds.) (1988). *Jüdisches Leben in Deutschland seit 1945.* Frankfurt am Main: Athenäum.

Butler, Judith (1990). *Gender Trouble: Feminism and the Subversion of Identity.* New York: Routledge.

Butwin, Frances (1973). *The Jews of America: History and Sources.* New York: Behrman House.

Carroll, David (1987). "Narrative, Heterogeneity, and the Question of the Political: Bakhtin and Lyotard." In *The Aims of Representation: Subject/Text/History,* ed. Murray Krieger, 69–106. New York: Columbia University Press.

Christian, Barbara (1985). *Black Feminist Criticism: Perspectives on Black Women Writers.* New York: Pergamon.

Cixous, Hélène (1975). *La jeune née.* Paris: Union Générale d'Editions.

——— (1976). "Schreiben, Feminität, Veränderung." Trans. Monika Bellan. *Alternative* 19 (June/August): 134–47.

——— (1980). "Laugh of the Medusa." Trans. Keith Cohen and Paula Cohen. In *New French Feminisms: An Anthology,* ed. Elaine Marks and Isabelle de Courtivron, 245–64. Amherst: University of Massachusetts Press.

Cixous, Hélène, and Catherine Clement (1986). *The Newly Born Woman.* Trans. Betsy Wing. Minneapolis: University of Minnesota Press.

Clifford, James (1988). "On Orientalism." In *The Predicament of Culture: Twentieth-Century Ethnography, Literature, and Art,* 255–76. Cambridge, Mass.: Harvard University Press.

Cocalis, Susan L., and Kay Goodman (Eds.) (1982). *Beyond the Eternal Feminine: Critical Essays on Women and German Literature.* Stuttgart: Hans-Dieter Heinz.

"The Combahee River Collective Statement" (1977). In *Home Girls: A Black Feminist Anthology,* ed. Barbara Smith, 272–82. New York: Kitchen Table/ Women of Color Press, 1983.

Coward, Rosalind, and John Ellis (1977). *Language and Materialism: Developments in Semiology and the Theory of the Subject.* London: Routledge and Kegan Paul.

Cowart, David (1989). *History and the Contemporary Novel.* Carbondale: Southern Illinois University Press.

Dallmayr, Fred R. (1981). *Twilight of Subjectivity: Contributions to a Post-Individualist Theory of Politics.* Amherst: University of Massachusetts Press.

de Lauretis, Teresa (1984). *Alice Doesn't: Feminism, Semiotics, Cinema.* Bloomington: Indiana University Press.

——— (1987). *Technologies of Gender: Essays on Theory, Film, and Fiction.* Bloomington: Indiana University Press.

——— (1989). "The Essence of the Triangle; or, Taking the Risk of Essentialism Seriously: Feminist Theory in Italy, the U.S., and Britain." *Differences: A Journal of Feminist Cultural Studies* 1: 3–37.

——— (1990). "The Practice of Sexual Difference and Feminist Thought in Italy: An Introductory Essay." In *Sexual Difference: A Theory of Social-Symbolic Practice,* by the Milan Women's Bookstore Collective, trans. Patricia Cicogna and Teresa de Lauretis, 1–21. Bloomington: Indiana University Press.

——— (Ed.) (1986). *Feminist Studies/Critical Studies.* Bloomington: Indiana University Press.

Deleuze, Gilles, and Félix Guattari (1986). *Kafka: Toward a Minor Literature.* Trans. Dana Polan. Minneapolis: University of Minnesota Press.

Dews, Peter (1987). *Logics of Disintegration: Post-Structuralist Thought and the Claims of Critical Theory.* London: Verso.

Diner, Dan (1989). "Austreibung ohne Einwanderung: Zum historischen Ort des '9. November.'" *Babylon* 5: 22–8.

——— (Ed.) (1987). *Ist der Nationalsozialismus Geschichte? Zu Historisierung und Historikerstreit.* Frankfurt am Main: Fischer.

Diner, Dan, Susann Heenen-Wolff, Gertrud Koch, Cilly Kugelmann, and Martin Löw-Beer (Eds.) (1986ff.) *Babylon: Beiträge zur jüdischen Gegenwart.* Frankfurt am Main: Neue Kritik.

Dinnerstein, Leonard (1973). "Atlanta in the Progressive Era: A Dreyfus Affair in Georgia." In *Jews in the South,* ed. Leonard Dinnerstein and Mary Dale Palsson, 170–97. Baton Rouge: Louisiana State University Press.

Dinnerstein, Leonard, and Mary Dale Palsson (1973). *Jews in the South.* Baton Rouge: Louisiana State University Press.

Duden, Anne (1982). *Übergang.* Berlin: Rotbuch.

———— (1985a). *Das Judasschaf.* Berlin: Rotbuch.

———— (1985b). *Opening of the Mouth.* Trans. Della Couling. London: Pluto Press.

Ecker, Gisela (Ed.) (1985). *Feminist Aesthetics.* Boston: Beacon Press.

Eggert, Hartmut, Ulrich Profitlich, and Klaus R. Scherpe. (Eds.) (1990). *Geschichte als Literatur: Formen und Grenzen der Repräsentation von Vergangenheit.* Stuttgart: Metzler.

Eisenberg, Dov (1979). *A Guide for the Jewish Woman and Girl: A Detailed Manual of the Jewish Laws, Customs, and Practices, as They Apply to, or Are Observed by Women and Girls.* 2d ed. New York: Berman.

El Saadawi, Nawal (1983). *The Hidden Face of Eve: Women in the Arab World.* Trans. Sherif Hetata. Boston: Beacon Press.

Engelmann, Bernt (1988). *Deutschland ohne Juden: Eine Bilanz.* Cologne: Pahl-Rugenstein.

Erenz, Benedikt (1986). "Berliner Adressen: Wo Himmler und Heydrich verfügten, Eichmann plante, Freisler richtete: Ein Weg durch die Ruinen des deutschen Alptraums." *Die Zeit* (Dec. 5).

———— (1987). "Mythos, Hitler, Spiel und Spaß: Über eine neue Art von Historien-Spektakel in Berlin und andernorts." *Die Zeit* (July 24).

Falk, Nancy Auer, and Rita M. Gross (Eds.) (1989). *Unspoken Worlds: Women's Religious Lives.* Belmont, Calif.: Wadsworth.

Featherstone, Mike (1982). "The Body in Consumer Culture." *Theory, Culture and Society* 1: 18–33.

Fernea, Elizabeth Warnock (Ed.) (1985). *Women and the Family in the Middle East: New Voices of Change.* Austin: University of Texas Press.

Foster, Hal (Ed.) (1984). *The Anti-Aesthetic: Essays on Postmodern Culture.* Port Townsend, Wash.: Bay Press.

Foucault, Michel (1977). *Discipline and Punish: The Birth of the Prison.* Trans. Alan Sheridan. London: Allen Lane.

Frank, Manfred (1984). *Was ist Neostrukturalismus?* Frankfurt am Main: Suhrkamp.

Frank, Manfred, Gérard Raulet, and Willem van Reijen (Eds.) (1988). *Die Frage nach dem Subjekt*. Frankfurt am Main: Suhrkamp.

Frederiksen, Elke (1989). "Literarische (Gegen-)Entwürfe von Frauen nach 1945: Berührungen und Veränderungen." In *Frauen-Fragen in der deutschsprachigen Literatur seit 1945*, ed. Mona Knapp and Gerd Labroisse, 83–110. Amsterdamer Beiträge zur Neueren Germanistik 29. Amsterdam: Rodopi.

Friedländer, Saul (1984). *Reflections of Nazism: An Essay on Kitsch and Death*. Trans. Thomas Weyr. New York: Harper and Row.

———— (1986). "'A Past That Refuses to Go Away': On Recent Historiographical Debates in the Federal Republic of Germany about National Socialism and the Final Solution." In *Wissenschaftskolleg-Jahrbuch 1985/86*, ed. Peter Wapnewski, 105–15. Berlin: Siedler.

Fuss, Diana (1989). *Essentially Speaking: Feminism, Nature and Difference*. New York: Routledge.

Futterknecht, Franz (1976). *Das dritte Reich im deutschen Roman der Nachkriegszeit: Untersuchungen zur Faschismustheorie und Faschismusbewältigung*. Bonn: Bouvier.

Gates, Henry Louis, Jr. (1986). "Introduction: Writing 'Race' and the Difference It Makes." In *'Race,' Writing, and Difference*, ed. Henry Louis Gates, Jr., 1–20. Chicago: University of Chicago Press.

Gättens, Marie-Luise (1989). "Die Rekonstruktion der Geschichte: Der Nationalsozialismus in drei Romanen der siebziger Jahre." In *Frauen-Fragen in der deutschsprachigen Literatur seit 1945*, ed. Mona Knapp and Gerd Labroisse, 111–30. Amsterdam: Rodopi.

Ghatan, Dr. H. E. Yedidiah (1986). *The Invaluable Pearl: The Unique Status of Women in Judaism*. New York: Block.

Gilbert, Sandra M., and Susan Gubar (1980). "The Parables of the Dark Cave." In *The Madwoman in the Attic: The Woman Writer and the Nineteenth-Century Imagination*, 2d ed., 93–104. New Haven: Yale University Press.

Gilman, Sander L. (1982). *On Blackness without Blacks: Essays on the Image of the Black in Germany*. Boston: Hall.

———— (1985). *Difference and Pathology: Stereotypes of Sexuality, Race, and Madness*. Ithaca: Cornell University Press.

———— (1986). *Jewish Self-Hatred: Anti-Semitism and the Hidden Language of the Jews*. Baltimore: Johns Hopkins University Press.

———— (1986–87). "Jewish Writers and German Letters: Anti-Semitism and the Hidden Language of the Jews." *Jewish Quarterly Review* 77: 119–48.

———— (1989). "Why and How I Study the German." *German Quarterly* 62: 192–204.

—— (1991). "German Reunification and the Jews." *New German Critique* 52: 173–91.

Golden, Harry (1965). *A Little Girl Is Dead*. Cleveland: World Publishing.

Greenberg, Blu (1981/5742). *On Women and Judaism: A View from Tradition*. Philadelphia: Jewish Publication Society of America.

Gubar, Susan (1982). "'The Blank Page' and the Issues of Female Creativity." In *Writing and Sexual Difference*, ed. Elizabeth Abel, 73–93. Chicago: University of Chicago Press.

Gumbrecht, Hans Ulrich (1985). "Posthistoire Now." In *Epochenschwellen und Epochenstrukturen im Diskurs der Literatur-und Sprachhistorie*, ed. Hans Ulrich Gumbrecht and Ursula Link-Heer, 34–50. Frankfurt am Main: Suhrkamp.

Gutstein, Linda (1988). *History of the Jews in America*. Seacaucus, N.J.: Chartwell.

Habermas, Jürgen (1987). *Eine Art Schadensabwicklung: Kleine Politische Schriften VI*. Frankfurt am Main: Suhrkamp.

Haeri, Shahla (1989). *Law of Desire: Temporary Marriage in Shi'i Iran*. Syracuse: Syracuse University Press.

Halverson, Rachel Jane (1989). "Historiography and Fiction: Siegfried Lenz and the *Historikerstreit*." Ph.D. diss., University of Texas, Austin.

Hartman, Geoffrey (Ed.) (1986). *Bitburg: In Moral and Political Perspective*. Bloomington: Indiana University Press.

Hartsock, Nancy (1985). *Money, Sex, and Power: Toward a Feminist Historical Materialism*. Boston: Northeastern University Press.

—— (1987). "Rethinking Modernism: Minority vs. Majority Theories." *Cultural Critique* 7: 187–206.

Hegel, G. W. F. (1971). *The Phenomenology of the Mind*. Rev. 2d ed. Trans. J. B. Baillie. New York: Humanities Press.

Heinemann, Marlene E. (1986). *Gender and Destiny: Women Writers and the Holocaust*. New York: Greenwood Press.

Heller, Agnes (1982). *A Theory of History*. London: Routledge and Kegan Paul.

Henning, Eike (1988). *Zum Historikerstreit: Was heißt und zu welchem Ende studiert man Faschismus?* Frankfurt am Main: Athenäum.

Herrmann, Claudia (1980). "Women in Space and Time." Trans. Marilyn R. Schuster. In *New French Feminisms: An Anthology*, ed. Elaine Marks and Isabelle de Courtivron, 168–73. Amherst: University of Massachusetts Press.

Heschel, Susannah (Ed.) (1983). *On Being a Jewish Feminist: A Reader*. New York: Schocken.

Higgins, Patricia J. (1985). "Women in the Islamic Republic of Iran: Legal, Social, and Ideological Changes." *Signs* 10: 477–94.

Hoesterey, Ingeborg (1988). *Verschlungene Schriftzeichen: Intertextualität von Literatur und Kunst in der Moderne/Postmoderne.* Frankfurt am Main: Athenäum.

Hohendahl, Peter Uwe (1988). "Marxistische Literaturtheorie zwischen Hermeneutik und Diskursanalyse: Fredric Jamesons *The Political Unconscious.*" In *Diskurstheorien und Literaturwissenschaft,* ed. Jürgen Fohrmann and Harro Müller, 200–220. Frankfurt am Main: Suhrkamp.

Honegger, Claudia, and Bettina Heintz (Eds.) (1984). *Listen der Ohnmacht: Zur Sozialgeschichte weiblicher Widerstandsformen.* Frankfurt am Main: Europäische Verlagsanstalt.

hooks, bell (1984). *Feminist Theory: From Margin to Center.* Boston: South End Press.

———— (1990). *Yearning: Race, Gender, and Cultural Politics.* Boston: South End Press.

Horkheimer, Max, and Theodor W. Adorno (1972). *Dialectic of Enlightenment.* Trans. John Cumming. New York: Herder and Herder.

Hull, Gloria, Patricia Bell Scott, and Barbara Smith (Eds.) (1982). *All the Women Are White, All the Blacks Are Men, but Some of Us Are Brave.* Old Westbury, N.Y.: Feminist Press.

Huyssen, Andreas (1981). "The Search for Tradition: Avant-Garde and Postmodernism in the 1970s." *New German Critique* 22: 23–40.

———— (1984). "Mapping the Postmodern." *New German Critique* 33: 5–52.

———— (1986). *After the Great Divide: Modernism, Mass Culture, Postmodernism.* Bloomington: Indiana University Press.

Huyssen, Andreas, and Klaus R. Scherpe (Eds.) (1986). *Postmoderne—Zeichen eines kulturellen Wandels.* Reinbek bei Hamburg: Rowohlt.

Iglitzin, Lynne B., and Ruth Ross (Eds.) (1976). *Women in the World: A Comparative Study.* Santa Barbara: Clio.

Irigaray, Luce (1980). "The Sex Which Is Not One." Trans. Claudia Reeder. In *New French Feminisms: An Anthology,* ed. Elaine Marks and Isabelle de Courtivron, 99–106. Amherst: University of Massachusetts Press.

Jaggar, Alison M., and Susan R. Bordo (Eds.) (1989). *Gender/Body/Knowledge: Feminist Reconstructions of Being and Knowing.* New Brunswick: Rutgers University Press.

Jameson, Fredric (1981). *The Political Unconscious: Narrative as a Socially Symbolic Act.* Ithaca: Cornell University Press.

JanMohamed, Abdul R. (1984). "Humanism and Minority Literature: Toward a Definition of Counter-Hegemonic Discourse." *boundary 2* 12/13: 281–99.

Kaes, Anton (1990). "New Historicism: Literaturgeschichte im Zeichen der Postmoderne." In *Geschichte als Literatur: Formen und Grenzen der Repräsen-*

tation von Vergangenheit, ed. Hartmut Eggert, Ulrich Profitlich, and Klaus R. Scherpe, 56–66. Stuttgart: Metzler.

Kamper, Dietmar (1985). "Die Körperlichkeit—Die Überholung des Körpers, mündlich und schriftlich." In *Das schnelle Altern der neuesten Literatur: Essays zu deutschsprachigen Texten zwischen 1968–1984*, ed. Jochen Hörisch and Hubert Winkels, 131–40. Düsseldorf: Claassen.

Kamper, Dietmar, and Christoph Wulf (Eds.) (1982). *Die Wiederkehr des Körpers*. Frankfurt am Main: Suhrkamp.

——— (Eds.) (1984). *Das Schwinden der Sinne*. Frankfurt am Main: Suhrkamp.

Kaplan, Caren (1987). "Deterritorializations: The Rewriting of Home and Exile in Western Feminist Discourse." *Cultural Critique* 6: 187–98.

Kaye/Kantrowitz, Melanie, and Irena Klepfisz (Eds.) (1986/5746). *The Tribe of Dina: A Jewish Women's Anthology*. Montpelier, Vt.: Sinister Wisdom.

Kelly, Joan (1984). "The Doubled Vision of Feminist Theory." In *Women, History, and Theory*, 51–64. Chicago: University of Chicago Press.

Klepfisz, Irena (1986/5746). "Secular Jewish Identity: *Yidishkayt* in America." In *The Tribe of Dina: A Jewish Women's Anthology*, ed. Melanie Kaye/Kantrowitz and Irena Klepfisz, 30–48. Montpelier, Vt.: Sinister Wisdom.

Koch, Gertrud (1990). "Corporate Identities: Zur Prosa von Dische, Biller und Seligmann." *Babylon* 7: 139–42.

Kocka, Jürgen (1987). "Hitler sollte nicht durch Stalin und Pol Pot verdrängt werden." In *"Historikerstreit,"* by Rudolf Augstein et al., 132–42. Munich: Piper.

Kocka, Jürgen, and Thomas Nipperdey (Eds.) (1979). *Theorie und Erzählung in der Geschichte*. Munich: dtv.

Koltun, Elizabeth (Ed.) (1976). *The Jewish Woman: New Perspectives*. New York: Schocken.

Koonz, Claudia (1987). *Mothers in the Fatherland: Women, the Family, and Nazi Politics*. New York: St. Martin's Press.

Koselleck, Reinhart (1979). *Vergangene Zukunft: Zur Semantik geschichtlicher Zeiten*. Frankfurt am Main: Suhrkamp.

Koselleck, Reinhart, and Wolf-Dieter Stempel (Eds.) (1973). *Geschichte— Ereignis und Erzählung*. Munich: Fink.

Kreuzer, Helmut (1987). "Vom 'Sein' zur 'Postmoderne': Streiflichter auf vier Dekaden der Literatur und Literaturwissenschaft im westlichen Deutschland." In *Zeitgenossenschaft: Zur deutschsprachigen Literatur im 20. Jahrhundert* (Festschrift für Egon Schwarz zum 65. Geburtstag), ed. Paul Michael Lützeler, 296–323. Frankfurt am Main: Athenäum.

Krieger, Murray (Ed.) (1987). *The Aims of Representation: Subject/Text/History*. New York: Columbia University Press.

Kristeva, Julia (1976). "Produktivität der Frau: Interview von Eliane Boucquey." Trans. Lily Leder. *Alternative* 19 (June/August): 166–72.

—— (1980). "Woman Can Never Be Defined." Trans. Marilyn A. August. In *New French Feminisms: An Anthology*, ed. Elaine Marks and Isabelle de Courtivron, 137–41. Amherst: University of Massachusetts Press.

—— (1982a). *Powers of Horror: An Essay on Abjection*. Trans. Leon S. Roudiez. New York: Columbia University Press.

—— (1982b). "Women's Time." Trans. Alice Jardine and Harry Blake. In *Feminist Theory: A Critique of Ideology*, ed. Nannerl O. Keohane, 31–53. Chicago: University of Chicago Press.

Krochmalnik, Daniel (1989). "9. November 1938, 14. Mai 1948: Zur Entmythologisierung von zwei historischen Ereignissen." *Babylon* 5: 7–21.

Kroker, Arthur, and David Cook (1988). *The Postmodern Scene: Excremental Culture and Hyper-Aesthetics*. London: Macmillan.

Kroker, Arthur, and Marielouise Kroker (Eds.) (1988). *Body Invaders: Sexuality and the Postmodern Condition*. London: Macmillan.

La Capra, Dominick (1987). *History, Politics, and the Novel*. Ithaca: Cornell University Press.

Lacks, Roslyn (1980). *Women and Judaism: Myth, History, and Struggle*. Garden City, N.Y.: Doubleday.

Laermann, Klaus (1988). "Von der APO zur Apokalypse: Resignation und Fröhliche Wissenschaft am Beispiel von Peter Sloterdijk." In *'Postmoderne' oder Der Kampf um die Zukunft: Die Kontroverse in Wissenschaft, Kunst und Gesellschaft*, ed. Peter Kemper, 207–30. Frankfurt am Main: Fischer.

Lander, Jeannette (1971). *Ein Sommer in der Woche der Itke K.* Frankfurt am Main: Suhrkamp.

—— (1972). *Auf dem Boden der Fremde*. Frankfurt am Main: Insel.

—— (1976). *Die Töchter*. Frankfurt am Main: Insel.

—— (1979). "Unsicherheit ist Freiheit." In *Fremd im eigenen Land*, ed. Henryk M. Broder and Michael R. Lang, 258–64. Frankfurt am Main: Fischer.

—— (1980). *Ich, allein*. Munich: AutorenEdition.

—— (1981). "Jeannette Lander." *Emma* 7 (July 1): 18–20.

Lanser, Susan S. (1981). *The Narrative Act: Point of View in Prose Fiction*. Princeton: Princeton University Press.

—— (1989). "Feminist Criticism, 'The Yellow Wallpaper,' and the Politics of Color in America." *Feminist Studies* 15: 415–41.

Laqueur, Thomas (1990). *Making Sex: Body and Gender from the Greeks to Freud*. Cambridge, Mass.: Harvard University Press.

Lavender, Abraham (Ed.) (1977). *A Coat of Many Colors: Jewish Subcommunities in the United States*. Westport, Conn.: Greenwood Press.

Lenk, Elisabeth (1983). *Die unbewußte Gesellschaft: Über die mimetische Grundstruktur in der Literatur und im Traum.* Munich: Matthes & Seitz.

Lennox, Sara (1984). "Geschlecht, Rasse und Geschichte in 'Der Fall Franza.'" Trans. Frank Mecklenburg. In *Ingeborg Bachmann,* ed. Sigrid Weigel, 156–79. Munich: text + kritik.

Levin, Tobe (1990). "Introducing Jeannette Lander to American Studies Scholars and the City of Her Growing Up, Atlanta." Presentation to the German Society for American Studies Annual Convention. University of Bonn, June.

Levinson, Pnina Navè (1989). *Was wurde aus Saras Töchtern? Frauen im Judentum.* Gütersloh: Gütersloher Verlagshaus Gerd Mohn.

Levy, Eugene (1974). "'Is the Jew a White Man?' Press Reaction to the Leo Frank Case, 1913–1915." *Phylon* 35: 212–22.

Lichtenstein, Heiner (Ed.) (1986). *Die Fassbinder-Kontroverse oder Das Ende der Schonzeit.* Königstein/Ts.: Athenäum.

Lifson, David S. (1965). *The Yiddish Theater in America.* New York: Yoseloff.

Lokke, Virgil (1987). "Introduction: Taxonomies Are Never Innocent." In *The Current in Criticism: Essays on the Present and Future of Literary Theory,* ed. Clayton Koelb and Virgil Lokke, 1–25. West Lafayette: Purdue University Press.

Lorde, Audre (1984). *Sister Outsider: Essays and Speeches.* Trumansburg, N.Y.: Crossing Press.

Lorenz, Dagmar C. G. (1991). "'Hoffentlich werde ich taugen': Zu Situation und Kontext von Brigitte Schwaiger/Eva Deutsch *Die Galizianerin.*" In *Women in German Yearbook: Feminist Studies and German Culture* 6, ed. Jeanette Clausen and Helen Cafferty, 1–25. Lanham, Md.: University Press of America.

Lützeler, Paul Michael (1986). *Zeitgeschichte in Geschichten der Zeit: Deutschsprachige Romane im 20. Jahrhundert.* Bonn: Bouvier.

——— (1987). *Geschichte in der Literatur: Studien zu Werken von Lessing bis Hebbel.* Munich: Piper.

McCormick, Richard W. (1991). *Politics of the Self: Feminism and the Postmodern in West German Literature and Film.* Princeton: Princeton University Press.

McGann, Jerome J. (Ed.) (1985). *Historical Studies and Literary Criticism.* Madison: University of Wisconsin Press.

Maier, Charles S. (1988). *The Unmasterable Past: History, Holocaust, and German National Identity.* Cambridge, Mass.: Harvard University Press.

Malti-Douglas, Fedwa (1991). *Woman's Body, Woman's Word: Gender and Discourse in Arabo-Islamic Writing.* Princeton: Princeton University Press.

Marcuse, Herbert (1980). "Protosocialism and Late Capitalism: Toward a Theoretical Synthesis Based on Bahro's Analysis." In *Rudolf Bahro: Critical Responses*, ed. Ulf Wolter, 25–48. White Plains, N.Y.: Sharpe.

Martin, Biddy (1982). "Feminism, Criticism, and Foucault." *New German Critique* 27: 3–30.

——— (1983). "Weiblichkeit als kulturelle Konstruktion." Trans. Cornelia Holfelder-von der Tann. *Das Argument* 25 (March/April): 210–15.

——— (1989a). "Lesbian Identity and Autobiographical Difference[s]." In *Lifelines: Theorizing Women's Autobiography*, ed. Bella Brodzki and Celeste Schenck, 77–103. Ithaca: Cornell University Press.

——— (1989b). "Zwischenbilanz der feministischen Debatten." Trans. Dorothea von Mücke. In *Germanistik in den USA: Neue Entwicklungen und Methoden*, ed. Frank Trommler, 165–95. Wiesbaden: Westdeutscher Verlag.

Martin, Biddy, and Chandra Talpade Mohanty (1986). "Feminist Politics: What's Home Got to Do with It?" In *Feminist Studies/Critical Studies*, ed. Teresa de Lauretis, 191–212. Bloomington: Indiana University Press.

Mattenklott, Gert (1982). *Der übersinnliche Leib: Beiträge zur Metaphysik des Körpers*. Reinbek bei Hamburg: Rowohlt.

——— (1988). "Körperpolitik oder Das Schwinden der Sinne." In *'Postmoderne' oder Der Kampf um die Zukunft: Die Kontroverse in Wissenschaft, Kunst und Gesellschaft*, ed. Peter Kemper, 231–52. Frankfurt am Main: Fischer.

Menke, Frank (1969). *The Encyclopedia of Sports*. 4th rev. ed. South Brunswick, N.J.: A. S. Barnes.

Menke, Timm (1986). "Anne Dudens Erzählband *Übergang:* Zum Verhältnis von Angst und Postmoderne in der Literatur der achtziger Jahre." *Orbis Litterarum* 41: 279–88.

Mernissi, Fatima (1987). *Beyond the Veil: Male-Female Dynamics in Modern Muslim Society*. Rev. ed. Bloomington: Indiana University Press.

Mohanty, Chandra Talpade (1984). "Under Western Eyes: Feminist Scholarship and Colonial Discourses." *boundary 2* 12/13: 333–58.

——— (1988). "Feminist Encounters: Locating the Politics of Experience." *Copyright* 1: 30–44.

Mohanty, Chandra Talpade, Ann Russo, and Lourdes Torres (Eds.) (1991). *Third World Women and the Politics of Feminism*. Bloomington: Indiana University Press.

Moi, Toril (1985). *Sexual/Textual Politics*. London: Methuen.

Mommsen, Hans (1987). "Suche nach der 'verlorenen Geschichte'?" In *"Historikerstreit,"* by Rudolf Augstein et al., 156–73. Munich: Piper.

Moraga, Cherrie, and Gloria Anzaldúa (Eds.) (1981). *This Bridge Called My Back: Writing by Radical Women of Color*. New York: Persephone Press; 2d ed., New York: Kitchen Table, 1983.

Morgan, Robin (Ed.) (1984). *Sisterhood Is Global: The International Women's Movement Anthology.* New York: Doubleday, Anchor Books.

Mosse, George (1985). *Nationalism and Sexuality: Respectability and Abnormal Sexuality in Modern Europe.* New York: Howard Fertig.

Müller, Heidy M. (1984). *Die Judendarstellung in der deutschsprachigen Erzählprosa (1945–1981).* Königstein/Ts.: Forum Academicum in der Verlagsgruppe Athenäum, Hain, Hanstein.

Nägele, Rainer (1977). "Heinrich Böll: Die große Ordnung und die kleine Anarchie." In *Gegenwartsliteratur und Drittes Reich,* ed. Hans Wagener, 183–204. Stuttgart: Reclam.

——— (1986). "The Scene of the Other: Theodor W. Adorno's Negative Dialectic in the Context of Poststructuralism." In *Postmodernism and Politics,* ed. Jonathan Arac, 91–111. Minneapolis: University of Minnesota Press.

Nashat, Guity (1980). "Women in the Islamic Republic of Iran." *Iranian Studies* 13: 165–96.

——— (Ed.) (1983). *Women and Revolution in Iran.* Boulder, Colo.: Westview Press.

Negt, Oskar, and Alexander Kluge (1972). *Öffentlichkeit und Erfahrung: Zur Organisationsanalyse von bürgerlicher und proletarischer Öffentlichkeit.* Frankfurt am Main: Suhrkamp.

——— (1981). *Geschichte und Eigensinn: Geschichtliche Organisation der Arbeitsvermögen, Deutschland als Produktionsöffentlichkeit, Gewalt des Zusammenhangs.* Frankfurt am Main: Zweitausendeins.

Newton, Judith, and Deborah Rosenfelt (Eds.) (1985). *Feminist Criticism and Social Change: Sex, Class and Race in Literature and Culture.* New York: Methuen.

Nicholson, Linda J. (Ed.) (1990). *Feminism/Postmodernism.* New York: Routledge.

Oguntoye, Katharina (1989). "Die Schwarze deutsche Bewegung und die Frauenbewegung in Deutschland." *Afrekete: Zeitung von afro-deutschen und schwarzen Frauen* 4: 3–5, 33–37.

Oguntoye, Katharina, May Opitz, and Dagmar Schultz (Eds.) (1986). *Farbe bekennen: Afro-deutsche Frauen auf den Spuren ihrer Geschichte.* Berlin: Orlanda Frauenverlag.

Omi, Michael, and Howard Winant (1986). *Racial Formation in the United States.* New York: Routledge and Kegan Paul.

Opitz, May (1986). "Afro-Deutsche nach 1945—die sogenannten Besatzungskinder." In *Farbe bekennen: Afro-deutsche Frauen auf den Spuren ihrer Geschichte,* ed. Katharina Oguntoye, May Opitz, and Dagmar Schultz, 85–102. Berlin: Orlanda Frauenverlag.

Opitz, May, Katharina Oguntoye, and Dagmar Schultz (Eds.) (1991). *Showing Our Colors: Afro-German Women Speak Out*. Trans. Anne V. Adams. Amherst: University of Massachusetts Press.

Orwell, George (1949). *1984: A Novel*. New York: Signet Classic.

Oswald, Niko (1991). "Judentum als Gegenstand von Wissenschaft: Eine Kritik des Faches Judaistik in Deutschland." *Babylon* 8: 45–71.

Ozick, Cynthia (1979/5740). "Notes Toward Finding the Right Question (A Vindication of the Rights of Jewish Women)." *Lilith* 6: 19–29. Rpt. in *On Being a Jewish Feminist: A Reader,* ed. Susannah Heschel, 120–51. New York: Schocken, 1983.

Peck, Jeffrey M. (1987). "The Institution of *Germanistik* and the Transmission of Culture: The Time and Place for an Anthropological Approach." *Monatshefte* 79: 308–19.

——— (1989). "Methodological Postscript: What's the Difference? Minority Discourse in German Studies." *New German Critique* (Special Issue on Minorities in German Culture) 46: 203–8.

Plaskow, Judith (1983). "The Right Question Is Theological." In *On Being a Jewish Feminist: A Reader,* ed. Susannah Heschel, 223–33. New York: Schocken.

——— (1990). *Standing Again at Sinai: Judaism from a Feminist Perspective*. San Francisco: Harper and Row.

Pratt, Minnie Bruce (1984). "Identity: Skin Blood Heart." In *Yours in Struggle: Three Feminist Perspectives on Anti-Semitism and Racism,* by Elly Bulkin, Minnie Bruce Pratt, and Barbara Smith, 11–63. Brooklyn, N.Y.: Long Haul Press.

Pullapilly, Cyriac K. (Ed.) (1980). *Islam in the Contemporary World*. Notre Dame, Ind.: Cross Road.

Rabinbach, Anson (1988). "The Jewish Question in the German Question." *New German Critique* 44: 159–92.

Rabinbach, Anson, and Jack Zipes (Eds.) (1986). *Germans and Jews since the Holocaust: The Changing Situation in West Germany*. New York: Holmes and Meier.

Reagon, Bernice Johnson (1983). "Coalition Politics: Turning the Century." In *Home Girls: A Black Feminist Anthology,* ed. Barbara Smith, 356–68. New York: Kitchen Table/Women of Color Press.

Reinig, Christa (1976). "Das weibliche Ich." *Alternative* 19 (June/August): 119–20.

Rich, Adrienne (1977). *Of Woman Born: Motherhood as Experience and Institution*. New York: Norton.

——— (1979). *On Lies, Secrets, and Silence: Selected Prose, 1966–1978*. New York: Norton.

——— (1984). "Notes Toward a Politics of Location (1984)." In *Blood, Bread, and Poetry: Selected Prose 1979–1985*, 210–31. New York: Norton, 1986.

Röll, Walter, and Hans-Peter Bayerdörfer (Eds.) (1986). *Auseinandersetzungen um jiddische Sprache und Literatur: Jüdische Komponenten in der deutschen Literatur—die Assimilationskontroverse*. Vol. 5 of *Kontroversen, alte und neue: Akten des VII. Internationalen Germanisten-Kongresses Göttingen 1985*. Tübingen: Niemeyer.

Rürup, Reinhard (Ed.) (1987). *Topographie des Terrors: Gestapo, ss und Reichssicherheitshauptamt auf dem "Prinz-Albrecht-Gelände," Eine Dokumentation*. 3d ed. Berlin: Arenhövel.

Rutschky, Michael (1980). *Erfahrungshunger: Ein Essay über die siebziger Jahre*. Cologne: Kiepenheuer & Witsch.

Ryan, Judith (1983). *The Uncompleted Past: Postwar German Novels and the Third Reich*. Detroit: Wayne State University Press.

——— (1990). "The Problem of Pastiche: Patrick Süskind's *Das Parfum*." *German Quarterly* 63: 396–403.

——— (1991). "Silting Up the System: A New Conception of History in the Contemporary Novel." In *"Was in den alten Büchern steht . . .": Neue Interpretationen von der Aufklärung zur Moderne* (Festschrift für Reinhold Grimm), ed. Karl-Heinz Schoeps and Christopher J. Wickham, 55–66. Frankfurt am Main: Peter Lang.

Said, Edward W. (1978). *Orientalism*. New York: Pantheon Books.

——— (1983). *The World, the Text, and the Critic*. Cambridge, Mass.: Harvard University Press.

Samuels, Charles, and Louise Samuels (1956). *Night Fell on Georgia*. New York: Dell.

Sangari, Kum Kum (1987). "The Politics of the Possible." *Cultural Critique* 7: 157–86.

Santner, Eric L. (1990). *Stranded Objects: Mourning, Memory, and Film in Postwar Germany*. Ithaca: Cornell University Press.

Sayers, Dorothy (1971). *Are Women Human?* Grand Rapids, Mich.: Eerdmans.

Scarry, Elaine (1985). *The Body in Pain: The Making and Unmaking of the World*. New York: Oxford University Press.

——— (Ed.) (1988). *Literature and the Body: Essays on Populations and Persons*. Baltimore: Johns Hopkins University Press.

Schick, Irvin Cemil (1990). "Representing Middle Eastern Women: Feminism and Colonial Discourse (Review Essay)." *Feminist Studies* 16: 345–80.

Schmelzkopf, Christiane (1985). "Zur Gestaltung jüdischer Figuren in der deutschsprachigen Literatur nach 1945." In *Juden und Judentum in der Literatur*, ed. Herbert A. Strauss and Christhaid Hoffman, 273–94. Munich: dtv.

Schmidt, Henry J. (1987). "What Is Oppositional Criticism? Politics and German Literary Criticism from Fascism to the Cold War." *Monatshefte* 79: 292–307.

Schmidt, Ricarda (1982). *Westdeutsche Frauenliteratur in den 70er Jahren*. Frankfurt am Main: Rita G. Fischer.

Schneider, Michael (1984). "Fathers and Sons, Retrospectively: The Damaged Relationship between Two Generations." Trans. Jamie Owen Daniel. *New German Critique* 31: 3–51.

Schneider, Peter (1987). *Vati*. Darmstadt: Luchterhand.

Schneider, Susan Weidman (1984). *Jewish and Female: Choices and Changes in Our Lives Today*. New York: Simon and Schuster.

Scholem, Gershom (1976). *On Jews and Judaism: Selected Essays*, ed. Werner J. Dannhauser. New York: Schocken.

Schulze, Leonard, and Walter Wetzels (Eds.) (1983). *Literature and History*. Lanham, Md.: University Press of America.

Seeba, Hinrich C. (1980). "Literatur und Geschichte: Hermeneutische Ansätze zu einer Poetik der Geschichtsschreibung." In *Akten des VI. Internationalen Germanisten-Kongresses Basel 1980*. Jahrbuch für internationale Germanistik, Reihe A, Band 8, 3: 201–8. Bern: Lang.

Showalter, Elaine (1982). "Feminist Criticism in the Wilderness." In *Writing and Sexual Difference*, ed. Elizabeth Abel, 9–35. Chicago: University of Chicago Press.

Silverman, Kaja (1983). *The Subject of Semiotics*. New York: Oxford University Press.

Sloterdijk, Peter (1983). *Kritik der zynischen Vernunft*. Frankfurt am Main: Suhrkamp.

——— (1984). "Cynicism—The Twilight of False Consciousness." Trans. Michael Eldred and Leslie A. Adelson. *New German Critique* 33: 190–206.

——— (1987). *Critique of Cynical Reason*. Trans. Michael Eldred. Minneapolis: University of Minnesota Press.

Smith, Barbara (1977). "Toward a Black Feminist Criticism." *Conditions* 2: 25–44.

——— (1979). "Notes for Yet Another Paper on Black Feminism, Or Will the Real Enemy Please Stand Up?" *Conditions* 5: 123–27.

Smith, Valerie (1989). "Black Feminist Theory and the Representation of the 'Other.'" In *Changing Our Own Words: Essays on Criticism, Theory, and Writing by Black Women*, ed. Cheryl A. Wall, 38–57, 221–23. New Brunswick, N.J.: Rutgers University Press.

Spanos, William V. (1984). "*boundary 2* and the Polity of Interest: Humanism, the 'Center Elsewhere,' and Power." *boundary 2* 12/13: 173–214.

Spelman, Elizabeth V. (1982a). "Theories of Race and Gender: The Erasure of Black Women." *Quest: A Feminist Quarterly* 5: 36–62.

—— (1982b). "Woman as Body: Ancient and Contemporary Views." *Feminist Studies* 8: 109–31.

—— (1988). *Inessential Woman: Problems of Exclusion in Feminist Thought.* Boston: Beacon Press.

Spivak, Gayatri Chakravorty (1987a). "Imperialism and Sexual Difference." In *The Current in Criticism: Essays on the Present and Future of Literary Theory,* ed. Clayton Koelb and Virgil Lokke, 319–37. West Lafayette: Purdue University Press.

—— (1987b). *In Other Worlds: Essays in Cultural Politics.* New York: Methuen.

—— (1990). *The Post-Colonial Critic: Interviews, Strategies, Dialogues,* ed. Sarah Harasym. New York: Routledge.

Stefan, Verena (1975). *Häutungen.* Munich: Frauenoffensive.

—— (1978). *Shedding.* Trans. Johanna Moore and Beth Weckmueller. New York: Daughter's Publishing.

Stephan, Inge, and Sigrid Weigel (1983). *Die verborgene Frau: Sechs Beiträge zu einer feministischen Literaturwissenschaft.* Berlin: Argument.

Stern, Frank (1991a). "The 'Jewish Question' in the 'German Question,' 1945–1990: Reflections in Light of November 9th, 1989." Trans. Bill Templer. *New German Critique* 52: 155–72.

—— (1991b). "Philosemitismus : Stereotype über den Feind, den man zu lieben hat." *Babylon* 8: 15–26.

Stierle, Karlheinz (1979). "Erfahrung und narrative Form: Bemerkungen zu ihrem Zusammenhang in Fiktion und Historiographie." In *Theorie und Erzählung in der Geschichte,* ed. Jürgen Kocka and Thomas Nipperdey, 85–118. Munich: dtv.

Suhr, Heidrun (1989). "*Ausländerliteratur*: Minority Literature in the Federal Republic of Germany." *New German Critique* (Special Issue on Minorities in German Culture) 46: 71–103.

Suleiman, Susan Rubin (Ed.) (1986). *The Female Body in Western Culture: Contemporary Perspectives.* Cambridge, Mass.: Harvard University Press.

Süskind, Patrick (1985). *Das Parfum: Die Geschichte eines Mörders.* Zurich: Diogenes.

—— (1986). *Perfume: The Story of a Murderer.* Trans. John E. Woods. New York: Knopf.

Swidler, Leonard (1976). *Women in Judaism: The Status of Women in Formative Judaism.* Metuchen, N.J.: Scarecrow Press.

Szondi, Peter (1986). "Hope in the Past: On Walter Benjamin." In *On Textual Understanding and Other Essays,* trans. Harvey Mendelsohn, 145–59. Minneapolis: University of Minnesota Press.

Tabari, Azar (1980). "The Enigma of Veiled Iranian Women." *Feminist Review* 5: 19–31.

Taguieff, Pierre-André (1990). "The New Cultural Racism in France." Trans. Russell Moore. *Telos* 83: 109–22.

Theweleit, Klaus (1987). *Male Fantasies. Volume 1: Women, Floods, Bodies, History.* Trans. Stephen Conway in collaboration with Erica Carter and Chris Turner. Minneapolis: University of Minnesota Press.

Thürmer-Rohr, Christina (1987). *Vagabundinnen: Feministische Essays.* Berlin: Orlanda Frauenverlag.

———(1989). "Frauen in Gewaltverhältnissen: Zur Generalisierung des Opferbegriffs." In *Mittäterschaft und Entdeckungslust,* ed. Christina Thürmer-Rohr, Carola Wildt, Martina Emme, Monika Flamm, Vera Fritz, and Sigrid Voigt, 22–36. Berlin: Orlanda Frauenverlag.

———(1991). *Vagabonding: Feminist Theory Cut Loose.* Trans. Lise Weil. Boston: Beacon Press.

Tohidi, Nayereh (1991). "Gender and Islamic Fundamentalism: Feminist Politics in Iran." In *Third World Women and the Politics of Feminism,* ed. Chandra Talpade Mohanty, Ann Russo, Lourdes Torres, 250–67. Bloomington: Indiana University Press.

TORKAN (1983). *Tufan: Brief an einen islamischen Bruder.* Hamburg: perspol-verlag.

———(1984). *Kaltland: Wah'schate Ssard.* Hamburg: perspol-verlag.

Trinh T. Minh-ha (1986–87). "Difference: 'A Special Third World Women Issue.'" *Discourse* 8: 11–37.

———(1989). *Woman, Native, Other: Writing Postcoloniality and Feminism.* Bloomington: Indiana University Press.

Tuchel, Johannes, and Reinhold Schattenfroh (1987). *Zentrale des Terrors: Prinz-Albrecht-Straße 8, Das Hauptquartier der Gestapo.* Berlin: Siedler.

Tuerk, Richard (1983). "Jewish-American Literature." In *Ethnic Perspectives in American Literature: Selected Essays on the European Contribution,* ed. Robert J. Di Pietro and Edward Ifkovic, 133–62. New York: The Modern Language Association of America.

Turner, Bryan S. (1984). *The Body and Society: Explorations in Social Theory.* Oxford: Basil Blackwell.

Utas, Bo (Ed.) (1988). *Women in Islamic Societies: Social Attitudes and Historical Perspectives.* Brooklyn, N.Y.: Olive Branch Press.

von Braun, Christina (1989). *Die schamlose Schönheit des Vergangenen: Zum Verhältnis von Geschlecht und Geschichte.* Frankfurt am Main: neue kritik.

Wagener, Hans (Ed.) (1977) *Gegenwartsliteratur und Drittes Reich: Deutsche Autoren in der Auseinandersetzung mit der Vergangenheit.* Stuttgart: Reclam.

Waines, David (1982). "Through a Veil Darkly: The Study of Women in Muslim Societies. A Review Article." *Comparative Studies in Society and History* 24: 642–59.

Wall, Cheryl A. (Ed.) (1989). *Changing Our Own Words: Essays on Criticism, Theory, and Writing by Black Women.* New Brunswick: Rutgers University Press.

Weed, Elizabeth (Ed.) (1989). *Coming to Terms: Feminism, Theory, Politics.* New York: Routledge.

Weeks, Jeffrey (1981). *Sex, Politics and Society: The Regulation of Sexuality Since 1800.* London: Longman.

Wehler, Hans-Ulrich (1988). *Entsorgung der deutschen Vergangenheit? Ein polemischer Essay zum "Historikerstreit."* Munich: Beck.

Weigel, Sigrid (1983a). "Die geopferte Heldin und das Opfer als Heldin." In *Die verborgene Frau: Sechs Beiträge zu einer feministischen Literaturwissenschaft* by Inge Stephan and Sigrid Weigel, 138–52. Berlin: Argument.

——— (1983b). "Ohne Schutzhaut." *Courage* 8 (June): 46–47.

——— (1984a). "Frau und 'Weiblichkeit': Theoretische Überlegungen zur feministischen Literaturkritik." In *Feministische Literaturwissenschaft,* ed. Inge Stephan and Sigrid Weigel, 103–13. Berlin: Argument.

——— (1984b). "Overcoming Absence: Contemporary German Women's Literature (Part Two)." *New German Critique* 32: 3–22.

——— (1985). "Double Focus: On the History of Women's Writing." Trans. Harriet Anderson. In *Feminist Aesthetics,* ed. Gisela Ecker, 59–80. Boston: Beacon Press. Originally published as "Der schielende Blick: Thesen zur Geschichte weiblicher Schreibpraxis." In *Die verborgene Frau: Sechs Beiträge zu einer feministischen Literaturwissenschaft,* by Inge Stephan and Sigrid Weigel, 83–137. Berlin: Argument, 1983.

——— (1986). "'Das Weibliche als Metapher des Metonymischen': Kritische Überlegungen zur Konstitution des Weiblichen als Verfahren oder Schreibweise." In *Kontroversen, alte und neue: Akten des VII. Internationalen Germanisten-Kongresses Göttingen 1985.* Vol. 6. *Frauensprache—Frauenliteratur?* ed. Albrecht Schöne. Tübingen: Niemeyer.

——— (1987a). "Die nahe Fremde—das Territorium des 'Weiblichen': Zum Verhältnis von 'Wilden' und 'Frauen' im Diskurs der Aufklärung." In *Die andere Welt: Studien zum Exotismus,* ed. Thomas Koebner and Gerhart Pickerodt, 171–99. Frankfurt am Main: Athenäum. Rpt. in *Topographien der Geschlechter: Kulturgeschichtliche Studien zur Literatur,* 118–48. Reinbek bei Hamburg: Rowohlt, 1990.

——— (1987b). *Die Stimme der Medusa: Schreibweisen in der Gegenwartsliteratur der Frauen.* Dülmen-Hiddingsel: tende.

——— (1991). "Der Körper am Kreuzpunkt von Liebesgeschichte und Rassendiskurs in Heinrich von Kleists Erzählung 'Die Verlobung in St.

Domingo.'" *Kleist-Jahrbuch 1991,* ed. Hans Joachim Kreutzer, 202–17. Stuttgart: Metzler.

Weiner, Marc A. (1991). *"Urwaldmusik and the Borders of German Identity: Jazz in Literature of the Weimar Republic." German Quarterly* 64: 475–87.

Weiss, Peter (1975–81). *Die Ästhetik des Widerstands: Roman.* 2d ed. Frankfurt am Main: Suhrkamp, 1983.

White, Hayden (1973). *Metahistory: The Historical Imagination in Nineteenth-Century Europe.* Baltimore: Johns Hopkins University Press.

—— (1978). *Tropics of Discourse: Essays in Cultural Criticism.* Baltimore: Johns Hopkins University Press.

—— (1987). *The Content of the Form: Narrative Discourse and Historical Representation.* Baltimore: Johns Hopkins University Press.

Wiesel, Elie (1972). *Night, Dawn, The Accident: Three Tales.* Trans. Stella Rodway. New York: Hill & Wang.

Winkels, Hubert (1988). *Einschnitte: Zur Literatur der 8oer Jahre.* Cologne: Kiepenheuer & Witsch.

Wittke, Carl (1976). *Tambo and Bones: A History of the American Minstrel Stage.* 3d ed. Westport, Conn.: Greenwood Press.

Yaeger, Patricia (1988). *Honey-Mad Women: Emancipatory Strategies in Women's Writing.* New York: Columbia University Press.

Zipes, Jack (1986). "The Vicissitudes of Being Jewish in West Germany." In *Germans and Jews since the Holocaust: The Changing Situation in West Germany,* ed. Anson Rabinbach and Jack Zipes, 27–49. New York: Holmes & Meier.

—— (1990–91). "The Holocaust, Modernity, and Tough Jews." *Telos* 86: 170–84.

—— (1991). "Die kulturellen Operationen von Deutschen und Juden im Spiegel der neueren deutschen Literatur." Trans. Angelika Schweikart. *Babylon* 8: 34–44.

Zorn, Fritz (1977). *Mars.* Munich: Kindler.

Index

Fatimeh, 74
Featherstone, Mike, 14
Federal Republic of Germany. *See* Germany
Feminist aesthetics: oppositional negativity, 41–42; and positionality, 42–43, 64–67, 127; and racism, 37–38, 113; and woman's body, xiii, 40–41, 135nn.20, 21; 151n.20, 160n.29
Feminist politics, 60
Feminists: African American, 61, 157n.14
Feminist scholarship: embodiment/disembodiment of women, 135n.20, 151n.20; essentialism, 67, 148n.13; identity politics, 60–62, 95–96, 159n.24; and language, 39–40; and postmodernism, 57; standpoint theory, 149n.14; and Third World women, 68–73, 152n.22. *See also* German feminist scholarship
Feminist theory, xiv, xv, 13, 16, 36, 38, 39–40, 57–67
Fischer, Michael M. J., 74
Foucault, Michel, 69, 131n.3; concept of the human body, 3; critical commentaries, 132n.8; *Discipline and Punish*, 12; relevance for feminists, 144n.18
Frank, Leo, 98, 161nn.30, 32
Frank, Manfred, 131n.3, 133n.10, 134n.16
Frankfurt School of Critical Theory, 2
Friedländer, Saul, 28
Fuss, Diana, 94, 148n.13; on black feminist criticism, 158n.19, 159n.21; *Essentially Speaking*, xiii
Futterknecht, Franz, 30

Gates, Henry Louis, Jr., 158n.19
Gender: production of, xiv, 58–59, 92–93, 124, 125–26
German cultural identity: alternative conceptualizations of, xvi; in critical scholarship, 91–92, 158n.16; since 1945, 97, 129
German feminist scholarship, 93, 124, 128, 142n.4, 151n.19; racial constructs, 92, 95
German literature: approaches to human body, xv, 30–36, 126, 127, 134n.18, 135n.19; "father books," 100, 162n.34
German Studies, xvi, 36, 93, 95, 96, 125
Germany: Historikerstreit ("Historians' Debate"), 28–29, 139n.38; racial constructs, 96–97, 159n.22
Geschichte und Eigensinn (Negt and Kluge): concept of subjective splinters, 8–9, 11, 17, 134n.16; on *Erfahrungsökonomie* (economy of experience), 17; on history, 10–11, 12; on identity, 7–9, 11; role of human body, 5–7, 41; subject-object relations, 41, 126
Giddens, Anthony, 136n.24
Gilman, Sander L., 122; *Difference and Pathology,* 26, 90
GIS. *See* Black GIS
Grass, Günter, 33
Greenberg, Blu, 116, 164n.46
Gubar, Susan, 42
Gumbrecht, Hans Ulrich, 139n.36
Gypsies, 88

Habermas, Jürgen, 28
Haeri, Shahla, 72
Halakhah, 101, 105, 106, 116
Harding, Sandra, 149n.14
Hartsock, Nancy, 149n.14

Hegel, G. W. F., 1
Heintz, Bettina, 80
Heller, Agnes: *Theory of History*, 23–27, 126, 139nn.36, 37
Henderson, Mae Gwendolyn, 147nn.6, 8
Heracles, 31, 32, 34
Heschel, Susannah, 105
Higgins, Patricia J., 72
Historikerstreit ("Historians' Debate"), 28–29, 139n.38
History: in contemporary social theory, 10–13; in literature, 34–36, 138n.34, 141n.42; postwar German interpretation, 27–29, 30–31; theory of, 22–27
Hohendahl, Peter Uwe, 134n.16
Holocaust, 27–29, 30–31, 53, 88, 89, 90, 97, 124
Homophobia, 13
Homosexuality, 10, 99, 113, 114
Honegger, Claudia, 80
hooks, bell, 149n.14, 151n.18, 158n.15
Horkheimer, Max, 1
Human body: in contemporary critical theory, 16–18; in contemporary German literature, xv, 30–36, 126, 127, 134n.18, 135n.19; in contemporary social theory, 3–15, 19–22; in feminist theory, 14–15; positionality, 19–22; and processes of cultural signification, 14–15; as site of contested identities, 97; as subject and/or object, 21
Huyssen, Andreas, 3, 133n.13

Identity politics. *See* Feminist scholarship
Iran: women's roles in, 73–75, 154n.30

Irigaray, Luce: "The Sex Which Is Not One," 40, 41
Islam: reductionist scholarship in, 71–75
Islamic identity, 67–86
Islamic law, 71
Islamic women, 71–72, 153n.27

Jaggar, Alison M., 135n.20
Jameson, Fredric, 134n.16
Jewish identity. See *Ein Sommer in der Woche der Itke K.* (A Summer in the Week of Itke K.)
Jewish Labor Bund, 102
Jewish women, 101, 105–7, 117, 162n.39, 163nn.43, 44
Jews: in postwar German culture, 90, 156n.7
Jews and Germany: altered representation, 87–93, 128, 156n.6
Johnson Bill, the 98
"Jude, Das," 162n.38

Kamper, Dietmar: on human body as subject/object, 13, *Das Schwinden der Sinne* (The Diminution of the Senses), 12; *Die Wiederkehr des Körpers* (The Body Returns), 12
Kaplan, Caren, 149n.14
Keddie, Nikki, 81
Kelly, Joan, 150n.15
Kluge, Alexander: *Öffentlichkeit und Erfahrung* (The Public Sphere and Experience), 10, 134n.15. See also *Geschichte und Eigensinn*
Kocka, Jürgen, 28
Koonz, Claudia, 152n.21
Koselleck, Reinhart, 138n.34
Kristeva, Julia, 3, 17, 41, 48
Kroker, Arthur, 135n.19
Kroker, Marielouise, 135n.19
Ku Klux Klan, 109